Teaching with
The Norton Anthology
of World Masterpieces

SEVENTH

VOLU

A Guide for

Teaching with The Norton Anthology of World Masterpieces

SEVENTH EDITION
VOLUME 1

A Guide for Instructors

Paula Berggren
BARUCH COLLEGE
with the Editors

W · W · NORTON & COMPANY ·
New York · London

The text of this book is composed in Fairfield Medium
with the display set in Bernhard Modern.
Composition by Publishing Synthesis, Ltd.

ISBN 0-393-97356-5 (pbk.)

W. W. Norton & Company, Inc., 500 Fifth Avenue, New York, N.Y. 10110
www.wwnorton.com

W. W. Norton & Company Ltd., 10 Coptic Streeet, London WC1A 1PU

1 2 3 4 5 6 7 8 9 0

Contents

Masterpieces of the Ancient World

GILGAMESH 1

THE BIBLE: THE OLD TESTAMENT
Genesis 5
Job 11
Psalms 13
The Song of Songs 14
Jonah 15

HOMER
The Iliad 16
The Odyssey 22

SAPPHO OF LESBOS 29

AESCHYLUS
The Oresteia 30

SOPHOCLES
Oedipus the King 39

EURIPIDES
Medea 48

ARISTOPHANES
Lysistrata 57

PLATO
The Apology of Socrates 61

ARISTOTLE
Poetics 68

PLAUTUS
Pseudolus 70

CATULLUS 72

VIRGIL
The Aeneid 74

OVID
Metamorphoses 82

PETRONIUS
The Satyricon 87

THE BIBLE: THE NEW TESTAMENT 90

LUCIAN
A True Story 94

AUGUSTINE
Confessions 97

Masterpieces of the Middle Ages

THE KORAN 101

BEOWULF 105

THE SONG OF ROLAND 108

MARIE DE FRANCE
Lanval *and* Laüstic 114

THORSTEIN THE STAFF-STRUCK 117

MEDIEVAL LYRICS: A SELECTION 119

MEDIEVAL TALES: A SELECTION 127

DANTE ALIGHIERI
The Divine Comedy 135

GIOVANNI BOCCACCIO
The Decameron 140

SIR GAWAIN AND THE GREEN KNIGHT 146

GEOFFREY CHAUCER
The Canterbury Tales 151

THE THOUSAND AND ONE NIGHTS 157

SIR THOMAS MALORY
Morte Darthur 160

EVERYMAN 163

Masterpieces of the Renaissance

FRANCIS PETRARCH 167

DESIDERIUS ERASMUS
The Praise of Folly 171

NICCOLÒ MACHIAVELLI
The Prince 174

LUDOVICO ARIOSTO
Orlando Furioso 178

BALDESAR CASTIGLIONE
The Book of the Courtier   184

MARGUERITE DE NAVARRE
The Heptameron   187

FRANÇOIS RABELAIS
Gargantua and Pantagruel   190

MICHEL DE MONTAIGNE
Essays   194

MIGUEL DE CERVANTES
Don Quixote   197

LOPE DE VEGA
Fuente Ovejuna   204

WILLIAM SHAKESPEARE
Othello   208

JOHN MILTON
Paradise Lost   212

INDEX   217

Masterpieces of the Ancient World

GILGAMESH

Backgrounds

The story of Gilgamesh moves through several distinct stages almost like acts in a drama. The first begins with Gilgamesh himself, or rather, the problem he poses, and ends with the solution the gods provide for him in the person of Enkidu. In an ancient and legendary time, the gods of Mesopotamia create a king for the great city of Uruk whose name is Gilgamesh. He is perfect in beauty and strength and is more god than man. The gods have, perhaps, been too generous in their gifts to him, although the poet does not say this explicitly. At all events, Gilgamesh's superiority makes him arrogant, and he serves his people badly. He fights wars that devour the young men of the city, and he takes women from their husbands and lovers for his own pleasure. His subjects complain of Gilgamesh's oppression, and the gods hear them. On humankind's behalf they implore Aruru, the goddess of creation, to produce a second being equal in strength and ferocity to Gilgamesh who will serve as a kind of counterbalance to him. This she does by first conceiving the image of the being who will satisfy their need and then making him of clay and water. The result is Enkidu, a creature who is half human and half wild animal. He falls to the ground in the wilderness, and at first he lives with wild beasts, hunting with them and eating only uncooked food. He knows nothing of the city and its people.

Enkidu becomes the king-protector of wild game, standing as much above them as Gilgamesh does above the people of Uruk. He is Gilgamesh's wild counterpart, except that he is a good king to animals, while Gilgamesh is a bad king to people. The first hunter to encounter Enkidu is terrified of him and asks his father what to do. His suggestion is to go to Uruk, to Gilgamesh, to request a prostitute from him. He recognizes that Enkidu is more man than animal and shrewdly determines to use the force of sexual attraction to lure him away from the wild kingdom. Once the prostitute has drawn Enkidu into the orbit of human society, she turns him over to the shepherds to complete the task of making a "man" of him. Enkidu soon becomes so human that the animals who were his companions shy away from him, and to show how complete his

1

transformation is, he now protects the shepherds' flocks rather than the wild animals.

When the prostitute sees that he is ready she brings him to Uruk, where he meets and battles with Gilgamesh, as Aruru has meant him to. Gilgamesh has already learned of his coming through a dream that his mother interprets as portending that he will find a true companion. When they meet, they fight, but are so evenly matched that only with great difficulty does Gilgamesh throw Enkidu to the ground. Once he has established his superiority, his anger vanishes, and they embrace as friends. The conflict between the civilized and the wild is a recurrent theme in Mesopotamian civilization. Here the two are united by a special alchemy into the first great male friendship in human literature.

Aruru's solution now becomes the start of another cycle that focuses on the quest for immortality. Gilgamesh's only reason for undertaking the slaying of Humbaba is to gain the immortality of fame. The heroes are successful in their adventure, but it seems a hollow triumph. The monster is pathetic in defeat, begging for mercy and then cursing them before he dies. Enlil, the god of wind and storm, is enraged by the slaying of his creature. He, too, curses the heroes, and denies them the reward of their victory—the seven splendors that had been Humbaba's.

Their second adventure is provoked by Ishtar. She desires Gilgamesh as her lover, but he rejects her insultingly and draws attention to how shabbily she has treated her former husbands. She sends the Bull of Heaven against the people of Uruk in retaliation, and Gilgamesh and Enkidu must destroy it. Ishtar demands vengeance for its death, and the gods grant that one of the two heroes, Enkidu, must die. Enkidu is enraged by his fate at first and curses all those who transformed him from a wild creature into a man, but he softens when Shamash, the sun god, reminds him of the glory he has enjoyed as a man.

Enkidu's death is a terrible blow to Gilgamesh, and it forces him to confront his own mortality. If Enkidu could find comfort in having moved upward in the scale of being, from an animal-like existence to that of a superhuman, Gilgamesh cannot. He yearns to advance beyond the limits of mortality, and when he learns that one human, Utnapishtim, has that gift, Gilgamesh decides to undertake a journey in search of him. This journey takes him out of the human realm into a region that seems to exist between his world and that of the gods. He begins it by first abandoning the city and passing through the wilderness, regaining, perhaps, some of the magical energy that he lost with the death of Enkidu. Then he must pass the fierce lions who guard the entrance to a dark tunnel that goes on for days. When he emerges, it is as though he had been reborn into a new world. He finds himself in a paradisial garden that seems to be the prototype for all those that follow it in Western literature. Then he makes a puzzling and perilous voyage to Dilmun—an island that lies beyond the reach of human voyaging. Although he is discouraged at every step, Gilgamesh perseveres and at last finds his way to Utnapishtim, who tells him the story of how he won the gratitude of the gods. When he learns that Gilgamesh, too, desires immortality, he tests him by asking him to stay awake for six days and seven nights. Sleep is often spoken of as a "little death" or the sister of death. If Gilgamesh cannot conquer sleep, how can he hope to conquer death? He fails this test, but by way of consolation, Utnapishtim offers him the secret of a plant that will ensure him perpetual renewal—not immortality, but something very like it. The plant lives at the bottom of the sea at a place where fresh and salty waters come together. Gilgamesh finds the plant, but carelessly allows the serpent to steal it from him—the first literary occurrence of the snake as an enemy of human happiness. Discouraged and defeated, Gilgamesh returns at last to Uruk empty-handed. His consolation is the knowledge that his worldly accomplishments will endure beyond his own lifetime. He has learned the essential lesson of mortality—although he is greater than Enkidu, and greater than all men, he cannot escape death. Only his name will outlive his body.

Classroom Strategies

Suggested assignments:

1. Prologue and parts 1, 2, and 3
2. Parts 4, 5, 6, and 7

Topics for Discussion

The Sandars translation smoothes out many rough spots in the original, but the text is still full of puzzles. There are so many gods, and all of them new. The names have a puzzling and comic sound (Utnapishtim). It is not always clear what is happening in the narrative, as is the case with the expedition to the forest to kill Humbaba, and so on. It may be helpful to point out that the gods are not organized in a clear hierarchy as is true with the gods of the Greeks and Romans. They are more like a large and noisy family, with no generally acknowledged patriarch to pull them together, or an alliance of semi-independent chiefs—a neighborhood association rather than a divine senate. Despite the occasional obscurities in the text, however, certain themes stand out quite clearly and are linked with individual sections of the work.

In the first, the arrogance of power offers itself for discussion, as does the thin line that divides enmity between men from deep friendship. There are also suggestive parallels between the account of the creation of Gilgamesh and Enkidu and Genesis 1–3. The process of civilizing Enkidu, of bringing him out of the wild and into the urban world opens up a discussion of the relation of civilization to nature. After all, Enkidu both gains and loses by his transformation, and it is surely worth noting that even at this very early stage of human history, the settled lived in conflict with the wild. The roles of hunter and shepherd as figures who stand between the two spheres are worth exploring, as is that of the prostitute who is principally responsible for Enkidu's transformation. She may be a temple prostitute here and not simply the Mesopotamian equivalent of a "hooker."

The campaign against Humbaba opens up a discussion of the importance of fame as conferring immortality and also the mixed results that
come about when the goal of an adventure is a selfish one. Humbaba
poses no threat to Uruk, and his death brings no benefits, at least as the
story is told here. Gilgamesh's encounter with Ishtar shows how risky the
relations of humans to gods can be, at least for humans. He has the right
to reject her advances, and good reason for doing so, but he oversteps
himself in rejecting her so insultingly. He pays a heavy price for his bad
manners.

The remainder of the poem focuses on the tragedy of mortality—a
tragedy made more poignant by the absence of a well-developed belief in
an afterlife.

Topics for Writing

1. Compare a passage from the Sandars translation with one that has
   ironed out fewer of the rough spots (Delaney, Kovacs, Pritchard).
   Are her solutions to the problems of a fragmentary text convincing
   to you? What else might she have done?
2. Dreams are so recurrent in Gilgamesh and so important. They serve
   as a vehicle of communication between gods and mortals, anticipating events symbolically but accurately. What narrative function do
   they serve? That is, why is it useful to know what is going to happen
   before it does?

Comparative Perspectives

1. Cities have important functions in the heroic works of the ancient
   and premodern world. What characteristics do these cities—places
   like Uruk and Troy—share? How would you contrast the attitudes
   toward urban life expressed in ancient texts to those you encounter
   in our contemporary world?
2. Gilgamesh depends on the advice of his mother, Ninsun, "one of
   the wise gods." Consider other heroes who have similarly close relationships with (sometimes divine) mothers: what does this imply
   about the kinds of strength a man needs to be able to summon in
   times of need? Cf. Achilles and Aeneas.
3. Gilgamesh has the earliest version of the flood story that appears
   later in the Old Testament of the Bible (Genesis 6–9). Discuss how
   each version has very different emphases and draws a different
   moral.
4. As the earliest human epic *Gilgamesh* also invites comparisons with
   later epics like the *Odyssey* and the *Aeneid*. Each, for instance, provides a different goal as an organizing principal—the return home,
   the founding of a state, the search for immortality. The involvement
   of the gods in human affairs also differs among them. Finally, the
   Aeneid is consciously and explicitly derived from Homer, but
   Homer shows no awareness of *Gilgamesh*. How is that apparent?

Further Reading

See also the reading suggestions in the anthology, p. 18.

Delaney, Stephanie. *Myths from Mesopotamia: Creation, the Flood, Gilgamesh, and Others.* 1989. Contains translations, with commentary, of a number of myths that illuminate the context of *Gilgamesh.*

Kirk, G. S. *Myth: Its Meaning and Functions in Ancient and Other Cultures.* 1970. Contains an extended discussion of both Mesopotamian and Greek mythology and the similarities between *Gilgamesh* and some Greek myths. Begins with a useful discussion of structuralism and myth.

Kovacs, Maureen Gallery. *The Epic of Gilgamesh.* 1989.

Pritchard, James Bennett, ed. *Ancient Near Eastern Texts.* 1955. The earliest complete translation together with a number of other, related texts.

Tigay, Jeffrey A. *The Evolution of the Gilgamesh Epic.* 1982. A detailed, informative discussion of the various stages in the evolution of the epic.

THE BIBLE: THE OLD TESTAMENT

Genesis

[THE CREATION—THE FALL; THE FIRST MURDER; THE FLOOD; THE ORIGIN OF LANGUAGES]

Backgrounds

The Creation of the world in seven days: light and darkness on the first day; the sky (firmament) on the second; on the third, land and sea and also vegetation on the land; on the fourth, sun, moon, and stars; on the fifth, fish and birds; on the sixth, animals and man (Adam). On the seventh day God rested. Adam, in the garden of Eden, is given permission to eat the fruit of any tree except the tree of knowledge of good and evil. He is also given a mate, Eve, who, tempted by the serpent, persuades Adam to eat the forbidden fruit. They are punished by expulsion from the garden and must now work to live; they must also face the inevitability of death: "dust thou art, and unto dust shalt thou return."

In the next generation, violent death comes into the world: Cain murders his brother Abel. Their descendants become so wicked that God is sorry he ever created the human race and decides to destroy it. But one just man, Noah, is allowed to survive the Flood, with his family and specimens of all the animals, fish, and birds. So the Earth is repopulated, but humans, in their pride, begin to build a tower as high as Heaven. God prevents this by confusing their speech; before, there was one universal language, but now the builders of the tower speak different languages and cannot understand one another.

Though Genesis is traditionally assigned to the prophet Moses, it bears the marks of a document that has a long history of revision, addition, and reinterpretation over a period of time. (There are, for example, two different accounts of the Creation that do not agree in detail.) The book probably preserves ancient oral tradition but shows signs also of priestly revision at a later stage. Its original language is Hebrew, and Genesis and the next four books of the Old Testament form the Torah (the Law) of the Jewish faith.

Classroom Strategies

The selections are short but have matter enough in them to form one assignment. Refer students to the headnote (pp. 47–50 in the anthology) for some of the problems raised by these texts.

The main difficulties for modern students are the following.

- The concept of God that underlies the stories of Adam, Noah, and Babel. You should explain that the punishments inflicted by God are in each case just: Adam disobeys the one prohibition imposed on him, the Flood is sent to punish almost universal wickedness, and the builders of the tower are encroaching on God's space. But in every case, justice is tempered with mercy: Adam and Eve are not destroyed, only expelled from the garden; Cain is not killed but condemned to be a wanderer on the face of the Earth; Noah and his family are saved, to repopulate the Earth, and God makes a covenant with him never to destroy the human race again; the builders of the tower are not destroyed or even hurt, they are simply divided by language. You can point out that these stories, like myths in many societies, have an explanatory function: they answer questions. Why do we have to work to live and eventually die? Why don't we all speak the same language? Why does the serpent crawl? And why do we feel revulsion when we see it?
- The subordinate role of Eve and her responsibility for the Fall. A difficult subject, but you can point out that this story is the creation of a firmly patriarchal society in which sons were more highly regarded than daughters and authority was the prerogative of the male. (We are told the names of Noah's sons, for example, but not the name of his wife.) It can be pointed out, too, that the Hebrews were not alone in this attitude; the Greek myth of Pandora has exactly the same moral: it's all the woman's fault.

Topics for Discussion

1. The significance of the fact that God forbids eating the fruit of the tree of knowledge. Why should the knowledge of "good and evil" be forbidden? *Are* there kinds of knowledge that it is risky for human beings to have?

2. The role of the serpent (refer ahead to *Paradise Lost*, where the serpent has become Satan). Is the serpent a way of passing the buck—of saying it's not *our* fault?
3. Cain and Abel, symbolic of two different ways of life, farmers and pastoral nomads.

Comparative Perspectives

What attitude toward city life is expressed in the story of the Tower of Babel? Does this differ from the view of Uruk in *Gilgamesh*? How would you compare the view of urban experience and architecture in other ancient works such as the *Illiad*, the *Odyssey*, or the *Aeneid*?

[ABRAHAM AND ISAAC]

Backgrounds

Noah has three sons—one of them, Shem, the ancestor of the Semitic peoples, including the Hebrews. One of the descendants of Shem, Abraham, is called by God to leave his home and eventually settle in Palestine. With the introduction of Abram (not yet Abraham) in chapter 12 (not in the anthology), the focus of Genesis shifts from universal history to the beginnings of monotheism. Abraham (so dubbed by God when He makes a covenant with him) will be the founder of the Jewish people.

The first of the three Patriarchs of Jewish legend, Abraham is married to Sarah, who is childless. She gives Hagar, her female Egyptian slave, to Abraham, and when Abraham is eighty-six years old, he fathers his first son, Ishmael, by Hagar. But God promises Abraham that His Covenant will be established with a son to be born of Sarah; this prophecy prompts both husband and wife to laugh. Yet when Abraham is one hundred years old and Sarah is ninety, she bears Isaac, whose name means "he who laughs."

A pattern adumbrated by the story of Cain and Abel is repeated in the history of Abraham's two sons, when the first-born is found inadequate to serve the divine purpose. Hagar and her sixteen-year-old son are banished by Sarah, who believes that they laugh at her. In chapter 21 of Genesis (not in the anthology), Abraham follows God's instructions to grant Sarah's request, sending Hagar and Ishmael away, furnished with bread and water. As their supplies dwindle, it appears that they will die in the wilderness, and Hagar moves away from her son, lest he die before her eyes. At this desperate moment, God's messenger calls to Hagar, and she sees a well of water. They are saved, and God promises to make Ishmael (whose name means "God will hear") the founder of a nation.

In chapter 22 of Genesis, the obedient Abraham takes his "only son Isaac"—his only legitimate son, by the wife he loves—away from home. The narratives complement each other and in their different emphases measure the special burdens that the Covenant will impose on the Jewish people, the descendants of Isaac (the descendants of Ishmael will populate the Arabian peninsula. Thus Muslims are also the children of Abraham).

Classroom Strategies

A close reading of this chapter famously demonstrates the narrative genius of Genesis, although the elegance of the King James translation sometimes obscures its power. Three times Abraham speaks the same single word in Hebrew, *hineni*, here rendered as both "here I am" and "here am I." For three days, he walks with two servants and his son (and the relentless repetition of "his son" insists on the terrible demand that God has made on Abraham, so ready to do His bidding).

In his influential comparison of the Hebrew Bible and Homeric epic, Erich Auerbach speaks of the silences and repressions in this text, "fraught with background." You may want to ask your students how the spareness of dialogue and description suggests what the impact of this journey on father and son must have been. Commentators note that Abraham is careful to carry the dangerous implements (the fire and the knife—better translated as "cleaver," to imply the butchery that is to take place) himself, while he leaves the wood to Isaac. This protective instinct makes all the more agonizing the consciousness with which the father proceeds to fulfill his task, as the narrative carefully spells out the preparations for the sacrifice after being so laconic about everything that leads up to the moment of truth.

[JACOB AND ESAU]

The wives of the three Patriarchs are the four Matriarchs, the second of whom is Rebekah. This strong-willed woman, Isaac's wife, plays the dominant role in deciding which of her children will gain the paternal blessing. Like Sarah, she is barren until her husband petitions God to give her children. In this second instance of two sons competing for favor, both are children of the same wife. The story of Jacob and Esau is consequently especially complex.

In chapter 25 of Genesis, Esau is portrayed as a coarse and unpromising person, not fit to fulfill the terms of God's Covenant with his grandfather. Hungry and careless, he "despised his birthright." The narrative conveys this sense of his indifference with a rapid succession of verbs: "he did eat and drink, and rose up, and went his way." The description of Esau as a baby who came from the womb "red, all over like a hairy garment" recalls the description of Enkidu in *Gilgamesh*, a reminder that it is always helpful to consider the Mesopotamian sources behind the often problematic tales told in Genesis. (The commentaries in E. A. Speiser's edition of Genesis, the first volume in *The Anchor Bible* mentioned in the bibliography in the headnote, are particularly useful in this area.) As in the fates of Isaac and Ishmael, political motives can be discerned. Edom, a trans-Jordanian kingdom that springs from Esau, will rival the Kingdom of Israel. But the story of the stealing of Jacob's blessing cannot be reduced to a national allegory.

In chapter 27, the narrative sympathy lies with Esau; nevertheless, Genesis in its entirety demonstrates that the divine imperative transcends individual claims and personalities. Rebekah eavesdrops on the feeble Isaac's conversation with her first son and hastily arranges the ruse by which her favorite will prevail. The blind old man relies on his remaining senses to perceive the world, and Rebekah brilliantly foresees the need to transform her younger son into a physical simulacrum of his hunter brother. You will probably want to challenge your students to explain the superiority of Jacob's claim to the paternal blessing. Although Jacob is portrayed here as a trickster, later chapters of Genesis underscore why he is to become the progenitor of the Twelve Tribes of Israel (he later acquires the name Israel). For like all the great heroes of the Hebrew Bible, many of whom demonstrate serious moral flaws, he has tenacity and resourcefulness; above all, whatever his shortcomings, he is capable of intimacy with God and of intellectual and spiritual growth.

It is worth reading this chapter for many reasons, not least that it prepares for the longer narrative of Joseph that follows. Rebekah helps Jacob trick his father with a change of garment and "the skins of the kids of goats." Just so will Joseph's brothers bring his garment back to their father (the aged and infirm Jacob, or Israel), stained with the blood of a kid, so that he will believe his son has died. The Bible teaches that our actions have consequences. Only in experiencing these consequences and learning to accept them do human beings fully enact the meaning of free will.

The poignancy of Esau's response in chapter 27 of Genesis is quite contrary to his coarseness in the earlier one, and the significance of Jacob's name is more fully explained. Rebekah's second twin son, who emerged from the womb holding his brother's heel is called *Ya'aqob*, for the root of the word that means heel—*'aqeb*. But change one vowel and the word *'aqob*, or "crooked," also can be understood as the source of his name.

Topics for Writing

1. How important is primogeniture in Genesis? What evidence can you see that more than simple birth order determines the legitimacy of an heir?
2. In the Shakespearean English of the King James translation of Genesis, we read that "Jacob sod pottage." This simply means that he made a stew. What is the importance of food in this selection? Why does Jacob decide to cook a meal?

   [Presumably this reflects his competitive instinct, since Isaac prefers his first to his second son because of the venison he prepares.]

Comparative Perspectives

1. When Abraham raises his knife against Isaac, a ram caught in a thicket is substituted and sacrificed. Compare the substitution of a human being for an animal in the events prior to the Trojan War that are described by the Chorus in *Agamemnon*. Why was sacrifice so important in the ancient world? Discuss the different views of divinity and the purpose of sacrifice expressed in the Greek and the Hebraic narratives.
2. Compare the brief biblical story of the binding of Isaac with *The Sacrifice of Isaac*, a twelfth-century poem by Rabbi Ephraim ben Jacob printed in the anthology's selection of medieval lyrics. How

does the comparison clarify the importance of interpretation in reading biblical texts?

3. Like Isaac, Telemachus is the son of a great man. Contrast the tests by which Telemachus proves himself in the *Odyssey* with those by which Isaac is defined in youth and old age in chapters 22 and 27 of Genesis. What do the differences tell us about the values of the ancient Greeks and Hebrews?

[Isaac essentially must obey and accept; Telemachus must learn to assert himself.]

[THE STORY OF JOSEPH]

Backgrounds

Jacob has thirteen sons; his favorite is one of the youngest, Joseph, to whom he gives a coat of many colors. (Modern scholars translate the phrase "a long robe with sleeves," but the coat of many colors is now proverbial in the English language.) Joseph has dreams that he interprets to mean that he will be the greatest of the brothers. His brothers are enraged and leave Joseph to die in a dry cistern in the outland pastures. They smear his coat with goat's blood and convince Jacob that his son has been killed by a wild beast.

But Joseph is rescued by passing merchants who sell him as a slave to Potiphar, the captain of the guard of Pharaoh, the ruler of Egypt. Joseph rises rapidly in his master's esteem and soon is entrusted with great responsibilities. Potiphar's wife tries to seduce him; rejected, she accuses him of an attempt at rape, and Joseph is sent to prison. There he interprets the dreams of fellow prisoners, and one of them, released and restored to his post as Pharaoh's butler, remembers Joseph when the Pharaoh has some disturbing dreams. Joseph interprets them as a prophecy of seven years of plenty followed by seven years of famine; he suggests storing food as a reserve. Pharaoh puts him in charge of the program; he becomes Pharaoh's chief minister.

The seven lean years begin as predicted; the Egyptians are provided for, but in Israel there is famine. Jacob sends his sons to Egypt to buy grain; they come to Joseph, whom they do not recognize. He denounces them as spies and tells them to come back, this time with the youngest of the brothers, Benjamin. Jacob is unwilling to let Benjamin go, but in the end he has to yield. Once in Egypt, the brothers are entertained royally; their sacks are filled with grain. But in Benjamin's sack Joseph has his servants, in secret, put his own silver cup. When it is found there after a search he tells the others to go home; he will keep Benjamin with him in Egypt. They beg him to let Benjamin go, saying that Jacob will die of grief. Joseph can conceal his feelings no longer and reveals his identity. He sends for Jacob, and so the Israelites settle in Egypt. After many years, when a later Pharaoh begins to oppress them, they escape from Egypt (the Exodus) led by the prophet Moses.

The story has some historical plausibility: for two centuries (1720–1550 B.C.) Egypt was under the domination of the Hyksos, a non-Egyptian people, and Semitic settlers were favored. Joseph's rise to power and influence could in such circumstances have happened. The sophisticated literary form of the story may owe something to a model: an Egyptian tale of a man who rejected the advances of his brother's wife, who then falsely accused him and almost caused his death at his brother's hands (see Thomas in "Further Reading"). The belief that dreams foretold the future, taken for granted in the Joseph story, is common to most of the civilizations of the ancient world; the teacher can refer forward, for example, to Penelope's dream in the *Odyssey* (XIX.572ff.). The basic mechanism of the plot, the hero in disguise (compare the scene between Joseph and his brothers), is also found on a larger scale in the *Odyssey.*

Classroom Strategies

One assignment. No special difficulties.

Topics for Discussion

1. Discuss Joseph's statement to his brothers: "So now it was not you that sent me hither, but God" (chapter 45).
2. "This dreamer cometh": Joseph as visionary and a man of action.

Topics for Writing

1. Discuss the function in the story of one of the following recurrent motifs: Joseph's clothes or dreams and their interpretation.
2. Recast the story as a play in five acts.
3. Why do you think Joseph put the silver cup in Benjamin's sack?
4. Does the "success story" of Joseph differ in any way from its modern counterparts in which an awkward, clumsy, ugly, or despised person makes good?
5. Genesis ends with the story of Joseph and begins with a story about free will, knowledge, and obedience. Discuss the importance and complexity of these three themes in the lives of the various biblical figures introduced in the anthology (Abraham, Jacob, Joseph). Does God want only obedience from those with whom He chooses to make His Covenant?

Job

Backgrounds

Satan—the Hebrew word means "the adversary"—challenges God to test the piety of Job, a rich and fortunate man famous for his devotion to the Almighty. How will his piety stand up in the face of calamity? God gives Satan permission to inflict any suffering short of physical harm on Job to see if, as Satan claims, he will curse God.

In the course of one day Job learns that all his servants, his flocks, and his sons and daughters have been killed, but he does not blame God. Satan demands and receives permission to inflict bodily harm; he covers

Job's body with sores. Job's wife tells him, "Curse God and die," but he rebukes her.

Now three friends (Job's comforters) come to sympathize with him. From this point on the story is cast in dramatic and poetic form until the short narrative conclusion.

Job wishes he had not been born, and the first of his friends replies: since Job has been punished, he must have sinned. Job's attitude is arrogant; he should show humility before God. The second friend suggests he may be paying for the sins of his children. The third returns to the theme of the first but more harshly: Job *must* be guilty or he would not be suffering. Job refuses to accept these arguments; the disasters inflicted on him are out of proportion to any sin he may unknowingly have committed. He appeals to God and wishes he could speak to Him directly and learn what the reason for his suffering is: "Behold, my desire is, that the Almighty would answer me" (chapter 31). His desire is fulfilled as God speaks from the whirlwind. His speech contains no justification for the suffering he inflicted on Job; it is a magnificent celebration of the power and greatness of God. Job accepts God's answer; he feels overwhelmed by God's personal intervention—now he has faith in him: "I have heard of thee . . . but now mine eye seeth thee" (42). God does not answer Job's question, but he does dismiss the beliefs of his friends: "ye have not spoken of me the thing that is right, as my servant Job hath" (42). And "the Lord gave Job twice as much as he had before" (42).

The basis of the work is an oral folktale, the story of the patient sufferer. Onto a Hebrew version of the tale has been grafted a poetic dialogue between Job and three friends and also the voice of God speaking from the whirlwind. The text probably was set in its present form some time in the sixth century B.C.

Classroom Strategies

Ideally this should be one assignment, but if necessary, it can be divided: 1–14 and 15 to the end.

Satan is a problem for most people new to this text. He is not the Devil of later literature but one of the "sons of God" (chapter 1). His name means "the adversary"; perhaps he is a sort of loyal opposition. Students can be told to watch for the transformation of this figure in later texts (especially Milton), his identification with the serpent of Genesis and the Evil One of the New Testament.

Topics for Discussion

Job (in chapter 31) makes the claim that his life has been virtuous and devoted to the worship of God, and so he does not deserve the calamities that have fallen on him. He asks God for an answer, but the voice from the whirlwind does not deal with his question at all. Why does Job accept God's assertion of divine power (42) and not press for an answer to his question? Why is he satisfied with what he is given? Do you find the end of the dialogue satisfactory?

The answer should be along the lines that Job is content with the fact that the Almighty has condescended to speak to him in person. Even if his question is not answered, he has the assurance that God cares for him enough to speak to him directly. Before this, he has known of God only by hearsay, but now he has direct experience (42). The question of justice in the world, of apparently undeserved suffering (and its opposite, the prosperity of the wicked) is not resolved; it is a question, too, that will be debated by the Greeks (the *Odyssey* 1.45ff. and *Oedipus the King*, for example).

Topics for Writing

1. Recast in your own (plain) language the core of the arguments offered by the three comforters. How do they differ from one another?
2. Discuss the statement that although God does not answer Job's complaint he "reveals himself personally to him and shares with him the vision of his cosmic responsibilities."

Comparative Perspectives

Look carefully at the use of figurative language in a few passages from these texts and try to explain how Hebraic parallelism functions. What do the comparisons chosen tell us about the mode of life and values of the original audience? Chapter 29 offers some particularly good examples of metonymy and synecdoche. You may want to spend some time talking about the indelible power of the King James Version. Give a moment to Job 7.6 ("my days are swifter than a weaver's shuttle, and are spent without hope") if you expect to teach Villon's *Testament* (which refers to this verse in lines 217–24) or Browning's *The Bishop Orders his Tomb* (see line 51). Depending on your choice of later texts, it can be useful also to point to differences between the more accurate modern translations and the King James Version. "Though he slay me, yet will I trust in him" (13), for example, another oft-quoted line, gives exactly the wrong impression; the meaning is rather, "Behold he will slay me; I have no hope." Or compare the exquisite but confusing "When I washed my steps with butter" (29) with Stephen Mitchell's vivid contemporary rendition: "when my feet were bathed in cream."

Psalms

Our selection offers five texts from what might be called the Hebrew hymnal, a collection of no less than 150 songs. (*Psalm* is a Greek word that describes the sound made by a plucked string, and many of these psalms have come down to us with musical directions attached—"for flutes," for example, or "with stringed instruments.") They are of various types; the selection offers specimens of hymns celebrating the majesty of God (Psalms 8, 19, and 104), songs of trust in the Lord (Psalm 23), and laments (Psalm 137).

Hebrew poetry is not based on strict metrical pattern alone (as in

Greek or Latin) or on metrical pattern and rhyme (as in English and many other modern languages); it works by what is known as "parallelism." A first statement is repeated or amplified in a different form—"The statutes of the Lord are right, rejoicing the heart: the commandment of the Lord is pure, enlightening the eyes" (19.8)—and this second form may echo the original thought, as in this example, build on it toward a climax, or contrast with it.

The Song of Songs

The headnote offers a fine summary of different interpretive approaches to these astonishing poems, and it would be worth working through some of the possibilities with your students. If the overall idea of allegory seems plausible, the wildly imaginative metaphors of particular lines may seem quite a way from expressing God's love for the Chosen People, or Christ's for his church. If you want to emphasize their allegorical possibilities, you may want to read the Song of Songs with your students as part of your discussion of biblical texts. It may be equally useful to assign the poem as a companion piece to other love lyrics encountered later in the semester.

In any event, detailed elucidation of the figures of speech in the Song of Songs is infinitely rewarding. Note, for example, the comparison of the beloved "to a company of horses in Pharoah's chariots" (chapter 1). Robert Alter clarifies this perplexing reference: "a mare in heat, let loose among chariotry, could transform well-drawn battle lines into a chaos of wildly plunging stallions." The male celebration of female sexuality as landscape is familiar to readers of later love poems, but the violence of this pictorially evocative image is startling and unusual.

The Songs of Songs is also remarkable for the frequency with which the woman speaks. The description of her lover as a sachet of perfume between her breasts (1), for example, so specific, unexpected, and witty, gives some sense of the liveliness of the Song of Songs.

Topics for Writing

Choose examples of the techniques of parallelism and intensification in Job, the Psalms, and the Song of Songs, noting whether the imagery used seems traditional or innovative.

Comparative Perspectives

1. How do the metaphors in the Song of Songs draw on the geography of the land of Israel and the way of life of its people? Compare and contrast the range of metaphors in other early love lyrics, such as Sappho's "Some there are who say that the fairest thing seen."
2. Echoes of the Song of Songs resonate throughout later literature. Discuss the ways in which three medieval poets, Hildegard of Bin-

gen, Judah Halevi, and Geoffrey Chaucer, borrow specific phrases from this biblical work to very different effects.

Jonah

Comparative Perspectives

1. Like Odysseus, Jonah is a reluctant traveler who takes refuge in sleep. Ancient writers use symbolic details like this to suggest delicate psychological states of mind. How would you interpret these characters' needs to abandon consciousness?
2. Jonah is allowed no answer to God's wry defense of Nineveh's right to exist. What do you take to be the import of the final line of the book? As you do your semester's reading, look for other examples of conclusions that reverse the audience's expectations.

Further Reading

See also the reading suggestions in the anthology, p. 50.

Alter, Robert. *The Art of Biblical Narrative.* 1981.

———. *The Art of Biblical Poetry.* 1985

——— *Genesis: Translation and Commentary.* 1996.

Bloom, Harold, ed. *The Bible.* 1987. This volume includes a number of provocative essays.

Eissfeldt, O. *The Old Testament: An Introduction.* 1965. Very full, authoritative discussion of every aspect of the problems posed by the Old Testament of the Bible by one of the greatest modern scholars in the field.

The New Oxford Annotated Bible (with the Apocrypha). 1977. The Revised Standard Version, which corrects misunderstandings in the Authorized and frequently translates a better text. It is equipped with helpful introductions to the different books and very useful footnotes. See "Characteristics of Hebrew Poetry" (pp. 1523–29) for help with the Psalms.

Olshen, Barry N. and Yael S. Feldman, eds. *Approaches to Teaching the Hebrew Bible as Literature in Translation.* 1989. Another useful volume in the MLA series.

Thomas, D. Winton, ed. *Documents from Old Testament Times.* 1961. Contains documents, translated by experts in the different fields from Babylonian, Egyptian, and other ancient Near Eastern texts, that parallel or throw light on the biblical accounts. See especially the Babylonian creation myth, the flood story in *Gilgamesh,* the Babylonian *Theodicy* (a dialogue on divine justice and human suffering, comparable in theme to Job), and the Egyptian *Tale of Two Brothers* (for comparison with the story of Joseph and Potiphar's wife).

HOMER

The Iliad

Backgrounds

In the tenth year of the Achaean siege of Troy, a rich city in Asia Minor, Agamemnon, the most powerful king among the Achaean allies, quarrels with the bravest of them, Achilles. Agamemnon had taken as his concubine the captive daughter of a Trojan priest of Apollo; at the priest's request, the god had sent a plague to devastate the army. Agamemnon agrees to give back the girl but demands compensation from the army for the loss of his share of the spoils of war. Achilles opposes this demand as unreasonable, and Agamemnon, at the end of a furious argument, announces he will take away Achilles' girl Briseis, whom Achilles had captured in a raid. Achilles draws his sword to kill Agamemnon but is dissuaded from violence by the goddess Athena, who promises that he will be amply recompensed for Agamemnon's insults at some future date. He goes back to his tent and pulls his men out of the fighting. But he also asks his mother, the goddess Thetis, to intervene. She is to use her influence with Zeus, the king of the gods, and ask him to inflict defeat and suffering on the Achaeans, so that they will turn against Agamemnon. She goes to Olympus and, in spite of the opposition of Zeus' wife, Hera (who favors the Achaean side), Zeus grants her prayer.

In books II–V (not included in the anthology) Agamemnon calls an assembly of the troops. In an attempt to test morale he suggests abandoning the war; the ensuing stampede for the ships is stopped only by Odysseus with the aid of the goddess Athena. The Achaeans then muster for battle and the poet describes each contingent in what is known as the Catalog of Ships; he then proceeds to list the Trojan forces. The two sides join battle, but Hector, the Trojan leader, proposes that the war be settled by a duel between Menelaus, the Achaean king, and Paris, the Trojan prince who had run off with Menelaus' wife, Helen. Both sides agree; Menelaus wins the fight and is about to kill Paris when the goddess Aphrodite, who protects Paris because he gave her the prize for beauty, rescues him and sends him to join Helen in Troy. Agamemnon tells the Trojans to give back Helen and all her possessions and also to pay an indemnity; it looks as if the two sides will make peace on those terms, but the gods, at the urging of Hera and Athena, prevent it. Athena persuades Pandarus to shoot an arrow at Menelaus during the truce. Menelaus receives only a light wound, but the truce is broken; the battle resumes. Zeus' promise is not fulfilled immediately; the Achaean hero Diomedes dominates the battle and the Trojans are hard pressed.

In book VI Hector goes to Troy to organize prayers to Athena; the poet gives us a glimpse of the rich, civilized city that the Achaeans will in the end destroy. Hector meets his mother, Hecuba; his brother Paris; and Helen, the cause of the war; he then sees, for the last time as it turns out, his wife, Andromache, and his infant son.

In books VII (not in the anthology) and VIII, the promise of Zeus is fulfilled. After an inconclusive duel between Hector and Ajax the Achaeans are driven back and the Trojans, who usually retire behind their city walls at night, camp out on the field, ready to deliver a decisive assault in the morning.

In book IX Agamemnon summons a council; they advise him to make amends to Achilles. He agrees and proposes not only to give a magnificent list of gifts but also to restore Briseis (whom he swears he has not touched) and to offer one of his daughters in marriage to Achilles after the war. This offer is made to Achilles by Odysseus, Ajax, and Phoenix, an old retainer of Achilles, but Achilles refuses outright. The insult to his honor is too great to be wiped out by gifts. He will go home, with all his men. Phoenix tries to persuade him, reminding him of the story of Meleager, who also withdrew from the fighting alliance in anger, was begged to return, and refused. When in the end he came back to the fighting, he had forfeited all of the gifts he would have been given if he had complied earlier. Achilles still refuses to fight, but he has been moved; he will stay at Troy. And the final appeal from Ajax moves him still more; he will not join the battle, he says, until Hector fights his way to the Greek ships and sets them on fire. Phoenix stays with Achilles; Odysseus and Ajax return to report the failure of their mission.

In book X (not in the anthology) Odysseus and Diomedes make a successful night raid on the Trojan lines, but this is the last Achaean success for some time. In books XII to XVII (not in the anthology, except for XVI), the tide of battle turns against the Achaeans. Paris wounds Diomedes with an arrow; Odysseus is wounded and withdraws; Machaon, the Achaean physician, is also wounded. Achilles, who is watching the fighting and rejoicing in the Achaean losses, sends his friend Patroclus to see if the wounded man he saw was indeed Machaon, and this, the poet says, "is the beginning of his evil." For Patroclus, moved to pity by the wounded men he sees in the Achaean camp and by Hector's assault on the wall the Achaeans have built to protect their ships, will appeal to Achilles on the Achaeans' behalf (books XIII–XIV). Achilles refuses to join the fighting himself but allows Patroclus, equipped with his own armor, to take the field. After driving the Trojans back, Patroclus is killed by Hector, who strips off the armor of Achilles and puts it on. After a desperate fight, the Achaeans recover the body of Patroclus and take it back to their camp (books XV–XVII).

When Achilles hears of the death of Patroclus, he resolves to avenge him by killing Hector, but he must wait until his goddess mother brings him new armor; it is forged by Hephaestus, the divine smith, and includes a marvelous picture shield. Achilles then (book XIX, not in the anthology) calls an assembly of the Achaeans, accepts Agamemnon's apology, and after mourning over the corpse of Patroclus, puts on the armor and goes into battle.

In the final battle (not in the anthology) even the gods take part, but Achilles drives all before him as he cuts the Trojan warriors down. He drives the Trojans inside the gates of the city but is distracted by the god Apollo, a protector of Troy who, taking the shape of a Trojan warrior, leads him on a futile chase. Hector, feeling responsible for the defeat of his people, stays outside the gate to face Achilles.

In book XXII the two great adversaries face each other at last. Hector is beaten but before he dies prophesies Achilles' imminent death. Achilles ties the corpse to his chariot and drags it out to his camp.

Book XXIII (not in the anthology) deals with the burial of Patroclus and the funeral games in his honor. Achilles distributes rich prizes to the winners of athletic events: chariot race, boxing, wrestling, foot race, armed combat, weight casting, and archery.

In the last book (XXIV) Priam, king of Troy and father of Hector, is led by a divine messenger, Hermes, to the tent of Achilles to offer a rich ransom for his son's body. Achilles has been told by Thetis that Zeus is angry with him for his desecration of Hector's corpse, and Achilles agrees to give it up. But he is not prepared to see Hector's father, king of Troy, a suppliant at his feet, and his pity for the old man puts an end to the inhuman fury that has ruled him since the death of Patroclus. He lets Priam take the body, gives him eleven days for the burial of Hector; on the twelfth day the war will be renewed. Hector's people lament for him and give him a magnificent funeral; the last line of the poem—"And so the Trojans buried Hector breaker of horses"—reminds us that the fighting will begin again at once and that Achilles, in his turn, will face the death he has inflicted on others.

Nothing is known about Homer's life or personality. It has even been thought that there was no one poet who composed the *Iliad,* that it was the creation of many generations of illiterate bards, the product of an epic tradition. That it comes out of some such background there can be no doubt; not only does it contain linguistic forms and refer to customs that predate the Greek adoption of literacy in the middle of the eighth century B.C., but it also shows in its repetition of epithets ("Achilleus of the swift feet"), phrases, lines, and even whole passages (compare I.13–16 and I.25–29 with I.439–41) the characteristic features of oral composition. The products of such a tradition are, however, usually much shorter than the *Iliad* and *Odyssey;* further, they rarely display the masterly construction and internal cross-reference that distinguish the Homeric poems.

Critical opinion now tends to assume a poet who was a master of the oral techniques and repertory but who exploited the new resource of the alphabet (adapted from a Phoenician script) for the construction of large-scale epics. This does not mean that overnight the *Iliad* and *Odyssey* became poems for reading; they were still performed by professional reciters, but the poem was no longer the creation, from memory and improvisation, of an individual bard; it was the dramatic recitation of a known and admired text. By the late sixth century B.C. public recitation of the poems was a highlight of the great festival of Athena at Athens, and the poems were also studied in schools. Scholars of the library at Alexandria in Egypt worked on the text in the third century B.C. and from that time on written copies for readers were the almost exclusive medium for Homer's survival to our own day.

Classroom Strategies

Suggested assignments:

1. Book I
2. Books VI,VIII, and IX
3. Books XVI and XVIII
4. Books XXII and XXIV

The longer assignments, 3 and 4, are possible because in the first two the student will have become familiar with the style and character of the work.

One thing that may puzzle the student is the organization (if it deserves that name) of the Achaean army. It should be explained first of all that the poem does not reflect any real historical situation; the oral tradition on which Homer draws is not concerned with historical fact but with stories of heroes who surpass ordinary human standards of courage and martial achievement. The Achaean army is an alliance of independent chieftains, each one in command of his own men, who have come together to help Menelaus recover his wife and punish the Trojans and also to share in the plunder that will result from the capture and destruction of Troy. Agamemnon's overarching authority is uneasy, open to challenge (as we see in book I), and based mainly on the fact that he is in control of the biggest contingent of armed men. On every important decision he consults his "council"—the chieftains of the separate bands; when he acts impulsively and without consultation, as in the quarrel with Achilles, he eventually comes to regret that action.

The political organization of the army is an imaginary, epic phenomenon, and the fighting is just as unrealistic. There are large numbers of nameless infantry who presumably fight with spear and shield, but we rarely hear about them; the poem concentrates on the duels of the chief heroes. These heroes have horse-drawn chariots, but they do not use them against the enemy infantry; they ride to the battlefield in them, then dismount to fight. This is not the way war chariots were in fact used, as we know from the art and historical literature of the ancient Egyptians and Babylonians; the epic poets had kept the memory of the chariots but forgotten how they were used. From the point of view of the epic bard, the chariots would in any case get in the way of his story, for time and time again he pits one hero against another not just in combat but in verbal exchanges of threats, insults, taunts, and boasts, which would not have been possible if they had been racing past each other in chariots.

This does not mean that Homer's picture of war is totally unrealistic; his descriptions of what happens when bronze weapons cut human flesh are all too accurate. But the realistic wounding and killing are set in a framework of single combat that allows the heroes to speak to each other before, during, and after the fighting and allows the poet to create dramatic tension out of these exchanges. See especially the speeches of Hector and Achilles, XXII.296–321 and XXII.390–432.

Topics for Discussion

1. Freedom and responsibility. To what extent are the decisions made by the heroes independent, individual decisions? Discuss, along these lines, Agamemnon's decision to take Briseis from Achilles.

   Agamemnon's decision is presented in book I as completely independent of divine persuasion or command (unlike Achilles' decision not to kill Agamemnon); his motives are anger (line 121), hatred for Achilles (lines 208ff.), a wish to assert his superiority (lines 219ff.). And when in book IX he regrets his action and wishes to be reconciled with Achilles, he blames his action as "madness" (line 138) and speaks of being "lost in my own inhuman rage" (line 143). It is noticeable, however, that he uses these words in a council from which Achilles is absent; the ambassadors to Achilles carry no apology from Agamemnon, only the offer of gifts. When finally, after the death of Patroclus, the two men meet, Agamemnon denies responsibility, claiming that his decision was not free. "But I am not to blame," he says (XIX.100); he blames his action on Zeus and Ruin, the daughter of Zeus, who took his wits away. In this case Homer shows us a man who evades responsibility for his free decision by blaming a god, but sometimes a god does affect human decision, as in book I when Achilles, after thinking over the alternatives, decides to kill Agamemnon (line 225) but is dissuaded by the goddess Athena.

2. Discuss the statement (from the period introduction, 4): "Morality is a human creation, and though the gods may approve of it, they are not bound by it."

   The fate of Troy depends on the will of the gods, and its final destruction is a product of a power struggle among them: Hera, Athena, and Poseidon are inexorably hostile to Troy, Apollo is its champion, and Zeus is swayed now by one side, now by the other. The fact that Troy is a civilized city besieged by soldiers bent on its destruction, the massacre of its men and the enslavement of its women and children, plays no part in the gods' decision, nor does the fact that, as Zeus says, Hector, the Trojan champion, worshiped Zeus with gifts and sacrifice ("the immortals loved Prince Hector," Zeus says, "best of all the mortals born in Troy," XXIV.81–82). Hera and Athena have no pity for Troy, even though the Trojans (in book VI) make offerings to Athena and pray for her help. They and their children will pay with their lives and freedom for the injury done to Athena's (and Hera's) pride when the Trojan prince Paris chose Aphrodite over them for the prize of beauty (XXIV.33ff.). However, in book XXIV, the gods (with the exception of Athena, Hera, and Poseidon) are appalled by Achilles' treatment of Hector's body and finally agree to order Achilles to give it up to his father, Priam.

Topics for Writing

1. Aristotle said that the man who is incapable of working in common, or who in his self-sufficiency has no need of others, is no part of the community, like a beast or a god. Discuss the figure of Achilles in the light of this statement.

2. In spite of the constraints imposed by the formulaic language of the oral tradition, Homer, according to one critic, "sees his people as individually distinct and makes us aware of their individuality." Discuss the ways in which Homer succeeds in presenting as differentiated individuals Hector, Nestor, Ajax, Odysseus, Agamemnon, Priam, and Phoenix.

3. Homer's preferred medium of poetic comparison is simile rather than metaphor, and his similes are "extended": the simile does more than establish a likeness between A and B; it goes on to describe B in great detail, some of the details not like A at all. Yet these details, the apparent development of B for its own sake, often do suggest points of comparison that lie below the surface, and often, too, they make significant comments on broader aspects of the situation in which they appear. Discuss the function of the extended simile in the following passages:

   XVIII.240–47   XXII.194–251
   XXII.31–38   XXIV.563–67
   XVIII.369–75

Further Reading

See also the suggestions in the anthology, pp. 102–03.

Chadwick, John. *The Mycenean World.* 1976. An up-to-date and critical survey of Mycenean civilization (including full discussion of the Linear B tablets and the light they throw on the period). Chadwick concludes that the Homeric poems preserve very little of the real facts of the Mycenean period.

Dodds, Eric R. *The Greeks and the Irrational.* 1951. Chapter 1, "Agamemnon's Apology," deals with the problem posed in the first topic under "Topics for Discussion."

Hogan, James C. *A Guide to the* Iliad. 1979. Based on the Fitzgerald translation. A volume similar to Willcock but based on a different translation: reference is more difficult but not impossible. It often explains passages Willcock passes over and also contains a valuable introduction.

Kirk, Geoffrey. *Homer and the Epic.* 1965. A masterly survey of the whole field of modern Homeric controversy distinguished by its firm grip on the historical background, the fairness of its critique of the various theories, and the reassuring moderation of its conclusions.

Lloyd-Jones, H. *The Justice of Zeus.* 1971. Chapter 1 makes a case for the Homeric gods as dealing justly with humankind. Relevant to the second topic under "Topics for Discussion."

Lord, A. B. *The Singer of Tales.* 1960. Lord explains the background and methods of composition of Yugoslav oral epic and compares the results of his researches to the Homeric text. This is the authoritative treatment of Homer as an oral poet.

Luce, J. V. *Homer and the Heroic Age.* 1975. A survey of all the archaeological and historical evidence for the Mycenean and Dark Age periods, evidence that may have some bearing on Homer; Luce is much less skeptical than Chadwick.

Owen, E. T. *The Story of the* Iliad. 1947. For ordinary readers, probably the most exciting account of the *Iliad* ever written. Brief but stirring.

Whitman, Cedric. *Homer and the Heroic Tradition.* 1965. Contains an excellent literary analysis of the *Iliad.*

Willcock, Malcolm M. *A Companion to the* Iliad. 1976. Based on the Lattimore translation. A detailed commentary that deals with difficulties in the text, explains mythological and historical details, and provides internal cross-references. An extremely useful volume for the teacher.

The Odyssey

Backgrounds

At a council of the gods on Olympus (book I), Athena pleads the case of Odysseus. It is now ten years since Troy was captured, but Odysseus, shipwrecked on his way home, is stranded on an island where the goddess Kalypso keeps him as her mate. The sea-god Poseidon—angry with Odysseus because the hero had blinded Poseidon's son, the Kyklops Polyphêmus—is absent from the council; Athena has her way, and Hermes, the messenger god, is sent to Kalypso with the order to release Odysseus. Athena goes to Odysseus' home in Ithaka to encourage his son, Telémakhos, whose household is occupied by the young and violent suitors of his mother, Penélopê; they are convinced Odysseus is dead and demand that she marry one of them. Athena, taking the shape of Mentês, king of a neighboring city, advises Telémakhos to visit old Nestor at Pylos and Menélaos at Sparta to see if they have any news of his father.

Encouraged by the goddess (book II), Telémakhos calls an assembly of the people of Ithaka and assails the suitors for their unlawful occupancy of his house; he announces that he is off to find news of his father. The suitors realize that this is no longer a timid boy but a resolute and dangerous man; when they find out that he has actually left, they decide to set an ambush for him at sea and kill him on his way back. At Pylos (book

III), Telémakhos meets old Nestor and hears from him how Agamémnon was killed by his own wife when he came home from Troy and how Menélaos, blown by adverse winds as far as Egypt, came home in the seventh year after Troy's fall. Accompanied by Nestor's son Peisístratos, Telémakhos goes to Sparta (book IV), where he is welcomed by Menélaos and Helen and told by Menélaos that, when last heard of, Odysseus was on the island of Kalypso, without ship or crew, longing to return home.

Meanwhile, the god Hermês arrives (book V) to bring Kalypso the command of Zeus. She accepts it with reluctance and when Hermês is gone makes one last attempt to keep Odysseus; she offers to make him immortal if he will stay with her. He refuses, and she helps him build a boat and sail off. The god Poseidon wrecks his boat, and Odysseus eventually crawls ashore naked and battered, on the island of Skhería, home of the Phaiákians. Here he meets the daughter of the king Alkínoös, Nausikaa (book VI), who has come down to the shore with her retinue of girls to wash clothes. She is charmed by him and sends him off to the palace, where he is hospitably entertained (book VII). The next day, at a banquet in the hall (book VIII), Odysseus, moved to tears by a minstrel's tales of Troy, is challenged to reveal his identity. He does so (book IX) as he tells the Phaiákans (and us) the whole story of his wanderings since he left Troy (books IX–XII).

Rounding the southern cape of Greece on his way to Ithaka he was blown out to sea, southwest presumably, but from this point on his itinerary leaves real geography behind. His first landfall is the country of the Lotus Eaters, from which he rescues those of his crew who have tasted the Lotus and lost their wish to return home. From the next trial, the land of the Kyklopês, he does not escape without casualties; four of his men are eaten by the one-eyed giant in his cave, and Odysseus would have been eaten, too, if he had not made the Kyklops drunk and then put out his one eye. After escaping from the cave, Odysseus, taunting the blind giant from shipboard as he prepares to leave, tells Polyphêmos his name, and the giant prays to his father, Poseidon, to make Odysseus' homecoming a hard one. On the next island (book X) he reaches Aiolos, King of the Winds, who gives him a bag containing all the winds except the one that will take him home. But, in sight of Ithaka, his crew, thinking the bag contains treasure, open it and the winds, let loose, blow the ship back to where it came from.

At his next landfall he loses all his ships but one to the Laistrygonians, giants and cannibals. He goes on to the island of Kirkê, who turns his advance party into swine, but dominated by Odysseus, she restores their human shape and entertains them all in royal style. They stay for a year but before they leave, Kirkê tells Odysseus that he must go to the land of the dead and consult the seer Teirêsias. There (book XI) he is warned by Teirêsias not to eat the cattle of the Sun when he lands on the island of Thrinakia; speaks to the shade of his dead mother, who tells him what is going on in his house at home; sees a procession of famous women; and then meets the ghosts of his companions at Troy—Agamémnon, Akhilleus, and Aîas.

Back on Kirkê's island (book XII), he bids farewell to her and passes the Seirênês, who lure men to their doom by their song; makes the passage between the monster Skylla and the whirlpool Kharybdis; and lands on the island of Thrinakia, where, in spite of his appeals, his men eat the sacred cattle of the Sun. Once again at sea, the ship is sunk in a storm, the crew lost; only Odysseus survives, to land at last on Kalypso's island.

The Phaiákians take Odysseus home to Ithaka (book XIII); Poseidon, with the consent of Zeus, punishes them for helping his enemy. Odysseus meets the goddess Athena, and they plan a stealthy approach to his house in disguise: if he goes home in his own person the suitors may kill him. She transforms him into an aged, ragged beggar, and he goes to his swineherd, Eumaios, for hospitality (book XIV). He tells his generous host a tall tale of wanderings in Egypt and the story of Odysseus at Troy. Meanwhile, Telémakhos returns from Sparta (book XV), avoiding the suitors' ambush. While Eumaios tells Odysseus how he was kidnapped as a child and sold to Odysseus' father as a slave, Telémakhos makes his way to the swineherd's hut. Without letting Eumaios know the truth, Odysseus reveals his identity to his son (book XVI); together they plot the overthrow of the suitors.

Odysseus and Telémakhos make their separate ways to the palace (book XVII). As Odysseus comes into the palace yard Argos, his dog, on the point of death from old age, recognizes his master. Odysseus goes begging bread from the suitors; Antínoös, the most violent of them, throws a stool at him. Odysseus is challenged by a real beggar, Iros (book XVIII), but beats him in a fight and wins the exclusive right to beg at the palace. Another prominent suitor, Eurýmakhos, insults Odysseus and throws a stool at him. Later that night (book XIX) Penélopê sends for Odysseus to see if the beggar has any news; he tells her of meeting Odysseus on the nearby mainland and assures her he will soon return. The old nurse Eurýkleia, told to wash his feet before he goes to bed, recognizes him by a scar on his leg, but he silences her.

Penélopê decides to announce for the next day an archery contest that will decide which of the suitors may claim her hand. The suitors feast and revel (book XX); one more of them, Ktésippous, throws something at Odysseus, a cow's hoof this time. They all start to laugh hysterically; the tension is mounting. The archery contest is set up (book XXI); the bow of Odysseus is brought out, but none of the suitors can string it. Telémakhos tells Eumaios to give it to Odysseus, who strings it and kills Antínoös (book XXII), Eurýmakhos, and then—with the help of Telémakhos, Eumaios, and some loyal servants—all the rest of the suitors. Only the poet-minstrel Phêmios is spared. When Penélopê is told the news she cannot believe it (book XXIII); she tests Odysseus' knowledge of a detail in their bedroom (the fact that the bed could not be moved since it was carved out of a standing olive tree) and accepts him as her husband.

But trouble is brewing in Ithaka. As Odysseus goes off to the country to see his father, Laërtês, and the ghosts of the suitors go to the land of the dead (book XXIV) to be interrogated by Agamémnon and others, the relatives of the suitors gather to attack Odysseus and his family. But their attack is thwarted by the goddess Athena, and the two sides make peace.

There was a theory in the ancient world that the *Odyssey* was a work of Homer's old age and that this accounts for the more mellow tone and the happy ending. Modern scholars have claimed that it must be later than the *Iliad* on other grounds: they discern a closer connection between human morality and divine judgment (in, for example, the speech of Zeus in I.45ff.) and assume that a higher morality must belong to a later age. Others have based the same later dating on the wanderings in books IX–XII, seeing in them a reflection of the early days of Greek colonization. Since, however, the geography of the wanderings suggests fairyland rather than the real western Mediterranean, this thesis, like the other, is controversial. There have been many attempts to identify the island of the Kyklopês and the land of the Lotus Eaters, but none of them has won general acceptance. The ancient critics were skeptical on this point: the great Greek geographer Eratosthenes of Alexandria (third–second centuries B.C.) said that you would be able to place the site of Odysseus' wanderings when you had found the cobbler who sewed up the leather bag containing the winds.

It is true, however, that the *Odyssey* takes for granted a knowledge of the *Iliad* on the part of the audience; it is remarkable that in all the tales told about Troy and the heroes of the war, by Odysseus, Menélaos, Nestor, Demódokos, and the ghost of Agamémnon, not one single episode is duplicated in the *Iliad*. Such a complete avoidance of the material treated in the *Iliad* suggests knowledge of it in something like its present form.

Classroom Strategies

The obvious assignments are I–IV (Telémakhos), V–VIII (Odysseus and the Phaiákians), IX–XII (the wanderings), XIII–XVI (at the hut of Eumaios), XVII–XX (the beggar in the palace), and XXI–XXIV (revenge and reunion). If you desire shorter assignments, take two books at a time.

If there is not time to read the whole poem, an Odyssean core (the wanderings) can be used: I, III–VI, VIII, IX–XII, XXI–XXIV. In this case, you will have to supply the bridge between VI and VIII, e.g., "Odysseus follows Nausikaa's instructions and is received as a guest in the palace by her mother, Arêtê, and her father, Alkinoös, who promises to help him return home."

Perhaps the main possibility of misunderstanding for today's students lies in the nature of the heroic ideal presented in the *Odyssey*. Odysseus is not an Achillean character (see the headnote, p. 100), but he is bound by a heroic ethic just the same. Lies and stratagems are his natural weapons, since most of the time he is pitted against superior force; he is a survivor, one who fights "to save his life" (I.9), but there are limits to what he will do to save it. On Kirkê's island, for example, he will not abandon his advance party, which has not returned, even though the rest of his crew urge him to leave. He fights not only "to save his life" but also "to bring his shipmates home" (I.9). In this he fails, but at least in the case of those who killed the cattle of the Sun, this is no fault of his.

In the famous contrast between Odysseus and Achilles in the lower world, many critics have seen a repudiation of the heroic ideal of the *Iliad*; Achilles would rather be alive and a slave to a peasant than a king over all the dead. Yet when told of the heroic achievements of his son Neoptólemos, he goes off "glorying" (XI.604), and in book XXIV the shade of Agamémnon contrasts the glory of Achilles' funeral with the ignominy of his own death and burial. As for Odysseus, in the last books of the poem, he exemplifies one heroic ideal in spectacular fashion. The hero avenges insults to his honor, and Odysseus' slaughter of the entire younger generation of the nobility of Ithaka is a heroic revenge on a grand scale.

Topics for Discussion

1. The heroic ideal in the *Iliad* and the *Odyssey.* See "Backgrounds."
2. Hospitality as a criterion of civilization in the *Odyssey.* Polyphêmus and Kalypso as opposite extremes—no hospitality at all and too much; the Phaiákians as ideal hosts; courtly hospitality at Pylos (Nestor) and Sparta (Menélaos and Helen); hospitality abused (the suitors), etc. Students should discuss the startling fact that the Phaiákians, the most civilized hosts in the epic, are punished for it by Poseidon and Zeus, who make sure they will not help travelers again. Does this conform to the picture of divine good intentions thwarted by human wickedness offered by Zeus in his speech in book I?
3. Telémakhos' growth to manhood. Analyze the stages of his assumption of responsibility and the recognition of the fact by others. His mother's reaction is surprise; Nestor and Menélaos recognize him as Odysseus' son (whereas Athena in book I professes not to); the suitors recognize his attainment of maturity by planning to kill him—*now* he is dangerous. He helps Odysseus kill the suitors; does he risk becoming his father's rival?

Topics for Writing

1. Two ancient Greek critics, Aristophanes of Byzantium and Aristarchus, thought that Homer ended his poem on the lines "So they came / into that bed so steadfast, loved of old, / opening glad arms to one another" (XXIII.298–300). In other words, they thought book XXIV unnecessary. What in fact does book XXIV contribute to the epic?

   [The ending at XXIII would have been a romantic ending: husband and wife reunited, nothing else matters. In fact there are still a great many problems to be solved, especially the consequences of Odysseus' slaughter of the suitors. Homer sees that Odysseus, who has established himself as master in his own house by violence, still has to be accepted by the community—the succession of his line

depends on the community's goodwill. The epic ends with a reconciliation, engineered by Athena, but before the threat of conflict is
removed, we are shown three generations of Odysseus' family—
father Laërtês, Odysseus, son Telémakhos—standing side by side,
ready for battle. Odysseus has been reintegrated in his family as he
shortly will be in the community of Ithaka.]

2. Woman's role in the *Odyssey*.

   [Faithful consort (Penêlopé, Arêtê) or temptation (Kirkê, Kalypso,
   the Seirênês, even Nausikaa). Helen has been one and is now the
   other. How "female" is Athena?]

3. Odysseus and Athena. Compare their relationship with that of Job
   and God. What does this suggest about the religious attitudes of the
   Hebrews and the Greeks?

   [For Odysseus-Athena, analyze carefully the long interview
   between them in XIII.267ff.]

4. From the moment he hears from Athena in XIII how things stand in
   his own home, Odysseus, in his disguise as a beggar, puts everyone
   to the test, to see if they are loyal to him or even whether they are
   decent human beings. List the incidents in which he puts people to
   the test and the results in each case.

   [Eumaios with the story of the cloak at Troy in XIV; the suitors by
   begging—Antínoös in XVII, Eurýmakhos in XVIII, etc.]

5. List and differentiate the different recognitions of Odysseus,
   intended and unintended.

   [Intended: Telémakhos in XVI; the suitors in XXII; Eumaios and
   Philoétios in XXI; Penélopê in XXIII; Laërtês in XXIV. Unintended:
   Argos in XVII; Eurýkleia in XIX.]

6. Penélopê and Telémakhos: a complicated relationship between
   mother and son. Analyze the process of Telémakhos' assertion of
   independent manhood and Penélopê's reluctant acceptance of it.

   [Telémakhos' first action after Athena encourages him is to contradict his mother (I.386–96); she "gazed in wonder and withdrew"
   (line 397). Telémakhos forbids Eurýkleia to tell his mother he is
   going to Sparta (II.391–95). Penélopê is distressed when she hears
   he has gone: "Why has my child left me?" (IV.740–43, 852–58).
   Athena inspires Telémakhos with suspicions about Penélopê's
   intentions—or does he have them anyway (XV.14ff.)? Telémakhos is
   afraid she has already married one of the suitors (XVI.38–40). Their
   meeting after his return (XVII.43ff.). She reproaches him
   (XVIII.242ff.). Penélopê on Telémakhos (XIX.567–71); Telémakhos
   on Penélopê (XX.137–40). Telémakhos sends her out of the hall
   (XXI.359–70). Telémakhos berates her for not recognizing Odysseus
   at once (XXIII.97–104).]

Comparative Perspectives

1. Hospitality is one of the chief virtues of ancient and heroic cultures. Consider why this should be so, paying attention to the expe-

rience of Odysseus in his travels. How would you compare the nature and extent of the hospitality displayed in other narratives, including the *Aeneid*, which is consciously modeled on Homer's poems, and those which are not, such as *Beowulf* and *Sir Gawain and the Green Knight*.

2. Compare the reasons why Odysseus visits the Underworld and what he experiences there with, as appropriate, Gilgamesh's visit to Utnapishtim, Aeneas's in book VI of the *Aeneid*, and Dante's in *The Divine Comedy*.

Further Reading

See also the reading suggestions in the anthology, pp. 102–03.

Finley, M. I. *The World of Odysseus*, rev. edition. 1978. A historical-anthropological approach to Homeric "society" (in fact, to the "society" of the *Odyssey*) based on a study of the function of the gift in primitive societies. Stimulating, like everything Finley writes, and extremely good background for a discussion of the "economic" aspect of Homeric hospitality.

Kirk, Geoffrey. *Homer and the Epic*. 1965. A masterly survey of the whole field of modern Homeric controversy, distinguished by its firm grip on the historical background, the fairness of its critique of the various theories, and the reassuring moderation of its conclusions.

Lord, A. B. *The Singer of Tales*. 1960. Lord explains the background and methods of composition of Yugoslav oral epic and compares the results of his researches to Homeric text. This is the authoritative treatment of Homer as an oral poet.

Stanford, W. B. *The Ulysses Theme*. 1968. A rich and suggestive examination of the figure of Odysseus from Homer to James Joyce. Chapters II–V deal with Homer's hero. (Chapter V, "The Untypical Hero," is reprinted in Steiner and Fagles.)

Steiner, George, and Robert Fagles, eds. *Homer: A Collection of Critical Essays*. 1962. George E. Dimock's "The Name of Odysseus" is a brilliant discussion of the hero's identity, contained in a name he is proud to proclaim but must time after time conceal, a name that announces his nature and destiny. This volume also contains Erich Auerbach's famous but controversial essay on the scar of Odysseus (book XIX), which explores fundamental contrasts between Homeric and Old Testament biblical narrative, and W. B. Stanford's essay "The Untypical Hero," on the character of Odysseus.

Whitman, Cedric. *Homer and the Heroic Tradition*. 1965. Contains the chapter "The *Odyssey* and Change," which deals sensitively with differences of tone and feeling between the two epic poems.

Sappho of Lesbos

Backgrounds

In some ancient texts Sappho is referred to as a teacher, and the girls whose names recur so often in her poems are said to be her pupils; a papyrus fragment published in 1974 (it was written in the late second century A.D.) speaks of her as "teaching in peace and quiet the noble girls not only from the local families but also from families in Ionia." A fragment of one of her poems, addressed, we are told by the writer who quotes it, to an "uneducated woman," begins with the words "But when you die, you will lie there in the grave and no one will remember you afterwards or long for you." The context of her poetry may have been a more or less formal circle of aristocratic girls whose same-sex bonding and instruction in music and dance prepared them for marriage.

Many of Sappho's poems were *epithalamia,* marriage songs, composed presumably for her favorite pupils; others were heartbroken laments for the loss of a loved companion. " 'Honest, I want to die,' " runs one fragment. "That's what she said to me, when in tears she was leaving me. 'Oh, what we have suffered, Sappho. It's not by my choice that I'm leaving you.' And I answered her: 'Go and fare well and remember me. For you know how we cared for you.' " And the second poem included in the anthology expresses a passionate reaction to the imagined sight of a beloved girl in conversation with a man. But Sappho's poetry is not always so tensely passionate; she can also treat the pangs of unrequited love with an ironic wit. The first poem in the anthology, for example, Sappho's invocation of the love goddess Aphrodite, starts out as a conventional appeal to a deity to come to the suppliant's help. It employs the usual formulas—"you came before, now come again"—but then it departs sharply from the established pattern. Instead of dealing with the present occasion, Sappho's need for help, it gives a vivid account of the goddess's previous visit. And we are told what Sappho's "griefs and bitternesses" are all about: she has been crossed in love, someone is rejecting her suit. On that previous occasion Aphrodite was gracious and promised her aid; Sappho now asks for the same promise: "accomplish all those things my heart desires to be done; appear and stand at my shoulder." The Greek for the final phrase means literally: "be my ally in battle."

The poem is a brilliant example of self-mocking wit. The whole religious terminology of a hymn, the appeal to a god, including the epiphany of the goddess concerned, is put in motion so that Sappho can win the heart of a recalcitrant girl, and furthermore, the poem shows us that this is not the first time Sappho has brought the goddess down from Olympus.

This ironic tone is, however, an exception; elsewhere Sappho is well aware of the awesome and terrifying powers of the goddess. "Once again," runs a fragment, "limb-loosening love makes me shiver, that bittersweet irresistible creature," and another speaks of love that shakes the heart "like the mountain wind when it falls on the oak trees."

Comparative Perspectives

1. Compare Sappho's rhetorical strategies to those of Catullus and Petrarch. How does she view the competition for a loved one? Is hers a sentimental poetry? What moments in erotic relationships does she focus on in these few poems?
2. Sappho's poems show an exquisite awareness of the body. Compare her appreciation for somatic textures with similar details in other love poetry.

Further Reading

See also the reading suggestions in the anthology, p. 515.

Greek Lyric, Vol. 1 (Loeb Classical Library). 1982. Contains the complete text of what remains of Sappho's work, with an English translation by David A. Cambell.

AESCHYLUS

The Oresteia

Backgrounds

The scene of the first two plays in the trilogy is the entrance to the palace of Agamemnon at Argos; the time is the tenth year of the Trojan War. A watchman on the palace roof sees the fire signal that announces the fall of Troy. A chorus of old men comes into the orchestra (the circular dancing floor in front of the stage area) and sings. They remember the departure of the army ten years before; adverse winds delayed the sailing, and at the command of the goddess Artemis, Agamemnon sacrificed his daughter Iphigenia to release the fleet. Clytaemnestra enters and tells the chorus the news—Troy has fallen. She describes the chain of signal fires across the sea from Troy and speculates about what is happening in that city now.

After her exit the chorus sings; the song begins as a hymn of victory for the Greek success but ends on a note of fear and foreboding. Enter a herald who has come to announce Agamemnon's arrival; he speaks of the suffering of the Greeks at Troy and also reveals that Agamemnon will come alone—Menelaus was blown off course and no one knows where he is. Another choral song begins with a meditation on the name and destiny of Helen but ends with a fearful vision of the recurrence of violence in one generation after another, as Agamemnon enters in a chariot. With him is a female figure who is not identified until later, but the audience knows, from Homer, that it is the Trojan princess Cassandra. Agamemnon, boasting exultantly of the destruction of Troy, is welcomed by Clytaemnestra in a speech full of menacing ambiguity. She invites him to walk into the palace on blood-red tapestries; at first reluctant, he eventually does so, after recommending Cassandra to her care. The choral song now is full of vague apprehension; they sense that something is wrong. Clytaemnestra comes on stage again to order Cassandra inside but meets only silence and departs.

Now Cassandra speaks. In a long exchange with the chorus she prophesies, at first in riddling images and finally in clear statement, all that is
to come—her own death, the murder of Agamemnon, and even the death
of Clytaemnestra at the hands of her son. She has been given the gift of
prophecy by the god Apollo, who loves her. But when she refused him her
love he added the proviso that though she could tell the future no one
would believe her—as the chorus refuses to believe her now.

She goes off to her death, and almost at once the chorus hears
Agamemnon's death cries from inside the palace. As they discuss what
action to take, the doors open and the bodies of Agamemnon and Cassandra are brought out; over them, Clytaemnestra makes a triumphant
speech of self-justification. But as the chorus, recovering from its initial
shock, rejects her defense and prophesies retribution, she retreats from
the high confidence of her opening speech and appeals to the "savage
ancient spirit of revenge" (line 1534) that plagues the house of Atreus to
let it end here, shed no more blood. At this point, its very embodiment,
Aegisthus, enters, with an armed bodyguard, and threatens the chorus.
Clytaemnestra prevents their coming to blows with her plea—"No bloodshed now" (line 1694)—and ends the play with her hope to "set the
house in order once for all" (line 1713).

[The second play, *The Libation Bearers*, is not included in the anthology but is fully summarized there. It treats the story of the next generation of the House of Atreus. Orestes, the son of Agamemnon and
Clytaemnestra, now a grown man, returns from exile and avenges his
father by killing his mother and her lover. That is, Orestes commits matricide at Apollo's command. Visually, the play links his deed with
Clytaemnestra's. At the climax, the house doors open, and Orestes
appears with the corpses of his two victims, as his mother did before him.
But the problems have, if anything, deepened. Orestes now loses control
of his emotions and his words; he is, he says, a charioteer with his horses
out of control. He starts to leave, bound for Delphi and Apollo's protection, but sees suddenly the Furies, the spirits of vengeance, "the
hounds / of mother's hate" (lines 1054–55). Only Orestes can see them
now, but in the final play we see them, too; they are its chorus.]

The scene changes for the opening of *The Eumenides*: it is the temple
of Apollo at Delphi. His priestess goes in to officiate but comes out terrified; she has seen, at Apollo's altar, a suppliant, Orestes, and the Furies
sitting round him waiting. The audience now sees the scene she
described: Apollo enters and sends Orestes off to Athens, where he will
find "judges of [his] case" (line 84). The ghost of Clytaemnestra (or is she
a dream in the Furies' heads?) spurs the chorus to action, and they
exchange taunts and threats with Apollo before rushing off in pursuit of
Orestes.

The scene is now Athens, where Orestes comes to clasp the statue of
the goddess Athena; the chorus follows, and after singing a song designed
to "bind" and paralyze him, they move on to take their prey just as Athena
arrives. After hearing both sides she determines to summon judges and
set up a court; she has shown such fairness that the Furies accept this

decision. They sing of their ancient duties, the punishment of criminals who would otherwise escape; they are confident they will win their case.

As the trial begins, Apollo arrives to speak for Orestes. Under the skillful questioning of the Furies, Orestes breaks down and has to turn to Apollo for help. Apollo proclaims the priority of the father over the mother: Orestes' duty to avenge his father outweighed his link to his mother. Athena addresses the jury, stressing the importance of this "first trial of bloodshed" (line 696), and repeats a theme of the Furies: that without fear there can be no order. She herself will vote for Orestes, since as a goddess born directly from her father, Zeus, without the intermediary of a mother, she favors the male.

The votes are evenly divided, and this, under Athenian law, means acquittal; Orestes goes free, but the Furies now threaten to turn their rage against Athens itself. Athena finally wins them over by an offer of a home and worship in her city, and the Furies, who have been outcasts even from the gods because of their function as executors of blood vengeance, accept her offer and become kindly protectors of the institutions and lands of Athens.

Aeschylus (524?–456 B.C.) belonged to the generation that saw the establishment of democracy at Athens (in the last decades of the sixth century B.C.) and the heroic defense of that democracy against a Persian expeditionary force at Marathon in 490 B.C. as well as the decisive Athenian contribution to the defeat of a full-scale Persian invasion on the sea at Salamis in 480 B.C. and on land at Plataea in 479 B.C. Aeschylus fought as an infantry soldier at Marathon and, probably, in the naval battle at Salamis: on his tomb at Gela in Sicily, where he died, a verse inscription commemorated his combat service at Marathon and did not even mention his plays. Yet his plays so impressed the Athenian public that they were revived after his death, to compete with the offerings of his successors at the Dionysiac festival—an honor accorded to no other dramatist in the fifth century. In *The Frogs*, a comedy produced in the last decade of the fifth century, Aristophanes staged a contest in the lower world between the ghosts of Aeschylus and Euripides, old-fashioned patriotic virtue versus newfangled intellectual fashions, and of course, Aeschylus was the winner.

How closely this nostalgic vision of Aeschylus the Marathon veteran as an arch-conservative corresponded to the reality we have no means of judging, but he was certainly an innovator in the world of theater. Aristotle, in the *Poetics* (in a portion that is not included in the anthology), says that he was the first to increase the number of the actors from one to two, a move that "reduced the role of the chorus, giving first place to the dialogue." It also made possible dramatic confrontation instead of the predominantly narrative mode that must have been characteristic of performance with a single actor. Aeschylus was far from conservative, too, in his treatment of myth and especially in his manipulation of mythical material to give it contemporary resonance; in this field he had no equal.

The Eumenides, for example, put the court of the Areopagus on stage shortly after its status had been the key issue of a political struggle that threatened to lead to civil war. The Areopagus, its ranks filled by ex-magistrates, had become in the years after the Persian War a powerful political force, a sort of senate of elder statesmen that was an obstacle to reformists who wished to make Athenian democracy more radical and egalitarian. Just a few years before Aeschylus' play was produced, the reformers, led by Pericles and Ephialtes, had taken away all the court's powers except its legal right to try cases of homicide; feeling ran so high on both sides that Ephialtes was murdered. Hence when Aeschylus dramatized the foundation of the Areopagus by Athena he was treading on dangerous ground.

Modern critics are divided in their assessment of his position: was he acquiescing in the reform by emphasizing the solemn antiquity of the court's judicial function or was his reminder of the divine origin of the Areopagus a protest against the reforms? The fact that there is no agreement on this point suggests that in fact he did not take a position one way or another: the point he emphasized, in the song of the Furies and the speech of Athena (lines 526ff., cf. lines 711ff.) was moderation, the avoidance of extremes—"Neither the life of anarchy / nor the life enslaved by tyrants, no, / worship neither. / Strike the balance" (lines 538–41)—and the civil war that extreme measures are likely to lead to. "Brutal strife," the Furies sing, "the civil war devouring men, I pray / that it never rages through our city" (lines 991–93).

In *Agamemnon*, Aeschylus was dramatizing a story known to the audience from Homer (cf. *Odyssey* I.42ff., III.248ff., IV.543ff., XI.425ff.), but the climactic action of *The Libation Bearers*, Orestes' murder of his mother, is not explicitly mentioned there. The action of the last play, *The Eumenides*, has no Homeric model at all; in fact, it has been thought that Aeschylus may have invented the story of the trial of Orestes at Athens. Cassandra is mentioned in Homer (she is the first to see Priam coming back to Troy with Hector's corpse [*Iliad* XXIV.819ff.] and is killed with Agamemnon by Clytaemnestra [*Odyssey* XI.463ff.]), but in neither passage is there any hint of her prophetic powers. Aeschylus' adaptation of the standard version is very bold; the Attic dramatists, who worked almost exclusively with traditional tales, were allowed, perhaps even expected, to present the familiar figures and situation in a new light. Both Sophocles and Euripides, for example, wrote plays called *Electra* that present the same action as *The Libation Bearers*, but though in both of them Clytaemnestra and Aegisthus are killed by Orestes, everything else is changed. Both dramatists, in contrast to Aeschylus, make Electra the central figure of the play, on stage throughout; but in Sophocles she is a heroic figure, while Euripides gives her a near-criminal mentality and has her collapse in bitter remorse after the murders. The fact that the poets used familiar stories did not rule out innovation and the element of suspense. The fact that the dramatists had to work with three actors was also not as much of a limitation on creativity as might appear. A change of mask and costume enabled an actor to reenter as a different character. *Agamemnon*, for example, has six speaking parts (Watchman,

Clytaemnestra, Herald, Agamemnon, Cassandra, and Aegisthus) and *The
Eumenides* five (Pythia, Apollo, Orestes, the Ghost of Clytaemnestra,
and Athena). In addition the leader of the chorus could play an important
speaking part, as he does in the trial scene of *The Eumenides.*

But the main function of the chorus is not the spoken word; it dances
and sings. The word itself in Greek suggests dancing above all (our word
choreography preserves this emphasis), and the long choral sections of
the texts must be imagined as delivered by fifteen dancers whose movements emphasized their words. This movement, however, could not have
been as athletic or complex as that of the modern ballet, for the chorus
also sang, in unison, and their words, unlike those of modern opera, had
to be intelligible to the audience, for they are vital to the significance of
the dramatic action. Unlike the actors, who by the time the *Oresteia* was
produced were professionals, the chorus consisted of citizen volunteers,
trained in their part, like the actors, by the playwright himself. The chorus is, as it were, the onstage representative of the citizen audience; it
observes and comments on the action and motives of the actors, reacts to
their announcements and commands, opposes or supports them, and
above all—and this is especially true of the chorus in *Agamemnon*—tries
to understand, to interpret. It is rare to find a chorus that, like that of
The Eumenides, assumes a decisive role in the action; this may have been
a characteristic of Aeschylean drama, for we find it also in his *Suppliants.*

Classroom Strategies

Two assignments.

For the modern student, perhaps the most disconcerting feature of the
trilogy is the trial scene in *The Eumenides,* particularly the argument put
forward by Apollo and approved by Athena, that "the woman you call the
mother of the child / is not the parent, just a nurse to the seed" (lines
668–69). This claim that the mother's role in the procreation of children
is purely passive, that she is a mere incubator for the male seed, is the
basis for Apollo's case that murder of a father is a more heinous crime
than matricide.

This strange biology is not peculiar to Aeschylus; it appears also in the
works of the philosopher Aristotle, who wrote a good hundred years after
the death of Aeschylus. It is a theory that reflects the masculine bias of
Athenian thought and feeling. The Greek city-state, and especially
Athens, excluded women from political action and even in private life
severely restricted their activities; they had no legal standing and were
kept, in respectable families, out of sight in a special section of the house
reserved for women and children. This male domination stemmed in part
from the fact that most city-states, and especially Athens, were at war
with their neighbors more often than they were at peace; treaties were
always made with a time limit, and even so, it was rare for the truce to
last the full term fixed in the treaty. War, which in the ancient world
meant close combat in which physical strength was a crucial factor, was
the exclusive business of men (cf. Hector's speech to Andromache in the

Iliad: "Go therefore back to our house, and take up your own work, / the loom and the distaff, and see to it that your handmaidens / ply their work also; but the men must see to the fighting," VI. 490-92.) As combatants who were often called on to risk their lives to save the city from destruction and its women and children from enslavement, men assumed the prerogatives of a ruling caste and developed an ideology of male supremacy to justify their dominance. (When Medea, in Euripides' play, makes her famous protest against a woman's subordinate position, she cites this military basis for male supremacy only to reject it.)

The goddess Athena explains her support for Apollo's position in mythological terms: she was born directly from the head of Zeus and had no mother. But it is understandable also in terms of contemporary realities. The goddess Athena, guardian and protector of Odysseus in the *Odyssey,* has another side to her nature: in the *Iliad* she is a relentless opponent of the Trojans, a warrior-goddess intent on the destruction of Troy and all its inhabitants. In Athens, the city that bore her name and worshiped her in the Parthenon on the Acropolis, she was thought of as the protector of Athens in war; her images in sculpture and painted on vases show her armed with a spear, shield, and helmet, sometimes actually in combat in the war with the Olympian gods against the Giants. "I honor the male," she says (line 754), as she casts her vote for Orestes, and later, when she urges the Furies to accept her offer of a home in Athens, she predicts a great future for her city: "As time flows on, the honors flow through all / my citizens" (lines 864–65). The source of such honor is made clear later in her speech: "Let our wars / rage on abroad, with all their force, to satisfy / our powerful lust for fame" (lines 874–76).

Topics for Discussion

1. The theme of conflict between the sexes dominates the trial scene of *The Eumenides,* but it is operative, sometimes openly, sometimes subtly, in *Agamemnon* as well. Trace its appearance and discuss its significance in both plays.

    [In the opening scene of *Agamemnon,* the Watchman calls Clytaemnestra "that woman" who "maneuvers like a man" (line 13), and later, when she persuades Agamemnon to walk on the crimson tapestries, we are shown how she works on his pride to bend him to her will. "Spoken like a man" (line 355), says the Leader of the Chorus to Clytaemnestra as she rounds off her vision of Troy's destruction with an ironic prayer for Agamemnon's safe return. Her lover, Aegisthus, plays the woman's part: "Coward," says the Leader of the Chorus, "why not kill the man yourself? Why did the woman . . . have to bring him down?" (lines 1680–82). Apollo, the male god par excellence, champions the father's rights against the Furies, female deities, champions of the cause of Clytaemnestra.]

2. The question (which will recur in the discussion of *Oedipus the King*) of the independence of the characters: how far are their

actions directed by the gods or by that Fate that seems even more powerful than the gods, until, at the end of the *The Eumenides*: "All-seeing Zeus and Fate embrace" (line 1062)?

[The main question here is Agamemnon's responsibility for the sacrifice of Iphigenia. The goddess Artemis demands it as the price for the release of the fleet from adverse winds. But, as in so many Greek stories of divine interference, Agamemnon is given a choice—he could abandon the expedition (indeed he mentions this possibility only to disregard it in *Agamemnon*, lines 213–16). Aeschylus, in a paradoxical phrase, characterizes Agamemnon's decision to sacrifice his daughter as a free acceptance of destiny: "He slipped his neck into the strap of Fate" (line 217). Once he took this step, however, his heart hardened, "he stopped at nothing, / seized with the frenzy" (lines 219–20) and gave the orders to gag his daughter and hold her ready for the knife in cold unfeeling words. Orestes too acts under orders from the oracle of Apollo and the threat, if he disobeys, of dreadful disease and a miserable death (in *The Libation Bearers*). But he goes on to reveal that he has his own motives for action that would urge him to kill his mother even without the gods' command. There is not only "mounting sorrow for father" but—a revealing detail—"the lack of patrimony presses hard" (*The Libation Bearers*, lines 306–7). His only route to the repossession of his father's kingdom and wealth lies through his mother's death.]

3. Many of the images of the *Oresteia* recur throughout the trilogy, gaining fresh significance with each new appearance (for an example see the discussion of the "net" imagery in the headnote, p. 520). Trace through *Agamemnon* and *The Eumenides* the pattern of images connected with (a) lions or (b) dogs.

[*Lions*. The lion is the heraldic device of the house of Atreus, as the lion gate at Mycenae reminds us. The choral parable of the lion cub that, brought up as a pet, turns savage when full grown (*Agamemnon*, lines 713–32), prepared for by the choral reference to Artemis as "so kind / to the ravening lion's tender, helpless cubs" (*Agamemnon*, lines 140–41) is the nexus of a widespread pattern of references to lions. This cautionary tale is offered by the Chorus as a comparison with Helen and the destruction she will bring to the Trojans who welcomed her. But in *Agamemnon*, the lion is used to characterize other figures as well: Agamemnon, who boasts of the slaughter at Troy as the work of "the beast of Argos . . . our bloody lion lapped its fill, / gorging on the blood of kings" (lines 810–14); Clytaemnestra appears in Cassandra's vision as "the lioness" who "rears on her hind legs" and "beds with the wolf / when her lion king goes ranging" (lines 1276–78); even Aegisthus is "a lion who lacks a lion's heart" (line 1236). They all began as "a captivating pet . . . like an infant just born" (lines 717–20) and ended as "a priest of ruin" (line 731). But the real lion cub is Orestes. In *The Eumenides*, when Apollo orders the Furies out of his temple he tells them where they should be: "your kind / should infest a lion's cavern reeking blood" (lines 192–93). To which they might have replied that the House of Atreus, whose last male descendant they are in pursuit of, is just such a lion's den.

Dogs. The Watchman on the roof in the opening scene of the *Agamemnon* keeps his vigil "propped on my arms . . . like a dog" (lines 3–4). He is a faithful dog, loyal to Agamemnon; we remember him when Clytaemnestra falsely claims that she is a "watchdog gentle to him alone, savage / to those who cross his path" (lines 604–5) and salutes the king as "watchdog of the fold" (line 887) as she plans his death. When Cassandra sings of the crimes committed in the House of Atreus the chorus recognizes her as "a keen hound . . . trailing murder" (lines 1094–95); but when she foresees the king's death at the hands of "that detestable hellhound / who pricks her ears and fawns" (lines 1241–42), the Chorus cannot connect her word with Clytaemnestra. And Aegisthus, when the Chorus defies him in the final scene of *Agamemnon,* calls them "insubordinate dogs" (line 1702): "We'll see if the world comes dancing to your song, / your absurd barking—snarl your breath away! / I'll make you dance, I'll bring you all to heel" (lines 1667–69). And in *The Eumenides,* when we see the Furies they are hounds, trackers of the scent of blood. Like hounds, they bay in their sleep (line 133) and like hounds they follow the prey: "blood of the mother draws me on—must hunt / the man for Justice. Now I'm on his trail!" (lines 229–30). This is their exit line in the scene set at Delphi; their entrance speech, delivered by the leader of the chorus when they reenter now at Athens, uses similar language: "At last! / The clear trail of the man. . . . / He's wounded— / go for the fawn, my hounds, the splash of blood, / hunt him" (lines 243–47).]

Topic for Writing

Zeus, so the Chorus sings, "lays it down as law / that we must suffer, suffer into truth" (*Agamemnon,* lines 178–79). Trace the steps by which the Chorus of *Agamemnon* comes through suffering and a series of misapprehensions to a true vision of the situation.

[At the beginning of the play it believes that the war against Troy was just (lines 66ff.); the kings are sent by Zeus. Yet it is clearly disturbed by Agamemnon's sacrifice of his daughter (lines 210ff.). The Leader reacts with joy to the news of Troy's fall (lines 269–70), which will of course mean Agamemnon's return. In its second choral ode it begins a victory hymn to celebrate the Greek triumph, but as it describes the process by which men are led to tread "the grand altar of Justice / down" (lines 385ff.)—though it claims it is singing about the Trojan Paris—its words are reminiscent of its description of Agamemnon's change of mind that enabled him to kill his daughter. The Chorus returns to the theme of the righteous war with an indictment of Helen (lines 403ff.) and expressions of sympathy for the grief of Menelaus (lines 411ff.) but soon turns to the grief of mothers and fathers who have lost their sons at Troy, "all for another's woman" (line 444). The image of the war god as a broker who exchanges living men for funeral ashes is in flagrant contradiction with the opening of the ode. The Chorus goes on to speak of the "people's voice" that is "heavy with hatred" (line 451), and the victory ode ends with a wish to be neither victor nor vanquished. But the sight of the herald who brings news from Troy raises its hopes again; it returns to the illusion that Agamemnon's return will put an end to its doubts and fears. The herald's tale of victory renews its confidence, and the Chorus sings of Helen and the destruction she wrought on the Trojans who greeted her arrival with such joy (lines 683ff.). And when Agamemnon enters, it greets him with enthusiasm. The Chorus tells him it was against the war at first, "But now from the depths of trust and love / I say Well fought, well won" (lines 789–90). But when its king, whose sacrifice of his daughter it has almost forgotten in its joy at his return, goes into the palace treading the blood-red tapestries like some proverbial man of pride destined for a fall, it sings in fear of some unknown terror; it senses that something is badly wrong. Cassandra tells the Chorus, first in riddling and then in plain terms, what it fears but dares not face: that Agamemnon must die, that according to that standard of Justice it has often invoked itself (lines 374ff., 751ff.) Agamemnon must pay for the blood of Iphigenia and perhaps for the blood of all those who fell at Troy (lines 455ff.). Cassandra tells it the truth in plain terms, but it cannot accept it; only as she goes into the palace to her death does it dare ask the question: "now if he must pay for the blood / his fathers shed, and die for the deaths / he brought to pass" (lines 1367–69). The answer comes at once; it is Agamemnon's cry of agony from inside the palace. Confronted with the corpse of the king and the defiant boasts of Clytaemnestra, the Chorus tries to lay the blame on Helen (lines 1485ff.), a patent evasion that Clytaemnestra bluntly rejects (lines 1495ff.); it then casts the blame on the spirit of vengeance that plagues the House of Atreus from generation to generation, a view that Clytaemnestra accepts, for she sees it as absolving her of responsibility. To this the Chorus reacts violently, but reminded of the murder of Iphigenia, it loses its bearing: "The mind reels—where to turn?" (line 1563). In the end it recognizes, at last, Agamemnon's guilt: "None can judge between them. Justice. / The plunderer plundered, the killer pays the price. . . . The one who acts must suffer" (lines 1593–96). It has learned, through suffering, to see the truth. But by that same law Clytaemnestra too must pay, and stung to fury by the sight of Aegisthus lording it in the house of Agamemnon, the Chorus calls on Orestes as its only hope for justice; it now understands, too late as always, the full meaning of Cassandra's vision of the future.]

Comparative Perspective

Most of the world's great dramatic traditions have their roots in religious rituals, yet not all of the world's great religions have nurtured drama. What role do the Greek gods play in the *Oresteia*? Compare the

way God in the Old Testament of the Bible and Allah in the Koran inter-
act with human beings and try to explain why neither Judaism nor Islam
gave rise to a classical theater.

Further Reading

See also the reading suggestions in the anthology, p. 521.

Aeschylus. *The Oresteia*. Trans. Robert Fagles. 1984. Contains a long and
stimulating introductory essay by Robert Fagles and W. B. Stanford, as
well as helpful explanatory notes on selected passages.

Kitto, H. D. F. *Form and Meaning in Drama*. 1956. In the first three
chapters, Kitto discusses the trilogy in an attempt to answer a series of
questions, for example: "Why in the *Libation Bearers* and the
Eumenides are Agamemnon's sins entirely forgotten even by his adversaries? Why does Aeschylus so arrange *Agamemnon* that the event earliest in time, namely Atreus' feud with Thyestes, comes at the end of
the play?" Kitto tackles these and many other puzzling aspects of the
trilogy with probing analysis; his answers may not persuade everyone,
but his great merit is to have recognized and explored the problems.

Knox, Bernard. *Word and Action: Essays on the Ancient Theater*. 1979. Contains the essay "Aeschylus and the Third Actor," which deals in some
detail with the Cassandra scene and also with the way the chorus comes
to understand and face, too late, the truth (see "Topic for Writing").

McCall, Marsh Jr., ed. *Aeschylus: A Collection of Critical Essays*. 1972.
Includes an important article on freedom and its limitations by N. G. L.
Hammond (see "Topics for Discussion") and a brilliant essay on sym-
bolism in the *Oresteia* by R. F. Goheen. There is also an interesting
survey of "tradition and method" in translating Aeschylus by Peter
Green.

Taplin, Oliver. *Greek Tragedy in Action*. 1978. A book on the ancient
staging of Greek tragedy by a scholar who has become perhaps the
foremost expert in this field. The book proceeds by subject rather than
play by play, but discussion of passages in the trilogy can quickly be
located from the index.

Winnington-Ingram, R. P. *Studies in Aeschylus*. 1983. Contains interpretive essays by a recognized authority on Greek drama: "Agamemnon
and the Trojan War," "Clytaemnestra and the Vote of Athena," "Orestes
and Apollo," and "Zeus and the Erinyes."

SOPHOCLES

Oedipus the King

Backgrounds

The city of Thebes is ravaged by a plague, and in the opening scene of
the play a delegation of its citizens comes to urge Oedipus, king of

Thebes, to find some remedy. They have confidence that he somehow can help them, for he has been their efficient and benevolent ruler ever since, many years ago, he came to Thebes and rescued the city from the Sphinx, a creature with a bird's body and a human female head, which preyed on the city's young men. Those who encountered it and failed to answer its riddle were killed. Oedipus volunteered to face the Sphinx and answer the riddle correctly; the Sphinx died, and Oedipus was given the reward proclaimed for the deliverer from the monster—the throne of Thebes and the hand in marriage of its recently widowed Queen Jocasta.

Her husband, Laius, had been killed on the way to Delphi in a quarrel over precedence at a junction of narrow roads; his killer was the young Oedipus, who does not realize that the man he killed in the fight was the former king of Thebes. Nor does he realize that Laius was his father and Jocasta is his mother. The play presents his discovery of this dreadful truth.

This situation is the result of a whole series of coincidences or perhaps the work of some power that guides the course of events. Laius and Jocasta heard a prophecy from the oracle of Apollo at Delphi that their son would kill his father and marry his mother. They sent a shepherd out to leave the newborn child on the mountainside to die of exposure; to make doubly sure that it would die, its ankles were pierced and fastened together. But the shepherd had pity on the child and gave it to another shepherd, one from the other side of the mountain range, the territory of Corinth. Knowing that his king and queen, Polybus and Merope, were childless, this shepherd took the baby down to them, and they adopted it. Because his ankles were swollen from the wounds, the boy was called Oedipus ("swollen-foot").

Oedipus grew up in Corinth, believing he was the son of Polybus and Merope. But as he grew to manhood, rumors began to circulate about his legitimacy; to know the truth, he went to Delphi to consult the oracle. All he heard there was a prophecy that he would kill his father and marry his mother; appalled, he resolved never to return to Corinth and set out in the opposite direction. At a place "where three roads meet" he was crowded off the narrow road by a man in a chariot; a fight broke out, and he killed the man and (he thought) all of his companions. (But in fact one escaped and brought the news back to Jocasta.) Oedipus kept on his way and at Thebes defeated the Sphinx, married Jocasta, and became king. Apollo's prophecy was fulfilled.

Now, many years later, the plague rages in the city, and Creon, Jocasta's brother, comes back from Delphi, where he was sent by Oedipus to ask what to do. The answer: find the killer of Laius, then kill or banish him. And Oedipus undertakes to find him. He puts a dreadful curse on the killer, cutting him off from all contact with his fellow citizens; he also sends for Tiresias, the blind prophet, who is believed to know all things. He does in fact know the truth but refuses to tell Oedipus; the king reacts with fierce anger, accusing him of betraying the city and then of conspiring with Creon to overthrow him. His anger blinds him to the truth that Tiresias, now angry in his turn, begins to reveal, although in riddling terms; he speaks clearly in the end, but Oedipus leaves in a fury, paying no attention.

In the next scene, Creon is directly accused of conspiracy and sentenced to death; at the request of the Chorus and Jocasta, who now comes on stage, Oedipus reluctantly retracts the death sentence. Wishing to calm Oedipus, Jocasta asks the reason for his rage; he replies that Tiresias accused him of the murder of Laius. She tells him to pay no attention to prophets, they know nothing more than ordinary men. To prove it she tells him of the prophecy that her son would kill his father and marry his mother. In fact the child, she says, died on the mountain, and Laius was killed by a stranger at the junction of three roads.

This detail terrifies Oedipus; he now tells her the story of his encounter at such a place. He is afraid he may be the killer of Laius, the cause of the plague, the victim of his own solemn curse. (He does not connect the prophecy with the one given him by Apollo, for he is sure that his father and mother are Polybus and Merope at Corinth.) But he knows that he was alone, and Jocasta spoke of "robbers" as the assailants of Laius. He needs an eyewitness to reassure him, and there is one: the survivor of the fight, whom Jocasta has sent away into the country to be a shepherd. It is the same man who took the baby Oedipus to the mountains to die, and when he comes he will bear witness to more than the death of Laius.

But meanwhile a messenger comes from Corinth: Polybus is dead, and the Corinthians want Oedipus to come back to reign over them. The news of Polybus' death is a great relief; Apollo's prophecy at Delphi was wrong—Oedipus did not kill his father—but he will not go to Corinth, because the second half of the prophecy, that he would marry his mother, will best be falsified if he stays in Thebes. The messenger now tells him there is nothing to fear; Merope is not his mother. The messenger, when he was a shepherd, was given the baby by another shepherd; its ankles were pierced.

By this time Jocasta has realized the horrible truth; she tries to stop Oedipus, to make him give up the search. But he insists he will know the truth, whatever it is. Jocasta rushes off stage (to hang herself, as we find out later), and Oedipus waits for the shepherd Jocasta sent for in the previous scene. When he comes, the man from Corinth recognizes him, and Oedipus forces the whole truth out of him. Then Oedipus too rushes off stage as the Chorus sings a despairing ode about the nothingness of men.

A messenger comes on to tell of Jocasta's suicide and Oedipus' self-blinding; soon the blind king himself comes stumbling on stage. His laments turn to stubborn resolution as he demands that the Chorus obey the oracle of Apollo and drive him out to die, on the mountain where he now wishes he had died as a child. Creon, now king of Thebes, comes on to take charge. Oedipus is allowed to embrace his two daughters, Antigone and Ismene, and then is ordered into the palace; about his eventual disposition Creon will consult the oracle.

The oracle of Apollo at Delphi was, in Sophocles' time, a powerful religious institution that wielded considerable political influence. Greek states and foreign kings consulted it about the future, as did also private individuals; their sacrifices and offerings made it one of the greatest concentrations of art and wealth in the Greek world. Apollo, through his priestess the Pythia (cf. the opening scene of *The Eumenides*) answered requests for advice; his advice was treasured because he was believed to know the future. During the last three decades of Sophocles' life, Athens was at war with Sparta; before declaring war, the Spartans had consulted the oracle and had been told that they would win (as they did).

But this belief that the gods know the future was no longer universally held in Sophocles' day; like many other features of traditional religion it was subjected to critical examination by the new philosophers, who speculated about the atomic constituents of matter, and by the Sophists, who applied the canon of probability to religious myth. The attack on the belief in divine prophecy was in fact the most dangerous of all the new attempts to reject tradition; if the gods do not know the future, they are no more in control of the universe than we are.

This intellectual conflict is reflected in the play. Jocasta sums up her argument that Oedipus should disregard the oracles with a contemptuous rejection: "So much for prophecy. It's neither here nor there. / From this day on, I wouldn't look right or left" (lines 948–49). The reaction of the Chorus is to call on Zeus, the supreme god, to make the prophecies come true, horrible as that will be for Oedipus; otherwise, it says, there will be no point in worshiping the gods at all: "Never again will I go reverent to Delphi . . . or Apollo's ancient oracle at Abae . . . unless these prophecies all come true" (lines 985ff.). Prophecies are despised and "the gods, the gods go down" (line 997). Later on, when he hears of the death of Polybus, Oedipus echoes Jocasta's disbelief: "Why, why look to the Prophet's hearth" (line 1054), and "all those prophecies I feared. . . . They're nothing, worthless" (lines 1062–64). And Jocasta draws the ultimate conclusion, that human life is a meaningless chaos, a chain of mere coincidences: "What should a man fear? It's all chance, / chance rules our lives. . . . Better to live at random, best we can" (lines 1069–72). They do not know it, but the truth of prophecy is about to be revealed, to Jocasta before the end of this scene, to Oedipus in the next. The play uses the myth to present the most controversial religious and philosophical issue of the day; it comes down decisively on the side of prophecy, divine knowledge and design—even though the ruin of a good man is part of that design.

The Oedipus story was of course well known, but it is likely that Sophocles reworked it along lines suitable for his own artistic purpose (as all the Greek poets did when they handled mythical themes.) In Homer's *Odyssey* the hero Odysseus sees, in the lower world, the mother of Oedipus (she is called Epikastê); she married her son, who had killed his father. The gods revealed the truth to humankind; Epikastê hanged herself, but Oedipus, though he suffered from the sorrows that the Furies of a mother bring to pass, lived on as king of Thebes (*Odyssey* XI.293–304).

There is no mention here of Oedipus' children, of his self-blinding and expulsion from Thebes, of Apollo's oracle, or of the Sphinx. All these details presumably came into the story later, in other epic tales or lyric poems, now lost. But we do know that Aeschylus produced a trilogy dealing with the house of Oedipus (we still have the final play, *The Seven Against Thebes*); from that play and the fragments of the others we know that the Aeschylean trilogy referred to the story of the Apolline oracle and the exposure of the child, the encounter where three roads meet, the self-blinding of Oedipus, and the part played by the Sphinx. This suggests that Sophocles could rely on audience familiarity with the main elements of the story to ensure appreciation of this masterly use of dramatic irony in the first two-thirds of his play.

We have only a version of the riddle of the Sphinx that comes from sources much later than Sophocles' time, but there is good evidence that it was known in this form in the fifth century. It is in hexameter verse; here is a literal translation:

> There is a two-footed thing on this earth, four-footed (but only one voice) and three-footed. It changes its form and is the only thing to do so of all the creatures that move on land, in the air or in the sea. Now when it walks supporting itself on most feet, the speed of its limbs is at its weakest.

There may be an allusion to the text of the riddle where Creon says "The singing, riddling Sphinx / She . . . persuaded us to let the mystery go / and concentrate on what lay at our feet" (lines 147–49). In any case, the fact that the answer is "man" is singularly appropriate for a hero who begins the play as a representative of humanity as master of its environment and ends it as a blinded outcast.

Classroom Strategies

One assignment.

Modern students will probably find themselves in difficulty when they move from the dramatic exchanges in the spoken scenes to the sometimes meditative, sometimes excited lyric poetry of the choral odes. Yet the choral poetry is not only, for most of its length, a profound meditation on the moral and religious themes of the play but also a reflection of the Chorus's reactions to and interpretations of the dramatic action. As in *Agamemnon*, the attitude of the Chorus is not fixed; it varies as the song expresses the hopes and fears of the citizens of Thebes before the words and deeds of their rulers. But whereas in *Agamemnon* the Chorus learns through suffering to see, at last, the truth of the matter, the Chorus of *Oedipus*, oscillating wildly between overconfidence and utter despair, serves Sophocles as a dramatic instrument for the creation of suspense, irony, and contrast.

The opening song (lines 168ff.) is a desperate appeal to the gods for relief from the plague. The Chorus does not yet know the message Creon has brought to Oedipus; they await the word from Delphi with apprehension. The vivid description of the sufferings caused by the plague in lines 190ff. reinforces the dramatic effect of the opening scene: Oedipus must act quickly and decisively if he is to save his city. As he comes out of the palace he hears the closing lines of the choral prayer, and Sophocles gives him an opening line heavy with dramatic irony: "You pray to the gods? Let me grant your prayers" (line 245). He will indeed grant its prayers, but only at the price of his wife's death and the loss of his own eyes.

The second choral song (lines 526ff.) follows the scene between Oedipus and Tiresias. The first half of it develops a vision of the man responsible for the plague, the murderer of Laius, as a fugitive in flight from the gods' pursuit—an outcast in the wilds, in "bristling timber . . . rocks and caves" (lines 542–43). Evidently, the Chorus does not accept Tiresias' identification of Oedipus as the killer; as it goes on to discuss the prophet's charge, it confesses to bewilderment. For all its respect for Tiresias, it can see no reason why a prince from Corinth should quarrel with and kill the king of Thebes. It rejects this assault "without proof" on the reputation of the man who once before saved Thebes. Not that it rejects prophecy: "Zeus and Apollo know" (line 561). But a human prophet may err; it will not believe until it sees "these charges proved" (line 568).

But the next choral ode (lines 945ff.) comes after the quarrel between Oedipus and Creon (in which the Chorus intervened on Creon's behalf) and the revelations that followed; it has heard Oedipus tell how he killed a man at the crossroads and now fears that he may in fact be the killer of Laius—that Tiresias was right—and the Chorus has heard Jocasta reject prophecy altogether, including one that came from Delphi. It is deeply disturbed and sings of the immortal laws as it prays for reverence and purity; it denounces the tyrannical spirit that mounts too high only to crash in ruin. This seems to be a reference to political power (and so to Oedipus); the Chorus qualifies it immediately as it prays that the god will never put an end to the "healthy strife that makes the city strong" (line 969). But dark thoughts return: it sings now of one who has no fear of justice, no reverence for the gods, who "lay[s] hands on the holy things untouchable" (line 980). In that last phrase (and the suggestion is especially strong in the Greek) there might be a reference to incest. If such a man go unpunished, the Chorus asks itself, why join the sacred dance? The dance it is performing as it sings is such a dance; the theater is a place of worship of the god Dionysus. If such crimes go unpunished, the Chorus's words imply, why worship the gods at all? And it spells this implication out clearly in the final stanza. It will no longer go to Delphi or any other sacred site unless "these prophecies all come true" (line 989). They are ready to abandon their king if the condition of his survival is the failure of divine prophecy.

But the next choral song (lines 1195ff.) is a jubilant speculation about the birth of Oedipus. The Chorus knows now that he is not the son of the royal pair at Corinth; as it waits for the arrival of the Theban Shepherd who carried the baby Oedipus long ago to the slopes of Mount Cithaeron, it indulges in pleasing prospects: Oedipus may be the child of

a god, of Pan by a nymph, of Apollo, Hermes, or Dionysus. It is not long
before the dreadful truth is revealed, to Oedipus and to the Chorus, that
now sings despondently of the fate of humankind: "generations of men
. . . adding the total / of all your lives I find they come to nothing" (lines
1312–14). Oedipus is the example; in his rise and fall the Chorus finds
the proof of this gloomy estimate of the human condition. Yet the last
scene of the play suggests that just as it went too far before in joyful
expectation, it has now gone too far in despair. For in the last scene, the
blind Oedipus emerges from his initial abject misery to reassert himself
as a man; he refuses to accept the Chorus's condemnation of his self-
blinding: "What I did was best—don't lecture me" (line 1500). The impe-
rious tone is certainly not that of a man who feels he is nothing, and he
uses the same tone to Creon later: "I command you—I beg you" (line
1584). This return to self-confidence is based on a feeling that his cruel
destiny marks him as unique and that, for some purpose undeclared, he
has been singled out among humankind: "I have been saved / for something great and terrible, something strange" (lines 1597–98). That
"something strange" is the subject of the last play Sophocles was to write,
Oedipus at Colonus.

Topics for Discussion

1. The theme of sight and blindness; its importance in a play that
   turns on human ignorance of the truth.

   [Tiresias the blind prophet can see the truth (as Oedipus begins
   to fear, line 823). Oedipus, who has the use of his eyes, moves
   blindly toward the revelation of the truth. He sees clearly only when
   he is physically blind. Compare the emphasis on Oedipus' sight
   throughout the first part of the play (lines 17, 28, 70, 96, 119, 394,
   427, 597, 830, 885, 1042, 1147, 1153, 1185, and 1190) and contrast the references to the vision of Tiresias (323, 359–60). Also
   Oedipus' sarcastic references to the blindness of Tiresias (lines 396,
   423, 425ff., 440–42, and 469) and Tiresias' references to the blindness of Oedipus (lines 419, 470–71, 517ff.; cf. 879, 1082, 1095,
   1360, 1406ff., 1567, and 1625ff.).]
2. Oedipus is a figure representative of human confidence that our
   intelligence makes us master of our world.

   [Oedipus is a man of action and experience (cf. lines 55–56), but
   he himself emphasizes that his action is based on thoughtful analysis ("groping, laboring over many paths of thought . . . painful
   search," lines 79–80). And he boasts that he alone was able to
   answer the riddle of the Sphinx: "the flight of my own intelligence
   hit the mark" (line 453). Here he prizes his own human intelligence
   above the prophetic skills of Tiresias, which are the gift of the gods.
   His intelligence is displayed in the frequent cross-questioning to
   which he subjects witnesses in the course of his investigation, an
   investigation that starts as a search for the murderer of Laius and
   ends as a search for his own identity. His questioning of Creon

(lines 112ff.), Jocasta (lines 804ff.), the messenger (lines 1114ff.), and the shepherd (lines 1229ff.) are models of logical pursuit of the truth. And it is through these intellectual efforts that he finally brings about the catastrophe, learns the truth about himself.]

Topic for Writing

Trace the pattern and discuss the significance of the following images throughout the play: (a) Oedipus as hunter, (b) Oedipus as plowman, and (c) Oedipus as sailor-helmsman.

[All three of these images reinforce the central idea of Oedipus as the symbolic representative of human progress, for the conquest of the wild beasts, the discovery of agriculture, and the mastery of the sea are important stages in our long development from "savagery" to "civilization." (That the Greeks were conscious of this historical view of human progress is clear from the choral ode in *Antigone*, lines 376ff., where mastery of the sea, the soil, and the animals are the first accomplishments of "man the skilled, the brilliant.")

Oedipus as hunter. The investigator of the crime is easily seen as a hunter, and this image is pervasive throughout the opening scenes of the play. "Where to find it now," he asks when Creon tells him that Apollo demands the punishment of Laius' murder, "the trail of the ancient guilt so hard to trace?" (lines 123–24). "What stopped you," he asks Creon, "from tracking down the killer / then and there?" (lines 146–47). He will take up the chase himself and later claims that if he had been present at the time "there would have been . . . no long hunt / without a clue in hand" (lines 250–51). Later Tiresias will tell him "I say you are the murderer you hunt" (line 413), but it will be a long time before he realizes this is the truth. The Chorus envisions the murderer of Laius as a hunted animal: "that man who left no trace— / after him, hunt him down with all our strength!" (lines 540–41). It does not realize that Oedipus is both the hunter and the prey.

Oedipus as plowman. The agricultural images are heavily loaded with significance in this play, because in the Greek language such words as "plow" and "sow" are familiar expressions for the begetting of children (as they were in the seventeenth-century English of the Bible—"the seed of Abraham," "the fruit of the womb," for example). Quite apart from their clear reference to the incestuous begetting of children by the royal pair, these images are strikingly appropriate to the dramatic situation. For the plague in Thebes affects the products of the soil as well as human beings (cf. "The fruits of our famous earth, they will not ripen" and "the women cannot scream their pangs to birth . . . children dead in the womb," lines 196–98). This sympathetic relationship between the fruits of the soil and the fruit of the womb is reflected in the transference of agricultural terms to the pollution of the marriage of Oedipus and Jocasta; what this suggests is the responsibility of that unholy marriage for the stunted crops and the plague. Oedipus' first statement about his relationship with Laius is made in terms of this metaphor. Not realizing the hideous ambiguities involved, he says, "I hold the throne that he held then, possess his bed / and a wife who shares our seed" (lines 295–96). What he means is simply that he and Laius have had children by the same wife, but the words suggest to the audience the hideous truth. The same image recurs when Tiresias prophesies that Oedipus will be revealed as his father's murderer and his mother's son: "He sowed the loins / his father sowed" (lines 522–23). After the revelation of the truth, the Chorus asks in horror: "How, how could the furrows your father plowed / bear you, your agony, harrowing on / in silence O so long?" (lines 1339–41) When Oedipus bursts into the palace, he asks, the messenger tells us, for "his wife, / no wife, his mother, where he can find the mother earth / that cropped two crops at once, himself and all his children" (lines 1388–90). He explains his own polluted state to his daughters with this same image: "I fathered you in the soil that gave me life" (line 1627) and "Your father killed his father, sowed his mother, / one, one and the selfsame womb sprang you— / he cropped the very roots of his existence" (lines 1640–42). The plowman has reaped a dreadful crop, the sower is not only the sower but also the seed.

Oedipus as sailor-helmsman. Oedipus as helmsman is a natural image, for as king he is thought of as guiding the ship of state (a common metaphor in Greek as in English). The city is compared to a ship in the opening speech of the priest—"our ship pitches wildly, cannot lift her head / from the depths" (lines 29–30)—and Creon, bringing news from Delphi, speaks of the "plague-storm" (line 114) that afflicts the city; he also refers to Oedipus' rescue of Thebes in earlier days with the phrase "you came and put us straight on course" (118). The Chorus takes up and elaborates this image when it asserts its loyalty to Oedipus after his quarrel with Creon: "You who set our beloved land—storm-tossed, shattered— / straight on course" (lines 765–66). And it exhorts him to do the same thing now: "Now again, good helmsman, / steer us through the storm!" (lines 766–67) But its wish is not to be granted; after Jocasta's mention of the three roads, Oedipus is distraught. The citizens, in Jocasta's words, are "passengers in the grip of fear, / watching the pilot of the vessel go to pieces" (lines 1010–11). Oedipus has not yet discovered the full truth. When he does he will understand at last the riddling question Tiresias asked him. "What haven won't reverberate? . . . That day you learn the truth about your marriage? . . . the lusty voyage home to the fatal harbor!" (lines 480ff.). Oedipus, like a navigator, had plotted his course by the stars: "I abandoned Corinth, / from that day on I gauged its landfall only / by the stars" (lines 876–78). But it brought him to an unspeakable destination. "One and the same wide harbor," sings the Chorus, "served you / son and father both / son and father came to rest in the same bridal chamber" (lines 1336–39).]

Comparative Perspective

What kind of correlation exists between the time covered by the action of the play and the time it takes to perform? Compare the management of time and event in other dramatic traditions. Speculate on the extent to which cultural attitudes toward time and human life influence the presentation of dramatic action.

Further Reading

See also the reading suggestions in the anthology, p. 599.

O'Brien, Michael J., ed. *Twentieth-Century Interpretations of* Oedipus Rex. 1968. Contains an essay by Eric Dodds ("On Misunderstanding *Oedipus Rex*") that with admirable clarity and concision draws on a lifetime of brilliant scholarship and teaching to deal with the difficulties students usually experience on reading this play. There are also essays by Francis Ferguson (on the play as theater), G. M. Kirkwood (on dramatic form), R. P. Winnington-Ingram (on the Old Testament of the Bible and Greek archaic thought), and Bernard Knox (on the ending of the play). The volume also contains useful short quotations from critics ancient and modern, including, for example, Plutarch, Voltaire, Bowra, Freud, and Marshall McLuhan.

Seale, David. *Vision and Stagecraft in Sophocles.* 1982. The title speaks for itself: the plays are explored primarily as theatrical performance (but with careful attention to content and imagery). One section deals with *Oedipus the King.*

Segal, Charles. *Tragedy and Civilization: An Interpretation of Sophocles.* 1981. Pages 207–48 offer a sensitive and rewarding reading of the play that makes use of modern structuralist approaches.

Sophocles. *Sophocles'* Oedipus Rex. R. D. Dawe, ed. 1982. This is an edition of and commentary on the Greek text of the play, but the introduction is an especially useful discussion of the problems raised by the intricacy of the plot.

Winnington-Ingram, R. P. *Sophocles: An Interpretation.* 1980. Pages 173–204 offer a profound and provoking exploration of the problems of fate in the play and of the moral implications of the "fall of Oedipus."

EURIPIDES

Medea

Backgrounds

The background for the events of the play is briefly sketched by Medea's old nurse, who delivers the prologue. The romantic idyll of Jason and Medea (see lines 1–10 and the footnotes to those lines) has long since come to an end; they are exiles in Corinth, and Jason has married the daughter of the king, abandoning Medea and his two sons by her. She is desperate, and the nurse is afraid of what she may do. The boys' Tutor brings news that the king (his name is Kreon, but he has no connection with the Creon of the Sophoclean plays) intends to expel Medea and her children from Corinth; he is afraid of her.

That his fears are justified is made clear in the next scene; Medea wins over the Chorus of Corinthian Women by her famous speech lamenting the subordinate position of women, and it promises not to betray her plans for revenge. Kreon arrives to expel her but is talked into granting her one day's reprieve. That is all she needs, she says, when he is gone; she plans to kill him, his daughter, and Jason (lines 371–72). At this stage she has not yet thought of killing Jason's sons. He now comes in to try to offer her financial help in her exile from Corinth, an offer she refuses with contempt in a speech of violent denunciation; he makes a cynical defense of his conduct, but she sends him away with sarcastic wishes for his enjoyment of his marriage and with veiled threats.

One obstacle to her plan for revenge is the fact that if she does succeed in killing Jason and the king and princess of Corinth she will have nowhere to go for refuge; no city will take her in after that. The problem is solved by the chance arrival of Aegeus, king of Athens. He is childless and has been to the oracle at Delphi for advice, but Apollo's reply to his request was obscure and he is on his way to a wise man at Troezen to ask for an interpretation. Medea tells him her troubles and begs him for a refuge in Athens, promising that through her knowledge of drugs she can cure his sterility. He offers her a home in Athens, and she makes him swear an oath to confirm this offer. (She does not tell him what she intends to do before leaving Corinth.)

Now she can plan her revenge. She will send the princess a wedding gift—a robe that will kill her and anyone that touches her. But she will also kill the children (line 776). Jason will be left wifeless and childless (lines 787ff.). She sends for Jason, and with feigned humility she plays the part of the submissive wife; Jason, deceived, leaves with the children, who carry the poisoned gifts for the princess. When the Tutor returns with the boys and announces that the gifts have been accepted, she prepares to kill her sons. In a famous monologue (lines 995–1054) she struggles with her own soul, changing her mind and then returning to her original resolution. After the messenger comes to report the hideous deaths of the princess and the king, she goes into the house to complete her revenge; she kills the children.

Jason comes on to save the life of his boys, for the king's friends will kill them otherwise (lines 1279–80), but Medea appears above the house in a chariot sent her by her grandfather the sun god. With her are the bodies of the children. She and Jason exchange reproaches and curses (she prophesies the manner of his death); finally, she leaves for Athens as Jason appeals to Zeus to bear witness to her slaughter of his sons.

Medea, with its concentration on the status of women, their sorrows and crimes, is not unique in Euripides' dramatic oeuvre; in fact he was famous (to some, infamous) for his emphasis on such themes. His *Hippolytus* deals with a stepmother, Phaedra, who falls in love with her stepson; in *Andromache* a barren, jealous wife plans to murder her husband's concubine and her son by him; the *Sthenoboea* had a plot similar to the story of Joseph and Potiphar's wife (see Genesis 39 in the anthology); *Aeolus* dealt with love of brother and sister, and *Auge* with a young woman who bore her illegitimate child in a temple. The comic poet Aristophanes, in his *Frogs,* staged a debate between Aeschylus and Euripides in the lower world (Euripides died just before the play was written) and had "Aeschylus" denounce "Euripides" for his *Phaedra* and *Sthenoboea* and some of his plots in the lines "His nurses go propositioning others / his heroines have their babies in church / or sleep with their brothers" (translated by Richmond Lattimore).

Long before Euripides produced *Medea* (in 431 B.C.), he had been attracted by the tragic possibilities of her story; his first offering at the festival of Dionysus (in 455 B.C.) included a play called *The Daughters of Pelias,* which dealt with Medea's role in the death of Pelias, king of Thessaly (*Medea,* lines 9–10 and the footnotes; lines 474 and 492). This incident was part of a long saga, the story of the Argonauts, which was well known to the audience that saw *Medea;* it is the background against which the drama of *Medea* is played out.

Jason's father, Aeson, was the rightful heir to the kingdom of Iolcus, in the north of Greece near Mount Pelion (line 3), but the throne was usurped by his half-brother, Pelias. Jason, who had been sent off to safety, came to Iolcus when fully grown to claim his rights. Pelias, who had been told by a prophet that his death would be brought about by one of his own kin, persuaded the young man to set off in quest of the fabulous Golden Fleece, which was guarded by a dragon in the eastern kingdom of Colchis (line 2), beyond the Hellespont, on the southern coast of the Black Sea. The king of Colchis, Aietes, was a son of Helios, the sun god (lines 403 and 930); he had a daughter, Medea, and a young son, Absyrtos.

Jason assembled a company of heroes (called Argonauts after the ship *Argo,* the first long-range ship ever built) and set off on his adventurous journey to the east; one of the many dangers he faced was a passage through the clashing rocks (the Symplegades, lines 2 and 423), which may be a mythical representation of the narrow passage of the Dardanelles, the entrance to the Black Sea. In Colchis, Jason had to face a series of ordeals before he could take possession of the fleece. He had to yoke a pair of fire-breathing bulls (lines 466–67), plow a field with them, and sow dragon's teeth. The crop would be armed men whom he would then have to fight. Medea, who had fallen in love with Jason, gave him an ointment that would make him invulnerable, and he came through successfully; he provoked the armed men into killing one another by throwing a stone that each side thought had been thrown by the other.

Aietes suspected Medea's complicity and planned to attack Jason and the heroes in the night. Medea came to warn them, led Jason to the dragon's lair, killed the dragon so that he could take the Golden Fleece (lines 468ff.), and embarked with Jason and the heroes in the night. When Aietes' ships came close in pursuit she killed her brother (line 165) and threw his limbs overboard one by one; Aietes' ships stopped to pick them up. After a long voyage Jason and Medea came to Iolcus, where Medea tricked the daughters of Pelias into killing their father. Jason did not, however, reap the rewards of Medea's action; Pelias' son drove Jason and Medea out of Iolcus, and they came to Corinth as refugees.

Classroom Strategies

One assignment.

Medea repeatedly refers to Jason as her husband (lines 227, 254, 259, 260, etc.) and herself as his wife (line 580), and Jason calls himself her husband (line 1312) and says she was married to him (line 1311). Yet he can abandon her and marry the princess of Corinth; though Medea protests passionately, Kreon and the princess find nothing objectionable in Jason's conduct, and there is apparently no violation of law on his part.

For the Athenian audience this would not have been seen as a contradiction; it was perfectly understandable as a reflection of conditions in their own society. At the time the play was produced, an Athenian citizen's sons could be recognized as citizens themselves only if born of an Athenian mother; "marriage" was a contract entered into by two Athenian families, the bride brought her husband a dowry (which had to be restored if he separated from her), and the purpose of marriage was officially defined as "the procreation of legitimate children." A marriage with a foreign woman was not a marriage in this sense at all; many Athenian men had, in addition to their legitimate wives, concubines who might well be of foreign birth and had no rights. What sort of a marriage ceremony Medea and Jason went through we are not told, but in the eyes of Athenian law it was not binding. Medea can call Jason to witness "the gods whose names you swore by" and "my right hand, and the knees which you often clasped / In supplication" (lines 481–85), but though it is true that he has broken his word, she has no legal hold on him.

Virgil will later make use of a similar situation in the *Aeneid*. Dido considers herself married to Aeneas by the pledge of his right hand (IV.409), but Aeneas does not recognize the bond as legal: "I never held the torches of a bridegroom, / Never entered upon the pact of marriage" (lines 443–44).

Medea has no legal recourse; she has to fall back on cunning and violence.

Topics for Discussion

1. Medea's plan for revenge is not clearly announced until fairly late in the play. Analyze the formation in her mind of the decision to kill the children.

   [The first formulation of Medea's revenge is vague; she asks the Chorus to aid and abet her by silence if she can find a means or devise any scheme "To pay my husband back for what he has done to me, / —Him and his father-in-law and the girl who married him" (lines 259–60). After she has won her day's grace from Kreon, she clarifies her intention: to kill all three of them, "father, the girl and my husband" (line 371). She does not know how yet; she talks of the sword (line 375) and of poison (line 381). But she cannot proceed without assurance of a refuge, a city to take her in after she has killed her enemies. When she is sure of such a refuge at Athens, promised by Aegeus and confirmed by an oath, her plan is complete. "I shall tell to you the whole of my plan," she tells the Chorus (line 756). She will pretend to give way, ask Jason to let the children take gifts to the princess, poison gifts that will destroy her and "all who touch the girl" (line 772). She hopes presumably that both Kreon and Jason will do so. But her revenge now includes the murder of the children. She speaks of this as specifically aimed against Jason; Jason, she says, "will pay me the price. . . . For those children he had from me he will never / See alive again, nor will he on his new bride / Beget another child" (lines 786–89). Jason, that is, will remain alive, to suffer the loss of his hopes—his sons who would prolong his line and preserve his name and memory; he will suffer also the loss of the hope of new children from his bride.

There has been no overt preparation for this drastic change of plan; Medea gives no reasons nor does she explain, as Euripidean characters often do, the psychological process by which she arrived at this decision. Yet Euripides has in fact prepared the ground carefully, so that the audience can accept this new and dreadful resolve. Right at the beginning of the play, when the audience hears her hysterical outbursts offstage, she wishes first for her own death (lines 96ff.), but then, when she sees the children brought into the house, she turns her despairing rage against them, Jason's sons. "I hate you, / Children of a hateful mother. I curse you / And your father. Let the whole house crash" (lines 112–14). And the nurse fears for the children's safety (line 118). When Medea speaks rationally and persuasively to the Chorus, her wild rage against the children is forgotten.

In her fierce exchange with Jason, however, she hears him speak with pride of his sons, of the plans he has for their future (which do not, of course, include her). He has left her, he says, in her best interests (and the children's). He wants to bring them up "worthy / Of [his] position (lines 550–51), give them royal stepbrothers by his new wife, a royal progeny to be brothers for the children he has now, "a sure defense to us" (lines 584–85). Jason sees the future of his house in these sons. The point is brought home sharply to Medea and the audience by the appearance of Aegeus, an old man who has no sons and who goes from the oracle at Delphi to the wise man at Troezen in search of some remedy for his childlessness, who will promise Medea a refuge in Athens when she offers to cure his sterility.

It is immediately after this scene that Medea announces her intention to kill the children. She will make Jason a man with no future in his line, a wreck of a man, like Aegeus. She does not announce this motive; she speaks instead of her inability to save the children after she has destroyed the king and his daughter (line 776). But when the Chorus asks her if she can really have the heart to kill them, she reveals her true motive: "Yes, for this is the best way to wound my husband" (line 801). In the false submission scene, the children's fate is sealed. For Jason shows how much he loves them, how much he counts on their future: "And of you, children, your father is taking care. / He has made, with God's help, ample provision for you. / For I think that a time will come when you will be / The leading people of Corinth" (lines 890–93). At this point Medea turns white and bursts into tears (line 898); Jason cannot understand why. "I was thinking about these children," she says (line 901).

We know what she was thinking. Jason's devotion to them, his rosy vision of their future career, to be men of influence and his support in old age—all this confirms Medea's feeling that this is in fact the best way to wound her husband. She wavers momentarily from her purpose (lines 1030ff.) but not for long; she kills the boys. And she savors her revenge in her last interview with Jason. She has left him childless, he says, (line 1301); "my life is over!" (line 1325). And she turns the blade in the wound: "The children are dead. I say this to make you suffer" (line 1345). And she reminds him that he will suffer more as time goes by. "I go," he says, "with two children to mourn for." And she replies: "Not yet do you feel it. Wait for the future" (lines 1370–71).]

2. Some critics (Denys Page, for example) refuse to see the play as, in part, a comment on woman's subordinate role in Athenian society; they point out that Medea is a dealer in supernatural poisons who escapes the consequences of her action on a magic chariot, that she is, in fact, an Oriental witch who cannot be regarded as representative of Athenian women. Is such a view justified?

[It is certainly expressed in the play; it is Jason's view: "There is no Greek woman who would have dared such deeds," he says (line 1314), and he calls her "a monster not a woman" (line 1317). It is true that she has at her disposal a poison that seems more magical than real and that she escapes in a chariot that flies through the air. It is also true that she swears by the goddess Hecate, "my mistress, / Whom most I honor and have chosen as partner . . . who dwells in the recesses of my heart" (lines 392–94). Hecate is the mistress of witches in Renaissance literature (she appears on the stage in this role in an interpolation made to Shakespeare's *Macbeth,* for example) and appears in Greek literature from the Alexandrian age (third century B.C.) on as the patron goddess of sorcery. But there is no text from Euripides' time or before to connect her with sorcery. She was a goddess particularly associated with women (and is often identified with Artemis, the protector of women in childbirth) and there was an image of her outside every Athenian house. Medea's invocation of Hecate carries no suggestion of witchcraft.

As for the robe and crown that burst into flames when put on, the audience is not likely to have read any hint of sorcery into it, since such devices are commonplace in mythical tales. In Sophocles' *Women of Trachis* the wife of Heracles sends him a similar robe (she does not realize its potency, but thinks it a love charm), which causes his death by fire, and in Euripides' *Ion* the Athenian princess Creusa uses a poison that is equally magical—a drop of the Gorgon's blood. Poison was in any case the natural recourse of a wronged wife driven to desperate action, for she could not hope to prevail in a contest of strength. The flying chariot is, of course, a gift from Medea's divine grandfather and points up the fact that the Odyssean figure with whom Medea is compared by the proponents of witchcraft, namely Circe, is not a witch at all but a goddess (cf. *Odyssey* X.233).

It is true that in other plays of the period, a lost play of Sophocles, for example, Medea is portrayed as a woman who works her will through drugs and poisons. But Euripides has been careful to avoid giving such an impression. It is noticeable that though his Jason, in the quarrel scene and in their final confrontation, pours out his contempt and loathing for her, he never uses this particular line of invective. Euripides did not want to undercut the effect of Medea's great speech on the position of women by any suggestion that she was not herself a wronged, abandoned woman. She tricks Kreon into giving her an extra day, Aegeus into offering her a refuge, and Jason into accepting the false gifts for his bride not through witchcraft but through purely human cunning and resolution.]

Topics for Writing

1. Medea is a woman, but Euripides has presented her as a figure previously thought of as exclusively male—a hero. Analyze her character in the play as an amalgam of the salient qualities of Achilles and Odysseus.

   [She expresses the heroic creed in lines 791–93: "Let no one think me a weak one, feeble-spirited, . . . but rather just the opposite, / One who can hurt my enemies and help my friends." Such a reputation ensures what Achilles values most—glory. "For the lives of such persons are most remembered," she says (line 794); so Achilles came to fight and die at Troy because his glory would be everlasting (*Iliad* IX.500ff.). When he goes to kill Hector even though he knows his own death will follow, he says: "Let me seize great glory" (XVIII.144ff.). Like Achilles (I.201, IX.791), Medea feels dishonored ("slighted," lines 20 and 26; "scorned," line 1329; "insulted," line 591). Like Achilles (I.330, IX.310, IX.828) she reacts with "anger" and "rage" (lines 94, 99, 174), which makes her, like Achilles, impervious to advice, to appeals to reason, or to pleas for moderation (cf. Achilles in *Iliad* IX and Medea at lines 29ff. and 827ff.). To others her rage seems like that of a wild beast ("wildness," line 103); she is "like a lioness guarding her cubs" (line 188). So Achilles makes his spirit "savage" (IX.769) and refuses to bend, "like some lion / going his own barbaric way" (XXIV.48–49). Both Medea and Achilles sacrifice the lives of their own people in their fury for revenge (Medea, the Children; Achilles, his fellow Achaeans), and both become inhuman in their rage (Achilles: "Would to god my rage, my fury would drive me now / to hack your flesh away and eat you raw," XXII.408–9; Medea: "O your heart must have been made of rock or steel," sings the Chorus, line 1254, and "A monster not a woman, having a nature / Wilder than that of Scylla in the Tuscan sea," says Jason, lines 1317–18—cf. *Odyssey* XII.331ff.).

The resemblances between Medea and Odysseus are clear and abundant. She from the beginning of the play and he from the moment he loses his crew are absolutely alone, dependent on their wits and courage; no help comes from their protecting gods either, until Odysseus reaches Ithaca and is met by Athena, and until Medea, her purpose accomplished, is given the winged car. Both play on the gullibility of their enemies, who do not realize that they are being deceived; Odysseus fools the Kyklops as Medea does Kreon and Jason. Both assume humiliating disguises: Odysseus as the beggar in his own house; Medea, in her second scene with Jason, the role of fulsomely flattering obedient wife. Both of them triumph over their enemies in a bloody revenge that more than compensates for their sufferings—seems, in fact, to go too far.]

2. Medea is a foreigner, an Oriental princess, and Jason, as well as some modern critics, attributes the ferocity of her revenge to the fact that she is a "barbarian." How does the contrast between barbarian and Greek function in the play?

[The idea that Medea is a "barbarian" is in fact peculiar to Jason; even Kreon, who fears her, does not speak of her in such terms. Jason, in the quarrel scene, reminds her that she owes him the privilege of living in a civilized society: "instead of living among barbarians, / You inhabit a Greek land and understand our ways, / How to live by law instead of the sweet will of force" (lines 524–26). Medea, of course, has no reason to congratulate herself on living "by law," a law that allows her husband to abandon her; she later reproaches herself for trusting "the words of a Greek" (line 785). And Jason will later lament the day he brought her to Greece. "Now I see it plain, though at that time / I did not, when I took you from your foreign home / And brought you to a Greek house" (lines 1304–6). He should not have married a barbarian: "There is no Greek woman who would have dared such deeds" (line 1314).

The Chorus, however—who is appalled at her intention to kill the children (lines 795ff. and 827ff.) and prays to Earth and Sun to stop her (lines 1225ff.)—never for one moment speaks of her as a barbarian. When she makes her opening appeal for its sympathy (lines 212ff.) she speaks as a Greek wife addressing Greek women; her problem is the Chorus's. And though the Chorus rejects the murder of the children (but not that of the king and his daughter), it understands the desperate rage that prompts it. Far from saying that no Greek woman would have done what Medea did, it mentions one, Ino, who "laid her hands on her children" (line 1258). She was, it says, the only one, but the audience would have thought of others, too: Agave, of the royal house of Thebes, who, under Dionysiac possession, helped tear her own son Pentheus to pieces; Procne, who, to punish her husband for raping her sister, killed her son Itys and served his flesh to his father.

Medea, who sacrificed family and country to save Jason's life, is labeled a barbarian—called unfit for civilized Greek society—by the very man she tried to help. His cynical betrayal raises grave doubts about the civilization he claims to speak for.]

Comparative Perspectives

1. The protagonists of ancient literature often struggle with the decision to murder a child.

    a. Compare the motives that lead Medea to kill her children with those that impel Agamemnon to sacrifice Iphigenia. How does the Chorus in *Agamemnon* treat his decision? How does the Chorus in *Medea* view hers?

    b. Consider the motives that cause Abraham to prepare to sacrifice his son in light of Medea's deliberations, and contrast the different means by which (and degree to which) Euripidean drama and biblical narrative permit access to the thought processes of these tortured parental figures.

2. Compare Jason's abandonment of his wife and family with Aeneas's abandonment of Dido. What ancient views of sexual passion may be perceived in *Medea* and the *Aeneid*? How would you contrast these views with those that dominate medieval romances such as Malory's *Morte Darthur*?

Further Reading

See also the reading suggestions in the anthology, p. 641.

Conacher, D. T. *Euripidean Drama: Myth, Theme and Structure.* 1967. Pp. 183–98. A challenging analysis of the play, which is discussed as "realistic tragedy," as opposed to "mythological tragedy," that is concerned with "the individual in relation to the gods."

Euripides' Medea. Introduction and commentary by Denys L. Page. 1938. This Greek text with commentary contains an eloquent introduction that puts the play in the context of its time and states the classic case for Medea as barbarian witch (pp. xvii–xxi).

Schlesinger, Eilhard. "On Euripides' *Medea.*" In *Euripides: A Collection of Critical Essays,* edited by Erich Segal. 1968. Pp. 70–89. An essay (translated from the German) that deals especially with the problems posed by the ending and uses a comparative approach (Goethe, Corneille, and Anouilh, for example, are cited) to throw light on the Euripidean play.

Aristophanes

Lysistrata

Backgrounds

Lysistrata, an Athenian wife whose name means "disbander of armies," comes on stage expecting the arrival of other Athenian women whom she has summoned to an important meeting. She also expects some women from Sparta, a city with which Athens has been at war for twenty years. When everybody has arrived she announces her plan: a sex strike of the women on both sides to force the men to make peace. In spite of their initial reluctance she persuades them to swear an oath to refrain from sex with their husbands.

Meanwhile, another group of Lysistrata's women friends has seized the Acropolis in Athens; the Athenian women on stage leave to join them while the Spartan women go home to organize the strike in Sparta. A Chorus of Men enters; it is on its way to the Acropolis to force an entry or, if repelled, to smoke the women out with the timber and fire pots the men are carrying. The Chorus is met, however, by a Chorus of Women carrying water to put the fire out; the contest between the two choruses is interrupted by a Commissioner of Public Safety, who takes charge of the operations against the Acropolis gates.

But Lysistrata comes out to parley, and in a spirited exchange with the Commissioner she gets the better of the argument. After another rowdy altercation between the two choruses, Lysistrata comes on again; her troops are trying to desert under various pretexts—what they really want is to go home to their husbands. She restores their morale, and they go back to the Acropolis.

At this point, an Athenian husband, Kinesias, arrives; he is in a visibly excited state and demands his wife, Myrrhine. In a ribald, comic scene Myrrhine teases Kinesias with the prospect of sexual enjoyment but in the end leaves him still frustrated. As he goes out, a Spartan Herald arrives, also visibly excited, looking for the Athenian Council of Elders; evidently the Spartan women have not let the side down. The Athenian Commissioner tells him Athens is ready to make peace; Sparta is to send ambassadors with full powers to negotiate.

After some more choral song, a delegation of Spartans enters; the Spartans too are in desperate condition. Under the guidance of Lysistrata, who prevents disputes over small points in the treaty from becoming major problems, peace is made and the end of the war celebrated with a banquet.

When this comedy was produced in 411 B.C. there was considerable war-weariness in Athens. The war, which began in 431, ended in a truce in 421, but this was not, in fact, the end of hostilities; Athens and Sparta fought each other indirectly through and sometimes directly with their allies, and in 415 Athens had launched a huge expedition westward with the aim of conquering the rich Greek colonies in Sicily. This expedition ended in disaster and inflicted huge losses in ships and men; the Spartans soon resumed hostilities against Athens as Athenian subject allies in the Aegean tried to secede from the empire.

This was not the first Aristophanic comedy to deal with the folly of the war and to express, in fantastically comic terms, a serious wish for peace. In 425 he had produced a play called *The Acharnians,* in which a citizen who is fed up with the war makes a separate peace with the Spartans and proceeds to enjoy, in the midst of the Athenian war shortages, an abundance of luxury imports, not to mention exemption from military service. In *The Peace* (421), produced as the first ten years of hostilities came to an end, an Athenian citizen flies up to Heaven on a giant dung beetle to demand that Zeus put an end to the war. *Lysistrata* plays on the same wish, which must have been widespread in Athens, for a return to more peaceful days.

Nevertheless, the war went relentlessly on; even when the Spartans, on several occasions, proposed a truce on unexpectedly favorable conditions, the political leaders of the democracy rejected them and Athens finally went down to complete defeat in 404 B.C.

Aristophanes' comedies are not to be regarded as political propaganda on behalf of a particular group or party. It was the function of comedy to provide a momentary relief from everyday cares through fantastic visions of freedom, abundance, and self-indulgence. The action was always something that could not possibly happen in real life: the private citizen making a separate peace, a ride to Heaven on a dung beetle, or concerted political action on the part of Athenian women, who had no public function at all and played a subordinate role in private life as well. Athenian comedy did, however, comment freely and satirically on public affairs, and it used humor to make its audiences think. It embodied the energy of Athenian democracy.

Classroom Strategies

One assignment.

The sexually explicit jokes and action (the Kinesias scene, for example) should not mislead the modern reader into thinking of the play in terms of pornographic shows or "adult movies." Comedy in Athens was part of a religious festival; the low jokes and obscene gestures of the comic actors were just as much a part of the celebration of the god Dionysus as the dignified language and formal movements of the tragic stage. Dionysus was originally a god of vegetation (and not just of the vine); tragedy perhaps represented the flowering and inevitable death of all things, comedy the fertility of the natural world.

The comic actor wore, as part of his costume, the ancient symbol of fertility, the *phallos,* a leather replica of the male sexual organ. The joking

remarks about the excited state of the Spartan ambassadors at the end of
the play had their visual corroboration on stage, and it is not hard to
imagine what a comic actor could do with this apparatus in the Kinesias
scene. This kind of horseplay was native to the comic genre. In Aristophanes it is used with keen wit and to dramatic and thematic effect.

Topic for Discussion

Both *Medea* and *Lysistrata* deal with, among other things, a conflict
between men and women and exploit the contrast between their situation and aspirations. But though the two dramatists develop many of the
same major themes (and even sometimes coincide in choice of minor
details) the two plays are worlds apart: the same basic material from
which Euripides produces his shocking tragic effect serves Aristophanes
for a series of comic scenes culminating in a happy ending—conciliation
and a return to normality.

[Both protagonists are women of courage, determination, and keen
intelligence. Medea's speech to the chorus, appealing to their consciousness of woman's unhappy condition, is as perfectly adapted to the situation as the repudiation of her reputation as a woman of intellect (lines
290ff.) in her plea to Kreon or as her assumption of the role of repentant
wife in her deception of Jason. Lysistrata displays the qualities of a leader
in her organization of the conspiracy in the opening scene and in her
argument with the Commissioner. Especially when she gives her recipe
for managing the affairs of Athens and "work[ing] out the snarls" of the
war (lines 657 ff.), she shows a statesmanlike intelligence beyond anything the fatuous Commissioner she opposes could even imagine. Both
heroines lament the subordinate lot of women—Medea in lines 229ff.
and Lysistrata when she details the effects of war on the women of the city
(lines 687–89)—but Medea's speech ends with her plea to the Chorus to
abet her in her bloody revenge while Lysistrata's argument leads up to a
ribald joke on the part of the Commissioner, in return for which Lysistrata
and the women's Chorus treat him like a corpse. Both Medea and Lysistrata speak of woman's nature as centered on love and sexual passion.
"Once she is wronged in the matter of love," says Medea, "no other soul
can hold so many thoughts of blood" (lines 264–65), and Jason sees
woman's nature in the same terms: "You women have got into such a state
of mind / That, if your life at night is good, you think you have / Everything; but, if in that quarter things go wrong, / You will consider your best
and truest interests / Most hateful" (lines 557–61). He does not realize
the meaning the audience will attach to these words: Medea will sacrifice
her "best and truest interests"—her children—to punish him. In *Lysistrata*
the same Greek cliché about woman's nature has no such tragic over-
tones, but is instead the base for coarse innuendo ("Nothing teeny, I trust?
/ Immense," lines 24ff.), for the wholesale desertion on the part of Lysistrata's supporters when she tells them her plan, and for the series of pre-
posterous excuses the women give as they try to escape from the Acropolis
and go home to their husbands: "I've got all this lovely Milesian wool . . .

and the moths will simply batter it to bits," "my flax! / I left and forgot to peel it," "I'm due—any second!" (lines 844–59).

Each play has a scene in which the heroine administers a solemn oath. Medea makes Aegeus swear by Earth and Sun, repeating the words after her, that he will give her refuge in Athens when she leaves Corinth (lines 730ff.). Lysistrata binds the women, by an oath on a cup of wine, to repeat after her a series of promises to refrain from all manner of sexual enjoyment (lovingly described in detail, in lines 230–60) until their husbands consent to make peace.]

Topic for Writing

In an earlier comedy Aristophanes has one of his characters draw attention to the underlying seriousness of the action by claiming that even comedy (in spite of its buffoonery) can deal with questions of right and wrong. What serious issues are being explored beneath the ribald surface of *Lysistrata*, and how are they expressed?

[The main issue, of course, is the folly of continuing a war between Greeks that has gone on indecisively for so many years. There are serious obstacles to making peace and Aristophanes, right in the middle of the burlesque scenes of the women's oath-taking, brings them to the fore. The Spartan woman Lampito is sure that she and her friends can persuade the Spartans to make a fair and just peace. "But take this rackety / passel in Athens" (lines 177–78), she says. It will be difficult, she says, to convince them: "Not long as they got ships kin still sail straight, / an' thet fountain of money up thar in Athene's temple" (lines 180–82). Lysistrata has already seen to the seizure of the Acropolis and the treasures stored there—the tribute from the subject cities of the Athenian empire. This, of course, is a joke; the fears of Lampito, however, do raise a serious issue.

Though Athens had been reduced to a position of military inferiority by its catastrophic losses of men and ships in Sicily, the Spartans on several occasions showed a willingness to negotiate a peace. The Athenian democratic leaders ("the rabble," as the Spartans thought of Athenian democracy) were unwilling to make the necessary concessions; they still considered their resources in ships and money sufficient to win them victory or at least a position in which they could negotiate from strength. It was in fact this attitude that brought them in the end to defeat and unconditional surrender. Later in the play Lysistrata answers the question—"Might I ask you where you women conceived this concern / about War and Peace?" (lines 569–70). She tells how the women would ask their husbands, " 'How was the Assembly today, dear? Anything / in the minutes about Peace?' " (lines 583–84). But all they heard was news of one stupid measure after another. The political content of all this is plain, and when Lysistrata is asked how women can stop all the confusion in the various states and bring them together, she makes her brilliant speech about "work[ing] out the snarls" as if the war were a tangled ball of wool and then goes on to give a recipe for cleaning up Athenian politics, including "comb[ing] . . . out / those lumps / that clump and cluster in knots and snarls to snag / important posts" (671–73).

The play ends in fact with a sermon delivered by Lysistrata to both sides, reminding them that they are all Greeks and that as they destroy each other, "the Persians sit by / and wait" (lines 1339–40). And so negotiations for peace begin and, although the give and take of territory between Spartans and Athenians is made wildly and obscenely funny by a series of double entendres, the fact is that the comic stage is presenting to the audience an image of a negotiated peace—something that no politician dared do in the Assembly.]

Comparative Perspective

Although students tend to think they will enjoy a comedy more than a tragedy, they sometimes learn, to their chagrin, that comedy is in many ways harder to understand. Discuss some of the topical allusions in *Lysistrata* and compare them to those in other comic and satiric works (the *Satyricon*, perhaps, or *Gargantua and Pantagruel*). What is the connection between social detail and laughter?

Further Reading

See also the reading suggestions in the anthology, p. 701.

Easterling, P. E., ed. *Greece*. Vol. 1 of *The Cambridge History of Classical Literature*. 1985. Pp. 355–414. Contains a masterly assessment, written for the classical scholar and the literate general reader, of the whole genre; pp. 370–91 focus on Aristophanes.

McLeish, K. *The Theatre of Aristophanes*. 1980. This is "an attempt to examine the plays from the point of view of a dramatic critic and to try to discover . . . what their effect may have been on their original audience." The approach is by subject, not by individual play, but the index lists all the relevant passages under useful headings.

Whitman, C. H. *Aristophanes and the Comic Hero*. 1964. An analysis of Aristophanes' achievement as the creator of "a new kind of hero, the comic hero, who parodies his two solemn older brothers of tragedy and epic, but at the same time challenges their supremacy in expressing human aspirations in the face of the world's dilemma." Chapter 6 deals with *Lysistrata*.

PLATO

The Apology of Socrates

Backgrounds

Apology is the Greek word for "defense"; this speech is Plato's version of the one in which Socrates defended himself in court against the charges brought by his adversaries. It is divided into three sections, which correspond to the three stages of the trial. The first (pp. 727–42) is the defense proper; at that point the jury decides on a verdict. Socrates is guilty; it is now up to the prosecutors and the defendant to propose what they think an appropriate penalty. The jury will choose one or the other; no compromise will be made. The prosecution asks for death; Socrates, in the second part of his speech, instead of proposing exile or imprisonment for a few years, makes the outrageous suggestion that he be rewarded as a public benefactor. But he then offers a small fine. He is condemned to death. The last section of his speech (pp. 743ff.) is his final address to the court.

In the first and longest part of the speech he deals with the general prejudice against him: the widespread impression that he is a philosophical agnostic and that he is a "sophist"—one who teaches new ideas and rhetorical techniques for high fees. None of this is true. The real reason for his unpopularity, he suspects, is that he has confounded so many Athenians in argument, shown them up as confused and ignorant. In doing so he claims that he was simply trying to test the truth of the god Apollo's statement that Socrates was the wisest of men. He found that men who thought they knew something did not, and so he was wiser than they, since he knew that he knew nothing.

So much for the general prejudice; he turns then on his accusers, who have claimed that he corrupts the youth of Athens, disbelieves in the gods of the state, and introduces new divinities of his own. He cross-questions Meletus, his main accuser, and shows that the charges are invalid. He then announces that he will continue, as he has always done, to question the Athenians about justice and knowledge; this is, he says, his mission in life, imposed by Apollo. This announcement evidently causes an outcry in court, for he asks those present not to interrupt (p. 738); the jury brings in a verdict of guilty. Socrates's refusal to bargain about the death penalty leads to his death sentence. Socrates prophesies that the Athenians will silence him but will have to listen to younger men who will carry on his mission. He accepts his death calmly, secure in his belief that "no evil can happen to a good man, either in life or after death" (p. 746).

Plato belonged to an aristocratic Athenian family (he was related by his mother's second marriage to Critias, the leading spirit of the "Thirty Tyrants" who ruled Athens for a short time after the surrender to the Spartans in 404); while still young (he was born in 429) he became one of the group of Athenian men who spent their time listening to and arguing with Socrates. Though Socrates did not, like the sophists, assume the role of teacher, Plato and his companions were in a real sense his pupils. The execution of his beloved teacher in 399 B.C. left an indelible mark on Plato's thought and writing; in all his philosophical dialogues except the last (The Laws) Socrates figures as one of the principals and, in most of them, as the protagonist. The Apology is Plato's version of the speech Socrates made before the Athenian court in 399. He was present at the trial (see p. 743), and though his version is hardly likely to be a verbatim transcript of Socrates' remarks on that occasion Plato could not afford to make radical additions or subtractions; he was writing for an audience that included the crowds who attended the trial, not to mention the five hundred members of the jury.

The speech defies the conventions of Athenian legal procedure and the rules recommended by the sophists, the professional teachers of rhetoric. Instead of a "set oration duly ornamented with words and phrases" (p. 728), Socrates proposes to defend himself in his "accustomed manner"—in other words, in the deceptively simple but actually disconcerting manner that has made him so many enemies among those whose ignorance and intellectual confusion he has often exposed. In fact, after disposing of the popular caricature of him as an atheistic philosopher who teaches immorality for high fees—the Socrates of Aristophanes' comedy *The Clouds* (423 B.C.)—he proceeds to defend the very thing his audience finds most aggravating about him: his habit of arguing with all the experts and proving them wrong. He knows that this has made him many powerful enemies but insists that it is a mission imposed on him by the god Apollo. So much for the actual charge brought against him by his accusers—that he does not believe in the gods the city believes in; to these charges he now turns, and in a skillful cross-examination of his chief accuser, Meletus, he demonstrates in his "accustomed fashion" that Meletus doesn't know what he is talking about when he claims that Socrates is corrupting the younger generation. From this point on, instead of trying to win the good graces of the jury, he alienates them by insisting, at great length and with unmistakable sincerity, that since what he has been doing all these years is by command of the god, he will continue to do so as long as he lives. To cease would be impious; it would also be dishonorable.

In the course of this defiant speech he also takes time to answer another unstated charge: that though he is so interested in other people's opinions he never speaks up in the Assembly, never plays his part, like a loyal citizen, in the discussion of public policy. His defense is that if he had done so he "would have perished long ago," for he would never have acted against his conscience, as a man in political life has to do. He cites two cases in which he had to defy in one case public opinion and in the other tyrannical power. Under the democracy, serving—as every Athenian had to sooner or later—on the steering committee of the Assembly, he refused to vote for what would otherwise have been a unanimous (and illegal) resolution, in spite of threats of impeachment. And under the dictatorial rule of the antidemocratic regime set up in Athens after the defeat in 404 he refused to obey an order to arrest a fellow citizen and escaped with his life only because the regime was overthrown soon after.

Plato does not mention the fact that there was a strong popular feeling against Socrates precisely on political grounds. Socrates mentions in his speech the fact that "young men of the richer classes, who have not much to do, come about me of their own accord" (p. 732); this innocuous phrase masks the fact that many of these rich young men were hostile to the democratic regime and one of them, Critias, was later the leading figure among the Thirty Tyrants, who, backed by the Spartan victors, imposed a reign of terror on Athens. This regime had been overthrown by the democrats in 403, but, to avoid a counterterror, the Athenians declared an amnesty (the survivors of the Thirty excepted); no prosecutions for political offenses committed before 404 were to be permitted. The resentment at what many saw as Socrates' responsibility for the education of such men as Critias could not express itself as a political charge; hence the vague indictment under a law against "impiety," which could be interpreted in more ways than one.

Socrates' defiance of the court in his apparently arrogant refusal to bargain by suggesting an acceptable penalty is not hard to understand, since the only penalty the court would have been likely to accept was exile: Socrates would leave Athens for some other city, and the Athenians would have been rid of him without having to put him to death (p. 743). This he refuses to do, just as later, in prison awaiting death, he will reject the offers of his friends to help him escape from Athens. He will remain true to his mission: "the difficulty . . . is not to avoid death, but to avoid unrighteousness" (p. 744).

Classroom Strategies

One assignment if possible; otherwise, divide at p. 736, just before the paragraph beginning "Some one will say."

The student may well get the impression from the *Apology* that Socrates' philosophical contribution is purely negative, that all he does is convince people they do not understand the words they are using when they talk about morality; he himself has no definition to offer, but claims only to know that he himself knows nothing. In the other books of Plato that, unlike the *Apology*, are cast in the form of dramatic dialogues, Socrates emerges in a different light. It is true that he rarely proposes a solution to the dilemmas he uncovers by his questioning, but the dialogues show that his probing questions about the nature of piety, justice, bravery, and all the other moral qualities people think they know the nature of are the necessary preliminary to a definition. Previous philosophers have simply announced their doctrines to the world; the world could take them on or leave them, read them or not. Socrates insisted that true knowledge could not be simply proclaimed and accepted (or rejected); learner and teacher had to find their way, through hard-won agreement on point after point, to definitions they could both accept and act on. This process—"dialectic," to give it its Greek name—is the so-called Socratic method, and it was, in its time, a startling contrast to the standard procedure of the sophistic teachers, who gave lectures and wrote books but did not expect to be questioned.

But Socrates' contribution was not merely a revolution in method. He was also responsible for a decisive shift in the area explored by philosophy, which had begun in the Greek city of Miletus as an attempt to understand the material universe (Thales, the first philosopher, thought that water was the basis of all matter). Some later philosophers had proposed more sophisticated and complicated answers (two philosophers almost contemporary with Socrates had in fact invented atomic theory), and others wrestled with the philosophical problems inherent in such concepts as being, becoming, and motion. But it was Socrates who brought philosophy to bear on the moral problems of human life, especially on the problem of justice in individual and collective conduct. Philosophy would after him still deal with cosmological, physical, and metaphysical problems, but the question of human conduct would bulk large in the works of Plato, Aristotle (author of the *Ethics*), and the later Epicurean and Stoic schools.

Though Socrates is no aristocrat (in fact his father was a stonemason and he himself, at the time of his trial, was penniless, pp. 738 and 743), he cites the example of Achilles for his refusal to be intimidated by the threat of death (p. 736) and, after his condemnation, looks forward to meeting, in the lower world, the heroes Palamedes and Ajax (p. 745). These epic figures seem at first glance strange company for a philosopher whose constant concern was to establish the primacy of justice and righteousness in human conduct, but in fact, in spite of the pride and violence such heroic names conjure up, they are not inappropriate in the context of the speech.

Palamedes was the cleverest of the Greek chieftains at Troy; he was credited with the invention not only of the alphabet and numbers but also of a game resembling checkers with which the Greeks amused themselves when all was quiet on the Trojan front. But he incurred the enmity of Agamemnon and Odysseus by speaking out against the long drawn-out war and calling for an immediate return home. Odysseus framed him: Trojan gold was buried in his tent while he was away and a forged letter from Priam produced to convict him as a Trojan agent. In spite of a brilliant defense at his trial, he was condemned and executed. The story was well known to Socrates' audience; both Sophocles and Euripides (and perhaps Aeschylus as well) had written tragedies on the subject.

The other sufferer from an unjust court cited by Socrates is, however, a very different case. Ajax was the best man among the Achaeans while Achilles was away, Homer tells us in the *Iliad*, and even his enemy Odysseus calls him the noblest of the Danaans after Achilles. When Achilles was killed and the Achaeans decided to award his arms and armor to the bravest among them, Ajax naturally expected to be chosen, but the judgment went to Odysseus instead. After an unsuccessful attempt to murder Agamemnon, Odysseus, and others whom he regarded as responsible, Ajax killed himself.

When Socrates speaks of talking to Ajax in the next world he is of course recalling to the minds of his hearers the famous passage in the *Odyssey* XI, where Odysseus addresses Ajax but gets no answer. Socrates, as a fellow sufferer, will not be treated so contemptuously. Yet it is a little disconcerting to find the gentle philosopher, whose sharpest weapon was the cut and thrust of his dialectic, associating himself with the primeval violence of Ajax. Just as surprising is his citation of Achilles, whom he actually quotes as an example to follow. Achilles would not let the prospect of certain death deter him from his purpose, which was, of course, to kill Hector and avenge the death of Patroclus: "Let me die forthwith . . . and be avenged of my enemy, rather than abide here . . . a laughing-stock" (p. 736). Socrates will not retreat in the face of death either: "wherever a man's place is, whether the place which he has chosen or that in which he has been placed by a commander, there he ought to remain in hour of danger" (pp. 736–37). Socrates remained in his place as a soldier, obeying the orders of the generals elected by the Athenians; now he will remain steadfast in the place ordained for him by the god Apollo, or rather, since this depends on his interpretation of the word of Apollo, in the place that he has chosen himself.

The snub-nosed, poorly dressed old man of seventy, facing adversaries determined to drive him out of Athens or kill him if he will not go, defies them and sees himself, not without reason, as one of the company of heroes whose memory all Greeks held in respect and whose burial places they recognized as holy ground. When he refuses to follow the usual practice of defendants in Athenian courts, to beg for mercy, to produce weeping children and relatives, he speaks in heroic terms, as a man who must be true, like Odysseus, to his reputation, to what the world expects of a hero: "Whether this opinion of me be deserved or not, at any rate the world has decided that Socrates is in some way superior to other men" (p. 741).

Topics for Discussion and Writing

Behind the actual terms of the indictment lay a real prejudice against Socrates as an opponent of democracy, and this was not due solely to his association with such figures as Critias. Can you find in his speech any grounds for such a prejudice?

[His abstention from political activity under a democratic regime that encouraged and depended on full participation by all the citizens. In his defense on this point he actually uses clichés of the opponents of democracy: "the truth is, that no man who goes to war with you or any other multitude, honestly striving against the many lawless and unrighteous deeds which are done in a state, will save his life" (p. 739).

Among the prominent figures he examined and found ignorant were politicians (pp. 730–31), that is, the orators whose speeches in the Assembly shaped public policy (cf. Lycon who has a quarrel with Socrates "on behalf of the rhetoricians," p. 732).

When he examines the artisans, he finds them, too, wanting: "because they were good workmen they thought that they also knew all sorts of high matters" (p. 732). In Athenian democratic theory an artisan was supposed to have just as much understanding of public policy and, therefore, just as strong a claim to direct it as, for example, a landed aristocrat.

When he proposes that he be rewarded instead of punished he speaks of himself as the man who "has been careless of what the many care for—wealth, and family interests, and military offices, and speaking in the assembly, and magistracies, and plots, and parties" (p. 742). There is clearly a certain dislike for the political life of Athens expressed in that list and in fact he continues: "Reflecting that I was really too honest a man to be a politician and live."

Plato himself was no admirer of the democracy that had put Socrates to death; his picture of Socrates may have been influenced by his own feelings. But it is quite understandable that a man with Socrates' insistence on universal moral standards should have been disgusted with the politics of Athens in the last years of the war; it must indeed have seemed as if the politicians and the assembly that supported them were bent on self-destruction.]

Comparative Perspectives

1. Socrates, as the headnote informs us, "wrote nothing," yet Plato's dialogues capture a defining moment in Greek culture, when oral traditions sustained by memorizing poetry like Homer's yielded to new styles of thought made possible by the writing of prose. What elements of Socratic dialectic seem, on the one hand, to reflect spoken discourse? What qualities of abstract thought expressed in that speech show, on the other hand, a shift away from the representation of thought through action characteristic of Homeric composition? [See, e.g., the opening of the *Iliad,* when the decision made by Achilles not to attack Agamemnon is attributed to the intervention of Athena, unseen by others, rather than to any process of internal rational analysis.]

2. Look at other philosophical texts of the ancient world (the Book of Job, The Sermon on the Mount, the Koran). Which seem primarily the record of oral discourse? How does the style of composition appear to affect the nature of the ideas being communicated?

Further Reading

See also the reading suggestions in the anthology, p. 727.

Guthrie, W. K. C. *A History of Greek Philosophy,* Vol. 4. 1975. Pp. 70–93. An authoritative discussion of the historicity, organization, and ideas of the speech. See also Vol. 3 (1969) on Socrates and the Delphic response (pp. 405ff.) and his political views (pp. 409ff.).

Havelock, Eric A. *The Muse Learns to Write: Reflections on Orality and Literacy from Antiquity to the Present.* 1986.

West, T. G. *Plato's Apology of Socrates.* 1979. A new translation with interpretation. A careful analysis of the speech section with helpful chapters on Socrates as a public man and Socrates as a private man.

West, T. G., and G. C. West. *Four Texts on Socrates.* 1984. Translations of *Euthyphro, Apology, Crito,* and Aristophanes' *Clouds.* The introduction deals with the *Apology.*

Aristotle

Poetics

Backgrounds and Topics for Discussion

The short selection from the work deals with tragedy. It begins with the famous definition of tragedy (for an explanation of the term *catharsis,* see n. 2, p. 747), which is explained, section by section, in the following paragraphs. Aristotle recognizes the importance of character in tragedy— the persons represented "must necessarily possess certain qualities of Character and Thought" (p. 747)—but places greater emphasis on the action, the plot. "It is not for the purpose of presenting their characters that the agents engage in action, but rather it is for the sake of their actions that they take on the characters they have" (p. 747–48). The plot has to have unity (which is not necessarily attained by telling the story of one individual) and the right "magnitude"—a length "sufficient to permit a change from bad fortune to good or from good fortune to bad to come about in an inevitable or probable sequence of events." Plots can be simple or complex; in complex plots the change of fortune involves a reversal or a recognition or both. (The prime example of change of fortune with both is the *Oedipus* of Sophocles.) Furthermore, the change of fortune should be from good to bad, and the victim of this reversal should not be a wholly bad man or a completely good one (for in the one case we would be pleased and in the other merely disgusted) but one "whose place is between these extremes . . . the man who on the one hand is not pre-eminent in virtue and justice, and yet on the other hand does not fall into misfortune through vice or depravity, but falls because of some mistake; one among the number of the highly renowned and prosperous, such as Oedipus" (p. 749). As footnote 7 on p. 749 of the anthology explains, the word translated "mistake" is often referred to as "flaw," which suggests a moral defect.

Aristotle's *Poetics* is the first treatise ever written on literary composition (the Greek word *poietes*—poet—means, literally, "maker"); many before him, Plato especially, discussed the nature and effect of poetry but a systematic treatise on the subject was unprecedented. It has had an enormous influence on modern critical approaches to tragic drama; particularly influential in the European Renaissance was the idea of the "tragic flaw," derived from the Greek word *hamartia,* which James Hutton's translation more correctly renders as "mistake." A classic version of this doctrine can be found in Shakespeare, in Hamlet's speech about the Danish nation and their penchant for drink: "So, oft it chances in particular men, / That for some vicious mole of nature in them" (1.4.23ff.).

The *Poetics,* however, was written long after the deaths of the three great tragic dramatists of the fifth century B.C. And Aristotle's view of the tragic character as one who "falls by some mistake" is, in most cases, not easily applicable to the plays of Aeschylus, Sophocles, and Euripides. This is a possible theme of discussion with the class: how far does *Oedipus,* for example, Aristotle's famous example of the well-made tragedy, fit the definition? Is Oedipus a man "not pre-eminent in virtue and justice" who "on the other hand does not fall into misfortune through vice or depravity, but falls because of some mistake"? If so, what is the mistake? His whole life seems to be a series of mistakes. It is hard to see how Medea can be understood along the lines of Aristotle's formulation, or Clytemnestra either, but perhaps a case could be made out for Agamemnon. Orestes, who knowingly commits the crime of matricide, escapes this view altogether.

Also essential to Aristotle's conception of tragedy is the recognition, which in what he considers the best type of plot is identical to the reversal of the protagonist's fortune. Oedipus is the classic example: he recognizes himself as the murderer he is searching for and also as a patricide and incestuous son; but recognition plays a part also in the *Oresteia*: when Clytemnestra recognizes her son's identity, her death is only moments away. Recognition of identity, though it frequently occurs in other Greek tragedies, plays no part in *Medea*; but in a metaphorical sense (one that Aristotle does not express but that he may have realized) recognition *is* essential to the tragic process. The tragic hero in the end is forced to dispense with illusions of power and claims to godlike superiority; in the reversal of fortune—often brought about, as Aristotle says, by his or her own actions, which produce the opposite of what is intended— he or she is forced to recognize the mortality and fallibility that are conditions shared with all humankind.

The class might also be asked to discuss the plays in the light of Aristotle's concept of unity—the avoidance of plots "in which episodes follow one another in no probable or inevitable sequence" in favor of a "plot so organized that if any one of [the events that are part of it] is displaced or taken away, the whole will be shaken and put out of joint." Many think that *Oedipus* has the most closely logical plot; comparison with *Medea* (how organic is the arrival of Aegeus?) should prove interesting, and all the plays can be examined to see if there is adequate motivation for new entries and developments.

Further Reading

See also the reading suggestions in the anthology, p. 746.

Aristotle's Poetics. Trans. S. H. Butcher. 1961. The introduction, by the outstanding modern critic Francis Fergusson, is a full interpretation of Aristotle's work for the modern reader.

Aristotle. *Poetics.* Ed. D. W. Lucas. 1968. An edition, with commentary, of the Greek text. The introduction contains a survey of Greek literary theory before Aristotle and valuable appendices: "Pity, Fear and *Katharsis*" and *"Hamartia."*

Aristotle on Poetry and Style. Trans. G. M. A. Grube. 1958. A translation of the *Poetics* and selections from the *Rhetoric*. The introduction deals succinctly and clearly with the problems raised by the text.

PLAUTUS

Pseudolus

Classroom Strategies and Topics for Discussion

You might want to begin by noting that the first two major comic works in the anthology are plays—*Lysistrata* and *Pseudolus*. It is important for students to understand how staging brings a verbal text to life and how funny Plautus's play is in performance. If you invite a small group of students to the front of the classroom to put on an impromptu short performance, you can make a serious point in the most natural and disarming way: without any prior rehearsal, even the most tentative enactment of a scene demonstrates the social nature of comic interaction. When a class becomes an audience, everyone experiences the power of comedy to bring members of a community together. Inevitably, one laugh begets more laughter, and you are launched on a discussion of why we laugh and why hearing someone else laugh makes us laugh more.

One reason we laugh, of course, is that we recognize the human reality that is exaggerated but not traduced by conventional type characters. Since Plautus, as the headnote points out, is the source of so many Western cultural conceptions about what is funny, you will probably want to examine why people who have no connection with ancient Rome continue to laugh at the definitions of behavior codified by Roman comedy. As always, it is a good idea to look both for the universal truths with which we can easily identify and for the culturally specific materials that require some contextualization. Some attention needs to be paid, therefore, to the satiric portrait of Rome that emerges from Plautus's work.

The play is dominated by the title character, and you should ask your students how they react to Pseudolus himself, perhaps by beginning with the detailed physical description that Harpax gives Ballio (4.7.215–18). Clearly, this is the Roman equivalent of a clown costume. It would be surprising if you have no natural clowns in your classroom, and it will be rewarding for everyone to consider why some people seem to be born with the gift of making others laugh. Why are some people good mimics? What gifts of observation seem to be required of a comic view of life?

This need not involve any profound delving; in fact, a point to make is that the stock figures of Plautine comedy demonstrate little in the way of individualized personality. Perhaps the most interesting psychological questions in this sort of drama involve the audience rather than the persons on the stage. Why does this scruffy-looking slave spend so much time talking to the audience? Pseudolus is only one of a long line of con artists who dare to take viewers into their confidence as they describe their mendacious plots and motivations. Audiences feel flattered by the implied compliment: you, the rogues seem to say, are smart enough to understand me; and, of course, I would never try to put anything over on anyone as smart as you!

In short, in the theater we become complicit with Pseudolus (whom in real life we would probably assiduously avoid) and root for him, even at the point when he is worried by the superior skills of Simia, whose virtuoso turn in Act IV is worth discussion. Other characters directly address the audience as well, notably Ballio in his whip-flourishing entrance. Your students should be asked why the audience is not seduced by the pimp's involving us in his contemptuous assessment of the members of his household—and why it is not offended. The genius of Plautine comedy is that it stylizes the seamy side of transactions such as these so that they do not threaten us.

Neither do the parents and children of the Plautine comic universe command the kind of audience interest or sympathy that we extend to the comic slaves. The *Pseudolus* actually offers rather an attractive version of the blocking father in Simo, not so much because of his paternal care but rather because of his amused acceptance of his clever slave's audacity. Calidorus is a sweetly hopeless youth, and perhaps the most remarkable fact about Phoenicium is that she can write.

It will be helpful to talk about the courtesan as a commodity in Roman comedy and Roman life. Although Plautine comedies center on sexual liaisons, *Pseudolus* contains no "love stories." Ballio is not simply a pimp but a slave trader. In threatening his stable of four "lovely ladies," he individualizes them only to the extent that three of them represent basic food groups: wheat, meat, and oil. Phoenicium, the fourth and the focus of desire in the *Pseudolus,* is identified simply with money. The real love interest of the play, then, is cash. If your students ask about the lines in which Ballio's teenage slaveboy wonders about homoerotic assaults (3.1), or note the way Ballio offhandedly assumes a sexual liaison between Harpax and his captain with the long name (4.7.145–46), you can simply note that these references show how relatively tolerant Rome (and Greece) were when it came to homosexual practices, which were understood as simply one phase of sexual expression rather than as an exclusive, self-defining carnal preference.

In fact, it could be argued that the most intense of bodily pleasures imagined in the *Pseudolus* involve food, not sex. Even in translation, the play's images emphasize gustatory preferences, from the Cook's celebration of spices to metaphors like "a lover who's been found / As empty as a rotten nut" (1.3.272–73) or "I'll bone and fillet him, the way / A cook prepares a slippery eel" (294–95). You may want to mention to your class that comic literature is full of characters whose whole existences, like the Cook's or the pimp's, seem penetrated by their professional activities, since one human foible at which we laugh seems to be tunnel vision. The comic protagonist generally possesses wide-ranging vision, sympathies, or resources; lesser characters are funny because they are stuck in one groove.

Food and sex are, of course, the staples of the rowdy, robust comedy that we associate with many of the authors in the anthology, emphatically including Aristophanes and Rabelais. We laugh at our appetites because we know how hard it is to control them and how they deflate our pretensions. In typical satiric style, bodily functions dominate the characters' experiences of themselves and each other. Ask your students what view of life emerges from the *Pseudolus,* with all its references to sweat, vomit, excrement, and fornication (the kind of references that are part of not only writers' but everyone's comic repertoire—we laugh at our bodies all the time).

Finally, you might consider with your students how the military is represented in the play and why a rigidly organized society like Rome's sanctioned the kind of festal rituals that produced the *Pseudolus.* How often do we get the chance to laugh at soldiers (even Ballio complains of the curtness of Polymachaeroplagides' epistolary manner)? What is the function of a safety valve? What does it mean to "let off steam"? After kicking up his big feet in the brilliant opening scene of Act V, Pseudolus heads "home," content to remain with his "old boss." Why?

In the end, the play is a tribute to the resourcefulness and sheer intelligence of two slaves. The dramatic medium makes it all the easier for Plautus to emphasize their wit. What is conveyed by the gusto with which they sing and dance and comment of their own performances? The headnote to the text provides a valuable discussion of the metatheatrical elements in this play, and you might conclude by asking your students to locate points in the text where they operate. In what sense is Pseudolus an artist? What kind of performer is required by this role?

Topics for Writing

1. Discuss the theatrical possibilities of Ballio's entrance with a whip, or of Pseudolus's final dance.
2. Food imagery in the *Pseudolus.*
3. The clever servant in classical comedy.

Further Reading

See also the suggestions in the anthology, p. 754.

Lowe, J. C. B. "The Cook Scene of Plautus' *Pseudolus.*" *Classical Quarterly* 35 (1985): 411–16. This learned article discusses the Plautine additions to a Greek source, making the interesting observation that, unlike the Greeks, the Romans enjoyed convivial meals at tombsites (which may account for the Cook's advertising the life-prolonging virtues of his cuisine).

Wright, John "The Transformation of Pseudolus." *Transactions of the American Philological Association* 105: 403–16

CATULLUS

Backgrounds

We know very little about Catullus; almost all that we do know is based on inference from the poems themselves. Luckily, the full collection of 116 poems that has survived the centuries contains many references to identifiable persons and events of his time. Many of them are addressed to men who were prominent in the cultural and political life of the Roman capital; it is clear that Catullus, though born in a provincial city, was well connected and fully at home in sophisticated society. He was also the leading figure in a literary movement, one of a group of young poets the orator and statesman Cicero refers to as "the moderns"; they turned their backs on what had so far been the characteristic media of Roman poetry, national epic, and tragedy, to produce shorter poems, modeled on the work of the Greek poets of Alexandria, full of learned allusions—elegant, witty, and compact. Catullus himself, however, surpasses his models; he can, on occasion, be learnedly allusive, even slightly pedantic, but he can also write about the humors and passions of everyday life with an energy and directness that have their equal only in the poetry of Sappho.

That the real name of his "Lesbia" was Clodia we know from the statement of a later writer, Apuleius (2nd century A.D.). What is not entirely certain is whether this Clodia was the famous—or rather, notorious—daughter of Appius Claudius Pulcher, a former consul and a member of one of the oldest patrician families of Rome. Clodia was married to another Roman aristocrat, Metellus Celer, but during his absence abroad as governor of a province her scandalous behavior was the talk of Rome. She took many lovers; there was even a rumor that she had an incestuous affair with her brother Publius Clodius Pulcher, who, in the last violent years of the Roman Republic's collapse into anarchy and civil war, distinguished himself as the most audacious and dangerous of the political gangsters who terrorized their opponents. When Clodia's husband died in 59 B.C. there were many who suspected she had poisoned him. Three years later she was instrumental in having one of her lovers who had broken with her, Caelius, prosecuted for a series of illegal actions. He was defended by Cicero, from whose speech in his defense, *Pro Caelio*, we know the details of the rumors that were circulating in Rome about clodia's morals. Cicero was delighted to accept the case, since he was one of the principal targets of clodia's brother and had suffered much at his hands. At one point in his speech he imagines that one of clodia's most famous ancestors, Appius Claudius, has come back from the dead to reproach her. "Was it for this that I built the first aqueduct to bring water to Rome, so that you could use it to wash after your debauches? Was it for this that I built a road [the Via Appia] so that you could travel on it with packs of other women's husbands?" Cicero does not forget, either, to make good use of the rumors that one of her lovers was her brother.

This trial took place in 56 B.C.; Clodia's liaison with Caelius had lasted about two years. The latest event mentioned in Catullus's poems occurred in 55 B.C.; it seems probable that he died in that or the next year. His affair with Clodia must then have taken place before 54 B.C. Though we cannot be absolutely certain of the identification, some of the things Catullus says about *his* Clodia (for example, the adulterous emotions described in poem 83 and the accusations of promiscuity in poems 8, 11, and 58) correspond well with Cicero's picture of the woman.

Topics for Discussion

1. Catullus had read and translated poems by Sappho. In what ways can one see evidence of a tradition of European love poetry in formation?

2. In poem 76, Catullus looks back on the pain of his love for Lesbia, using imagery of hunger and sickness, and tries to find some way to transcend his bitterness. In his own way, Catullus fuses convention and personal experience and produces verse that seems absolutely "sincere." What does this ability suggest about the function of poetry in Augustan Rome?

Further Reading

See also the reading suggestions in the anthology, p. 754.

Cicero. *The Speeches. Pro Caelio etc.* (Loeb Classical Library). 1958. Contains a translation of *Pro Caelio*; for Clodia, see pp. 445–53.

Kenney, E. J., ed. *Latin Literature:* Vol. II of *The Cambridge History of Latin Literature.* 1982. Pp. 198–200.

VIRGIL

The Aeneid

Backgrounds

Aeneas, a Trojan prince in flight from the Greek sack of Troy with his father, his young son, and the statues of his household gods, sails west in search of the new home promised him by the gods in a score of prophecies. Virgil opens his narrative at a moment when Aeneas has almost reached his goal—the plain of Latium in Italy, where he will eventually found a city, Alba Longa, from which will come after his death the founders of Rome. Aeneas and his fleet are off Sicily, almost in sight of their destination, when Juno (the Roman equivalent of Hera), who hates even the survivors of ruined Troy, sends a storm to scatter the ships.

Aeneas, with his ship, is driven south to the African coast, to the territory of Dido, queen of Carthage, a new city for which Juno plans a glorious future as master of the Mediterranean world (the same destiny Jupiter [Zeus] and Venus [Aphrodite] plan for Rome). Dido welcomes Aeneas as well as the crews of his scattered ships, who also come ashore; she offers Aeneas and the Trojans a partnership in the city that she is building. At a banquet she gives for them, Aeneas is prevailed on to tell the story of his wanderings since he left Troy.

He begins (book II) with the fall of the city: the Greek stratagem of the wooden horse; the lying story of Sinon that tricks the Trojans into admitting it to the city; the fate of Laocoön, who warned against it; and the night assault of the Greeks, led into the city by the Greek warriors concealed in the horse. Aeneas fights but in a losing battle; he sees Priam killed at the altar of his palace by Neoptolemus, son of Achilles, and returns to his own house, where he collects his father, Anchisës, his wife, Creusa, and his son, Iulus, and leads them out of the burning city. On the way, Creusa is lost; her ghost appears to him, urging him on and promising him a kingdom in the west. From Troy, Aeneas sets sail and, after a series of adventures like those of Odysseus (one of them in fact is a meeting with a Kyklops), reaches Sicily, where his father, Anchisës, dies. (These travels, the material of book III, are not included in the anthology.)

Book IV opens with Dido passionately in love with Aeneas; during a hunt they are overtaken by a storm and shelter alone in a cave. There they become lovers but, though Dido regards her union as a marriage, Aeneas will later insist that it is not binding. For meanwhile the gods who have imposed on Aeneas the responsibility for Rome's future have become impatient with his long stay at Carthage and his cooperation with Dido in the foundation of Carthage, a city that will one day be Rome's mortal enemy.

Jupiter sends Mercury (Hermes) to order him to put to sea. As he prepares to obey, Dido summons him, pleads with him, denounces him, and threatens him—all to no avail; he must obey the commands of Heaven, think of his son and the kingdom he is to inherit in Italy. As Aeneas puts out to sea, Dido, after cursing him and promising unceasing war between her descendants and his, kills herself. In book V (not in the anthology) Aeneas, back in Sicily, holds funeral games for Anchisës (like those Achilles held for Patroclus in the *Iliad*) and then sails for Italy. There, in book VI, he is led by the Sibyl down to the realm of the dead, where he sees, as Odysseus does in book XI of the *Odyssey,* the great sinners and great men of the past but also, unlike Odysseus, the great men of the future, who will impose Roman dominion on the whole of the known world.

In books VII and VIII (not in the anthology) the Trojans become involved in a war with the Italians, who are roused to battle by Juno, anxious to forestall the foundation of the city that will be the rival and conqueror of her favored Carthage. At the end of book VIII Venus brings to her son Aeneas, as Thetis brought to her son Achilles in the *Iliad,* armor newly forged by Vulcan (Hephaestus); on the shield (cf. the shield of Achilles) Vulcan has depicted the glorious exploits of the Roman descendants of Aeneas. Books IX–XI (not in the anthology) follow the ebb and flow of battle, which end (Book XII) with the death of Turnus at the hand of Aeneas and Juno's acceptance of the Roman destiny. She accepts on the condition that the Trojans, whom she still hates, abandon their language and nationality and merge their identity in the new Roman nation that is to conquer the world.

In book XX of the *Iliad* (not in the anthology) the Trojan prince Aeneas, whose mother was the goddess Aphrodite, fights with Achilles; he is rescued from certain death by the god Poseidon because "it is destined that he shall be the survivor." He is to found a royal house that will reign over the Trojans in time to come. Later poets developed this mysterious prophecy into a story of Aeneas's escape from Troy, carrying his old

father Anchisës on his back, and other poets made him the leader of a
westward voyage with his family and his household gods in search of a
place to found a new Troy. When in the third century B.C. the Romans
came into contact with Greece, they admired and imitated its arts and literature, but had to subdue the Greek cities by force of arms. The Roman
wish to find a place for themselves in the Greek epic and historical tradition without claiming kinship with the subjected and despised Greeks of
their own day was granted by the creation of the legend that Aeneas the
Trojan was the founder of the Roman nation. This story was given literary form in the epics (now lost) of the Latin poets Naevius and Ennius
(third century B.C.) and was in Virgil's time the authorized version of
Rome's origins. Augustus, the first Roman emperor and Virgil's patron,
had the temple of Athena at Troy rebuilt on a magnificent scale.

Virgil was recasting the traditional Roman story in what was to be its
enduring form, a restatement of national ideals, for the new age of peace
and prosperity under the rule of Augustus, who had finally brought peace
to a world that had been racked for over a century by civil war.

Augustus was intensely interested in Virgil's poem; we know that parts
of book VI (the visit to the underworld) were read aloud to him by the
poet himself and when Virgil, dying before he could put the last touches
on the work, ordered his friends to burn it, Augustus intervened to preserve the poem.

The poem is, in a sense, officially inspired, but it does not read like
propaganda. The sacrifices Aeneas has to make to fulfill his god-given
mission are so great that some readers have even seen the poem as a
muted repudiation of imperial Roman values. This is an exaggeration,
but there is no question about the sacrifice the imperial mission involves,
both for the hero and for the Roman people. Aeneas not only has to abandon the great love of his life but also will die before he has time to enjoy
the promised reward, the city from which will come the founders of
Rome. Dido's dying prayer to her gods will be answered. If, she says, he is
indeed destined to land in Italy,

>   yet all the same
> When hard beset in war by a brave people,
> Forced to go outside his boundaries
> And torn from Iulus, let him beg assistance,
> Let him see the unmerited death of those
> Around and with him, and accepting peace
> On unjust terms, let him not, even so,
> Enjoy his kingdom or the life he longs for,
> But fall in battle before his time and lie
> Unburied on the sand!
>
>   (IV.823–32)

Aeneas does indeed find himself hard beset in war; books VII–XII are
a Virgilian *Iliad* in which Aeneas and his Trojans fight against Turnus, a
new Achilles. He does indeed have to leave his son, Iulus, and go begging

for help from neutral Italian tribes. He loses allies in battle, chief among them young Pallas, for whose death he takes revenge on Turnus in the last lines of the poem. He accepts a peace that, if not unjust, is at least a compromise: the bargain made by Jupiter with Juno that the Trojan name will vanish in the fusion of Aeneas's people with the Latins. And after a few years at the head of his new kingdom he is to be killed in battle; his body will not be found. Greatness, Virgil is suggesting, calls for almost unbearable sacrifice. And the Romans who later carry on Aeneas' line will have to make sacrifices, too. Anchises, in the world of the dead, spells out the Roman destiny for Aeneas:

> Others will cast more tenderly in bronze
> Their breathing figures, I can well believe,
> And bring more lifelike portraits out of marble;
> Argue more eloquently, use the pointer
> To trace the paths of heaven accurately
> And accurately foretell the rising stars.
> Roman, remember by your strength to rule
> To pacify, to impose the rule of law,
> To spare the conquered, battle down the proud.
> (VI.848–57, not in the anthology)

The "others" who perfect the creative arts and sciences of peace are the Greeks; the Roman destiny is war and rule over peoples. The contrast is more emphatically expressed in the original Latin: the address to the Roman begins, *At tu romane memento* ("But you, Roman, remember"). The imperial destiny excludes the arts of peace. Virgil himself was an intellectual who studied philosophy, a poet steeped in the literature of Greece and Rome; his heart was with those "others," and he above all men realized what had to be given up if men were to become Romans.

Classroom Strategies

Suggested assignments:

1. Books I and II
2. Book IV
3. Books VI, VIII, and XII

or

1. Books I, II, and IV
2. Books VI, VII, and XII

Virgil, unlike Homer, thinks always in terms of history, of the rise and fall of nations and in particular of the rise of Rome. His characters and incidents have not only their dramatic present intensity, they are invested also with a wealth of symbolic correspondences to history, past and future. The student will need some background in Roman history to appreciate the significance, to take one example, of Dido's great curse on Aeneas. She appeals to her people, the Tyrians, the Carthaginians,

> besiege with hate
> His progeny and all his race to come:
> Make this your offering to my dust. No love,
> No pact must be between our peoples; No,
> But rise up from my bones, avenging spirit!
> Harry with fire and sword the Dardan countrymen
> Now, or hereafter, at whatever time
> The strength will be afforded. Coast with coast
> In conflict, I implore, and sea with sea,
> And arms with arms: may they contend in war,
> Themselves and all the children of their children!
>   (IV.834–44)

Every Roman who read these lines remembered the history of the wars that, after threatening the existence of Rome itself, extended Roman power overseas from Italy and launched the city on the path to world empire. They were called the Punic (that is, Carthaginian) wars, and there were three of them.

The first began in 264 B.C. as a Roman attempt to restrain Carthaginian expansion in Sicily. To win the war, however, the Romans, who had never had a navy, found themselves compelled to become a seapower to deal with Carthaginian control of the sea between Italy and Africa. They did so and, in what was mainly a naval war ("Coast with coast / In conflict . . . sea with sea"), they eventually forced Carthage to evacuate Sicily and pay an indemnity.

The war lasted twenty-three years; a little more than twenty years later (218 B.C.) the Second Punic War began. In the interim, the Carthaginians had built up a base in Spain; when the Romans tried to check their expansion there, the Carthaginian general Hannibal led his forces through Spain and southern France, over the Alps, and down into Italy. He defeated one Roman army after another and laid waste Italy with fire and sword ("rise up from my bones, avenging spirit! / Harry with fire and sword the Dardan countrymen"). But he was unable to assault the fortified city of Rome itself, or to break the loyalty of the Italian fortified cities to Rome, and in the end, when the Roman general Scipio drove the Carthaginians from Spain and then invaded North Africa, Hannibal came home to Carthage, only to be decisively defeated by Scipio in 202 B.C.

Carthage was forced to give up Spain (which became a Roman province), surrender its fleet, and pay an indemnity. But in the next few decades it began to gain strength again, and in 149 B.C. the Romans began the Third (and last) Punic War. Carthage was invaded, the city stormed and then (146 B.C.) utterly destroyed; the Romans ran plows over the ruins of the city. Africa became a Roman province.

All this, and more besides, was evoked for the Roman reader by the lines of Dido's curse, and this is typical of Virgil's poetic practice throughout. Dido herself, for example, would recall to the Roman reader another African queen, Cleopatra of Egypt, who had ensnared with her love Mark Antony, Augustus's rival for supremacy in the Roman world. Aeneas, abandoning his mission and helping to build Dido's Carthage, would remind the Roman readers of Antony, who, reveling in the delights of Cleopatra's Alexandria, lost a world for love; this would deepen their sense of the danger Aeneas was courting by his delay at Carthage. The subdued reference comes clearly to the surface when, on the shield of Aeneas in book VIII, we see Augustus, the descendant of Aeneas, facing in battle Antony, the renegade Roman who marshals against Rome the power of the East "And in [whose] wake the Egyptian consort came / So shamefully" (VIII.106–7).

Topics for Discussion

Virgil deliberately models his poem on Homer; the first six books are Aeneas's *Odyssey*, the last six his *Iliad*. Sometimes specific incidents from Homer are imitated; yet though the relation to the model is in every case clear, Virgil makes the material serve his own, different purpose. Discuss the nature and effect of the Virgilian adaptation of the following.

1. Odysseus' interview with Ajax in book XI of the *Odyssey* for Aeneas's interview with Dido in book VI of the *Aeneid*.
   [In both cases the hero makes an appeal for reconciliation with a suicide who has reason to feel wronged by him, but the appeal is rejected in silence. Odysseus, however, does not really admit that he was responsible; he wishes the Greeks had not given him the arms of Achilles as his prize but does not say that in fact they should have gone to Ajax. He blames the whole thing on Zeus ("no one bears the blame but Zeus," *Odyssey* XI.628). Aeneas too puts the responsibility on the gods (*Aeneid* VI.245), but in this case we know that he did indeed have direct orders from Jupiter, brought by Mercury, and furthermore that the fate and future of a great nation rested on his decision. For Odysseus the silence of the shade of Ajax is a minor matter: "Who knows if in that darkness he might still / have spoken, and I answered? But my heart / longed, after this, to see the dead elsewhere" (*Odyssey* XI.635–37). Odysseus and Ajax in life were fellow soldiers, rivals for rewards and glory, but Aeneas loved Dido, and her silent, hostile rejection of his plea brings him to shed the tears he held back when they parted at Carthage. Unlike Odysseus, who let Ajax go, "Aeneas still gazed after her in tears, / Shaken by her ill fate and pitying her" (*Aeneid* VI.263–64).]
2. Homer's description of the shield of Achilles in the *Iliad* (XVIII.572ff.) for Aeneas's shield in the *Aeneid* (VIII.24ff.).
   [The parallelism of the contexts is close; the mother goddess in each case brings armor made by the divine smith for her son to use against his enemy (Hector, Turnus), and each hero delights in the

splendor of the arms. But the shields present two different worlds. Achilles' shield is an image of human life as a whole, of cities in war and at peace, of work on the land and the dance at the palace—a world that has no past or future, a human condition that will never change. On Aeneas's shield the god has figured episodes from the early history of Rome—the three generations of Ascanius (Iulus, Aeneas's son) and the wolf-suckling Romulus and Remus, the builders of Rome. On goes the historical procession, through the early kings, to the expulsion of Tarquin (the last king) and the heroic defense of the city against his Etruscan allies. An incident from times still further in the future, the Capitol attacked by the Gauls, is followed by scenes from the lower world, the conspirator Catiline in torment, the virtuous Cato giving laws. These two men lived and died not too many years before Augustus established his imperial regime; the prelude to that period of peace and reconstruction was the defeat of Mark Antony and his eastern allies at the Battle of Actium in 31 B.C.—the central scene on the shield. All this lies far in the future, and it is beyond the comprehension of Aeneas, though "He felt joy in their pictures, taking up / Upon his shoulder all the destined acts / And fame of his descendants" (*Aeneid* VII.165–67).]

3. Odysseus' story of his wanderings at the court of Phaeacia for Aeneas's account of the fall of Troy and his subsequent wanderings, at Dido's banquet.

[Odysseus at the court of Alcinous is alone, a shipwrecked naked sailor befriended by a princess and cautiously concealing his identity until, moved by the song of the bard Demodocus, his tears betray him as one of the heroes from Troy. His tale, a spellbinding story of encounters with giants, monsters, and hospitable goddesses, of visits to strange lands, even to the land of the dead, wins him rich gifts and a passage home, and though the princess Nausicaa, with her father's consent, would obviously like to keep him as a husband, he insists on returning to Ithaca. Aeneas does not conceal his identity but reveals it to Dido, as she offers his ships' crews the choice of passage to Italy or a share in the new city she is building in Africa. At the banquet where he tells his tale, the queen, through the machinations of Venus, is already falling in love with Aeneas, and the tale of his sorrows and adventures wins her heart completely. But it is a very different story from that of Odysseus. The first half of it is the account of the destruction of Troy, the hideous death of Priam, and the loss of his wife, Creusa. In what follows, he is wandering—not, like Odysseus, to find his way home but in search of a site to found a new city. His tale is not romance but the tragic history of a great defeat, the end of a civilization and of the painful search for a place in which it can be re-created. Nausicaa's gentle hints to Odysseus become, in the Virgilian version, Dido's passionate pursuit of Aeneas; and Odysseus' delicate rejection of Nausicaa's offer (*Odyssey* VIII.481–86), Aeneas's "marriage" with

Dido in the cave. Odysseus on his travels becomes the lover of Circe and Calypso, but these are incidents with no consequences; Aeneas's love for Dido endangers the future of his race and of the world, and when he renounces it to follow his destiny he sows the seeds of the great Punic Wars of the future.

Topic for Writing

Discuss the character of Aeneas, which has often come in for harsh criticism. (Charles James Fox, the eighteenth-century English statesman, found him "either insipid or odious," and William Butler Yeats speaks of an Irishman who thought Aeneas was a priest.) The implied comparison is of course with epic heroes such as Achilles and Odysseus. How far is such an attitude justified?

[There is sufficient material in "Backgrounds" and "Classroom Strategies" to suggest an answer. The main defense of Aeneas is of course that, unlike Achilles and Odysseus, who have no responsibilities other than the maintenance of their own heroic reputations, Aeneas carries the burden of a nation's destiny. He is a man devoted to duty (this is the basic meaning of the word *pius*, which Virgil applies to him so often), and this does not make him as attractive a figure as the rebellious and wrathful warrior Achilles or the unscrupulous and calculating adventurer Odysseus. Yet he can, on occasion, act with the wild passion characteristic of the heroic temper of an Achilles (or a Medea); in the last book, where everything leads us to expect that he will spare Turnus, his defeated enemy, the sight of Pallas's belt worn as a trophy by his killer inflames Aeneas with rage. The poem closes not on the note of reconciliation that the divine agreement seemed to promise but with a typically heroic act of revenge.]

Comparative Perspectives

1. The ghost of Hector comes to Aeneas in a dream to urge that he flee Troy and build another city, where he will salvage his household gods. Ghosts and dreams are familiar phenomena in early literature; the ghost of Clytemnestra, for example, asks the Furies at the beginning of *The Eumenides* to wreak vengeance on Orestes, her son and murderer, demanding that right and order be restored. How would you compare their roles?

   [If the motive for her ghostly visitation is fundamentally personal, Hector's motive seems more altruistic. It is not vengeance that he seeks but salvation for his people.]
2. Dido is one of many lovelorn women in the literatures of the world. Compare the emotions that contribute to her extreme reactions to her situation with those of Medea or Ovid's Myrrha.

Further Reading

See the reading suggestions in the anthology, p. 816.

Commager, Steele, ed. *Virgil: A Collection of Critical Essays.* 1966. Contains the essays "Basic Themes" by Victor Poschl and "The Imagery of the Second Book of the *Aeneid*" by Bernard Knox, as well as a brilliant essay by Adam Parry, "The Two Voices of Virgil's *Aeneid,*" which deals with the imperial theme and the contradictory theme of human suffering and sadness.

Kenney, E. J., ed. *Latin Literature.* Vol. II of *The Cambridge History of Latin Literature.* 1982. Pp. 331–69 (R. D. Williams). An up-to-date discussion for the modern reader. It covers the Augustan background, the literary background, composition and structure, the chief characters, destiny and religion, and style and meter.

OVID

Metamorphoses

Background

Ovid's account of "bodies becoming other bodies" (I.3) runs, so his proem announces, "from the world's beginning to our day" (line 6). The transformation that occurred in his own day was the metamorphosis of the soul of Julius Caesar, assassinated in 44 B.C., into a star. Augustus was the adopted son of Julius Caesar, so the poem ends with a compliment to the reigning emperor, which is deftly capped by the wish that many years may elapse before Augustus too ascends to Heaven and becomes a god.

Ovid starts with the creation of the material world (not in the anthology) and proceeds to the birth of humankind and the history of our four ages—Gold, Silver, Bronze, and Iron—a tale of change from good to fair to bad to worse. The men of the Iron Age are so wicked that Jove (Jupiter) begins to fear for his throne and, deciding to wipe out the human race, he sends a cleansing flood. Finally, life comes back to the world.

Among the forms of life are serpents; one of them, Python, is killed by the god Apollo, who falls in love with Daphne, the daughter of the Peneus River. A virgin huntress, Daphne flees the god's advances. About to be overtaken, she prays for help to her father, the river god, who changes her into a laurel tree. The rivers of Greece come to console Peneus, all except Inachus, whose daughter Io is missing; he does not know whether she is alive or dead.

She has, in fact, caught the roving eye of Jove, who has pursued and caught her. When Juno catches him in the act, he changes Io into a white heifer. Juno, pretending not to know what has happened, begs for the heifer as a gift, and Jove must give way. Juno puts Io under the surveillance of Argus, who has a hundred eyes. Io finds her father and manages to identify herself by scratching her name in the dust, but there is nothing he can do. Jove takes pity on them and sends Mercury to kill Argus. He first lulls Argus to sleep with his magic wand, meanwhile playing on his reed pipes and telling a story.

It is the story of Syrinx, pursued by the god Pan but rescued from his embraces by being changed into a reed. Once Argus falls asleep, Mercury kills him. Jove takes his hundred eyes and sets them in the tail of the peacock. Juno also sends a fury to drive Io all over the world. Io's prayers to Jove induce him to swear to Juno that he will never touch the girl and Juno changes Io back again to human shape.

Ovid, whose reputation as a poet had been built on his playful, witty, and at times licentious love poetry, turns in the *Metamorphoses* to the epic genre; the meter of his verse, the hexameter, is the same as that of Virgil's *Aeneid*, and the opening lines of the poem announce the theme in solemn strains. This dignified tone is maintained through the account of the creation and the four ages, the account of the flood and the re-creation of humankind; but with the episode of Apollo and Daphne we are back in Ovidian territory.

But it is not only the subject matter that has changed; though the stories still deal with gods, the style modulates toward the playful wit that will be characteristic of Ovid's narrative for the bulk of the poem. The dialogue between Apollo and Cupid, for example (I.14ff.), makes no attempt at epic seriousness. Apollo's detailed appreciation of Daphne's charms as he pursues her (lines 72ff.) recalls the poet of the *Art of Love*. The embarrassment and subterfuges of Jove when caught redhanded by Juno (lines 245ff.) suggest social comedy rather than epic grandeur. Daphne is rescued from what she feared most, and Io is restored to human shape.

Ovid's poem pursues its course through more than twelve thousand lines; this "epic of the emotions," as it has been called, rings the changes on all the genres—comedy, tragedy, pastoral, didactic—as it creates a brilliant anthology of mythological tales (most of them Greek). Most of the mythical stories that have become household words in Western culture through their re-creation in later art and literature—Pygmalion and Galatea, Midas and the golden touch, Pyramus and Thisbe—owe their form to their appearance in Ovid's *Metamorphoses*.

At the end of the poem, however, Ovid returns to the serious tone of the opening. The doctrine of eternal change, the impermanence of all things human and material, the transformations brought by time impart a solid moral to the kaleidoscope of changing forms that, sometimes gruesome, sometimes comic, but always memorable, justifies Ovid's claim to immortality: "I shall be living always."

Classroom Strategies and Topics for Discussion

Ovid's treatment of the gods may puzzle some students. In the *Aeneid*, the gods, though subject to human passions—Juno's hatred of Troy, for example—are figures of immense dignity. Virgil's Juno may be simply jealous, but she is also terrifying in her wrath; Venus may trick Dido into falling in love with Aeneas, but her purpose is serious and the fate of empires is involved. In Ovid, however, these same gods are treated with lighthearted humor; even Jove himself appears in the likeness of an embarrassed husband caught philandering by his wife. Ovid's attitude toward the gods is not really a religious one at all. In his *Art of Love,* in fact, Ovid had expressed a cynical view: belief in the existence of gods is advantageous for society, so, he says, let us believe in them (*Expedit esse deos, et, ut expedit, esse putemus*). In that same passage, however, he goes on to recommend conformity with ritual—incense should be burned and wine poured on the altars. For Ovid the Olympian gods had become material for poetry, and lighthearted poetry at that; but there is no reason to think that his attitude was unusual. Pagan religion, in the early centuries of the Roman Empire, was for most people a question of conformity to custom, not of belief. It had little spiritual force with which to confront the new religions, Christianity in particular, which commanded fervent belief in its new visions of divine power and humanity's life in this world and the next.

Students will have little trouble perceiving how abundantly clear Ovid makes his skeptical view of the gods, since so many of the selections in the anthology show them intent on rape and, in their zeal to ravish, often memorably ridiculous. As you examine the very first episode in the sequence, ask the class how desire for Daphne undermines Apollo's vaunted divine attributes (the god of oracles can't predict the future; the god of medicine can't heal himself). As the headnote suggests, the poem openly invites us to laugh at Jove himself when he transforms himself into a bull: "majesty and love do not go hand / in glove—they don't mix well" (II.17–18).

When Jove undertakes a metamorphosis, of course, he assumes a new form temporarily; once he achieves his mission, he resumes his grandeur. and if he decides to become a bull, he becomes an adorable bull. Rarely do the gods' intended victims have the opportunity to return to their previous forms. The sufferings of Io, so poignantly detailed, are partially assuaged, but she never can be herself again. By elaborating on a process that is, at its most serious, about the eradication of identity, the poem responds subtly to a complex array of moral and psychological issues.

Ovid invests this long poem's repeated descriptions of "bodies becoming other bodies" with finely judged detail, appropriate to each individual case. Jove's transformation is never shown; he just becomes a bull, feeling no pain. Mortals, even when they welcome their metamorphoses, seem more pathetic as they pass from one form to another, as does Daphne (I.139–45). Myrrha, in her guilty exhaustion, hastens her metamorphosis (X.375–90) and Arethusa's sweating abets hers. When they struggle against punitive metamorphosis (as in the changing of the daughters of Pierus into magpies at the end of book V), the poem, like the process it illustrates, can seem cruel.

Read in its entirety, the poem's own transitions rival the transitions of those bodies, as topic leads to topic and a finely ironic sense of order is dimly revealed. The story of Ceres and Prosperina, for example, is told by the Muse Calliope. Embedded in a sequence of stories that involve impious human challenges to the power of the gods, Calliope's convoluted story bests the narrative efforts of the "stupid sisters" (V.21)—like the Muses, nine in number—who are turned to magpies for their insolence.

Thus cruelty is an important theme throughout. Embedded in the story of Ceres' heroic quest for her lost daughter,for example, is the episode in which she angrily transforms a young boy into a lizard because he laughs at her thirsty drinking of barley water proffered by his grandmother. (V.245–55) Similarly, Venus will turn Hippomenes and Atalanta into lions tethered to Cybele's chariot for failing to show their gratitude for her assistance (X.684–711).

Ovid's range is also notable for the way he interweaves familiar mythological materials, such as the aetiological story of Ceres and Prosperina that "explains" vegetation cycles, with others that he embroiders or invents to comment on fundamental human experiences. Books IX and X examine a group of stories about "impossible love" (a term used by Galinsky in his book mentioned in the headnote). The story of Iphis and Ianthe should particularly interest students, since (as noted in the headnote) its understanding of the way gender identity is shaped by environment seems extremely modern. At the same time, the last-minute sex change undergone by a resolutely heterosexual Iphis is a staple of literary history. (The story of Fiordispina, Bradamant, and Richardet in Ariosto's *Orlando Furioso*, which borrows from the Iphis-Ianthe story and elsewhere in the *Metamorphoses* as well, will give your class an opportunity to see a good example of Ovid's influence on later poets.)

In the same sequence of stories is the tragic tale of Myrrha, whose forbidden love of her father leads to incest. Preceding this story, which has many affinities with classical and neoclassical tragedy (note especially the nurse as confidante to the lovesick heroine, a relationship to be studied as well in *Medea* and in Racine's *Phaedra*, which is itself based, of course, on another play by Euripides, the *Hippolytus*), is the even better-known story of Pygmalion and Galatea, one that rewards extended inquiry in its richly ambivalent approach to another erotic dilemma.

As the headnote indicates, Pygmalion's inability to love a woman he has not created seems pathological. Linked to Myrrha's story in a typically Ovidian transition (the child of Pygmalion and Galatea is Myrrha's grandfather), Pygmalion may be considered another practitioner of incest. He is also, of course, an artist, and art is a central concern of Ovid's poem. Like Calliope and Minerva, gods who assert their artistic superiority to the efforts of mere mortals, Venus and not Pygmalion is the true creator in this story. Without her granting the sculptor's prayer, the statue would have remained ivory. The power to transform, to shape experience, is granted to the gods; the *Metamorphoses* begins, after all, with a creation story. But it is also the vehicle by which lesser beings express their passions—ask your students how Io manages to communicate with her father (I.297–99) or how Syrinx is transformed into a musical instrument (I.78–82).

The Ovidian narrator weaves in and out of his long poem, ceding to other narrators as will Shahrazad in *The Thousand and One Nights*, and as she might, he concludes by boasting that the power of his words will confer upon him immortality. When Venus turns Adonis into an anemone, the flower's evanescence is recalled. Yet your students will find evidence at every point along the literary continuum that follows of the longevity of the fragile, shifting forms that populate the *Metamorphoses*.

Topics for Writing

1. Ovid drew on the rich mythological literature for his stories of transformation, but he added a new element to these tales of changed forms. "By . . . fleshing out the story, by inspecting the emotions and psychological problems of the characters, . . . by weighing the reasons for the metamorphosis and the feelings of the human spirit inside the changed body, Ovid gave new life and meaning to the myth" (W. S. Anderson). Discuss this analysis of Ovidian technique for the transformation of Daphne, Io, Iphis, or Myrrha.
2. Pygmalion "falls in love with his own work." How would you evaluate him as an artist and a man? What implications does this episode have for our understanding of the nature of artistic creation?

Comparative Perspectives

1. Compare and contrast the involvement of the gods in human life in *Gilgamesh*, Genesis, the Homeric epics, and the *Metamorphoses*. What do the deities want from human beings? How do they treat them?
2. Ovid's narrative technique, as well as his narrative content, is metamorphic. Look closely at the way he manages transitions from one story to the next. How does this resemble the technique of other anthologies of popular stories, such as the tales of *The Thousand and One Nights*?

Further Reading

See also the reading suggestions in the anthology, p. 898.

Anderson, W. S., ed. *Ovid's* Metamorphoses, *Books 6–10*. 1972. An edition of the Latin text with introduction and commentary. Although it does not deal with the books printed in the anthology, the introduction gives many useful insights into Ovidian style and technique.

Duff, J. Wight. *A Literary History of Rome from the Origins to the Close of the Golden Age*. 1909. Pp. 598–605. A venerable but still suggestive discussion of the *Metamorphoses* and its place in Latin and European poetry.

Smith, R. A. *Poetic Allusion and Poetic Embrace in Ovid and Virgil*. 1997. The discussion of Pygmalion is particularly good.

Tissol, Garth. *The Face of Nature: Wit, Narrative, and Cosmic Origins in Ovid's* Metamorphoses. 1997. A close reading of the poem, emphasizing Ovid's puns. Even teaching from a translation, one can profit from this discussion of the tightly woven wordplay of several episodes, including that of Myrrha.

Wilkinson, L. P. *Ovid Recalled*. 1955. Pages 190ff. discuss the gods; pp. 203ff., mortals in the *Metamorphoses*.

PETRONIUS

The Satyricon

[DINNER WITH TRIMALCHIO]

Backgrounds

The selection in the anthology is an account of a dinner given by a vulgar profiteer, a freedman (ex-slave) called Trimalchio; the narrator, Encolpius, is an educated man, a student of rhetoric. The dinner proceeds with one wildly extravagant course after another as the guests, most of them tradesmen with Greek names, talk business and cheap philosophy in language that has a scurrilous vitality unequaled in all Latin literature. Trimalchio tells the story of his life, and with the late arrival of Habinnas (a man in the funeral monument business who is building Trimalchio's tomb according to his specifications) the party gets wild: Fortunata, Trimalchio's wife, arrives and shows off her jewelry, but when Trimalchio makes a pass at a handsome boy slave, she bawls him out and is treated, in turn, to a vicious stream of vulgar abuse from her husband. Finally, maudlin drunk, Trimalchio orders his burial shroud to be brought in for the guests to admire; the band he has ordered to play a funeral march makes so much noise that the neighborhood is aroused and the fire brigade, thinking Trimalchio's house is on fire, breaks in with water and axes, thus giving Encolpius and his friend Giton a chance to escape in the confusion.

The *Satyricon* has come down to us as a collection of fragments (the banquet of Trimalchio is the longest); we have only remnants of what was originally an immense narrative of perhaps twenty books (the fragments included in the anthology seem to come from books XIV–XVI). It was a sort of picaresque novel: the amorous and disreputable adventures of its young narrator, Encolpius. He is a penniless student of rhetoric, living by his wits (and occasionally by the lightness of his fingers) in the cities of southern Italy. He has a young companion-lover, Giton, who is a perpetual bone of contention between Encolpius and another of his shady companions, Ascyltus, who from time to time takes his place in Giton's affections.

The literary origins of such a work are hard to seek. The *Satyricon* may have drawn on licentious Greek narratives (the so-called Milesian tales) and does owe much to Roman satire (in one of his *Satires* the Augustan poet Horace, for example, describes a rich upstart's banquet much like that of Trimalchio), but the vitality and realism of Petronius's fiction is something new in ancient literature.

Its author was almost certainly an aristocratic member of the court of

Nero (emperor, A.D. 54–68), Titus Petronius, whose life and death are described by the historian Tacitus, writing some fifty years after the events he records (*Annals* XVI, chapters 18–19). Petronius, he says,

> was a man who spent his days sleeping and his nights working or enjoying himself. . . . He was thought of as a refined artist in extravagance. His conversation and actions had a freedom and an air of carelessness which appealed to people by its lack of affectation. Yet as governor in Bithynia and later as consul he showed that he was a man of energy and fully equipped to deal with business. Later, returning to loose habits (or perhaps pretending to do so), he became a member of the inner circle of Nero's companions where he was known as the Arbiter of Elegance; Nero's jaded fancy would find charm and finesse only in what passed Petronius' scrutiny.

This position of influence aroused the jealousy of the powerful commander of the praetorian guard, and as a result of his intrigues, Petronius was arrested on suspicion of treason. Rather than wait for Nero's sentence, he committed suicide by cutting his veins. But his suicide was a spectacular event:

> He had the veins, once severed, bandaged up, when he felt like it, and then opened them again, meanwhile talking to his friends, not on a serious note or with any intention of winning a reputation for a brave end. The conversation was not concerned with the immortality of the soul or philosophical doctrines but consisted of amusing songs and frivolous verses. Some of his slaves he gave rewards to, others he had whipped. He sat down to a banquet, drowsing a little, so that his death, though forced on him, would look natural. In his will he did not follow the usual routine of flattering Nero; instead he listed the names of Nero's sexual partners male and female, and followed that with detailed descriptions of the emperor's activities, specifying the novel features of each sexual encounter. This document he sent to Nero.

Classroom Strategies

One assignment.

The student may wonder about the social position of slaves in Roman imperial society; on the one hand Trimalchio owns a great many of them—there are at least forty "divisions" of slaves in his household (p. 952)—but he himself was a slave once, and so were some of his rich friends (one of them takes it on himself to reproach Ascyltus for laughing at Trimalchio [p. 953] and proclaims his pride in his status of "freedman," that is, liberated slave). There seems to be a certain social mobility in this society, and this does correspond to the facts of Roman history.

In Greece we hear very little about the transition from slave to free status; the one thing we do know is that a freed slave remained an alien in the city—he could not acquire citizenship. In Rome, however, he did. His status as *libertus,* "freedman," gave him citizen rights, and in the next generation his son would be not even a freedman but a citizen on a level with all comers. The Augustan poet Horace was, in fact, a freedman's son, and yet he moved easily in the exalted circle of the emperor Augustus.

Trimalchio's account of his rise from rags to riches (pp. 958–59), though Petronius's satiric intent is plain, has a ring of truth to it. He came from Asia—probably a Greek city in the Middle East—and was a slave for fourteen years, during which time he was the sexual favorite of his master (and incidentally obliged his mistress too). He became, as he says, "boss in the house"; he learned accounting and became steward— the indispensable servant manager. He was left, at his master's death, not only his freedom but a fortune. He bought freedom for his wife, Fortunata, too (p. 958), and went into business in the wine trade. With the proceeds he bought back all his master's old estates, built a house, and invested in slaves. Trimalchio's emancipation by his master's will was in fact a common occurrence; common enough so that the imperial government collected a tax on it.

Topic for Discussion

Although the *Satyricon* is unlike any other literary work that has come down to us from antiquity, it is nonetheless influenced by and conscious of its predecessors. In particular, since it is a long narrative, it frequently compares and contrasts itself with the noblest and most monumental narrative form in antiquity, the epic. The references are, of course, ironic; the business of the inhabitants of Trimalchio's world emerges in sharp relief from the implied comparison with Achilles and the heroes of the Trojan saga.

The name of the rhetoric teacher, Agamemnon, is one among the many deliberate references to the heroic past; the point is emphasized by the name of his assistant, Menelaus. But this Agamemnon is a flatterer who dignifies Trimalchio's inane remarks by admiring their wit (p. 952). The mural in Trimalchio's house includes representations of "The *Iliad*, and *Odyssey*, and the gladiatorial show given by Laenas" (p. 946), and in the conversation of the guests that goes on when Trimalchio has left to go to the toilet, the heroes of past time who are held up to admiration are not warriors but, for example, Chrysanthus, who "started out in life with just a penny" and "left a solid hundred thousand" (p. 948), and Safinius, who kept the price of bread down by terrifying the bakers: "he used to wade into some of them—no beating about the bush" (p. 949).

As for the heroes of the present day, chief among them is Titus, who, his friend Echion the rag merchant says, is about to give a gladiatorial show that will be "the best ever . . . cold steel, no quarter and the slaughterhouse right in the middle where all the stands can see it" (p. 950). Echion's son is "ahead with his Greek, and he's starting to take to his Latin," but his father wants him to pick up some legal training for home use: "There's a living in that sort of thing" (p. 951).

Trimalchio too has pretensions to culture; he has "two libraries, one Greek, one Latin" (p. 952), but he doesn't seem to have read the books. He remembers a story of Ulysses (Odysseus), "how the Cyclops tore out his thumb with a pair of pincers" (p. 952)—which he claims to have read in Homer. The only time he gets an allusion to the great literature of the past even remotely right is when he calls Fortunata, who has objected to his dalliance with a boy slave, a "Cassandra in clogs" (p. 958).

Topics for Writing

1. Discuss the following statement:

Trimalchio is a complex character; he now wallows in luxury and self-deception, but was once resilient and faced a hard world on its own terms. For all his coarseness and ostentation, he is not utterly unlikeable.

F. D. Goodyear

2. The same critic says of the characters who speak at the banquet when Trimalchio is absent: "they are characterized by what they say as well as by the way they speak." Discuss with specific examples.

Comparative Perspectives

1. What view of life emerges here? What cultural developments seem to precipitate this kind of satiric vision? Compare the elements of life emphasized in Rabelais's account of life in Paris or by Gulliver when he looks at the way the Yahoos live.
2. Dinner with Trimalchio, like the Aeneid and the Metamorphoses, shows how Roman writers had constantly to deal with the example set by them for the Greeks and how complicated were their attitudes toward their precursors. In both the Aeneid and the Satyricon, wall paintings take Homeric texts for their subjects. The one Aeneas sees in Carthage evokes an interpretation that would not be out of place in Petronius's work: what is satiric about the way he describes Achilles (I.85–86)?

Further Reading

See also the reading suggestions in the anthology, p. 944.

Kenney, E. J., ed. Latin Literature. Vol. I of The Cambridge History of Classical Literature. 1982. Pp. 635–38 (F. D. Goodyear). A short discussion of the Satyricon as a whole, with some perceptive remarks on the banquet of Trimalchio.

THE BIBLE: THE NEW TESTAMENT

Backgrounds

The selection in the anthology (from Luke and Matthew) begins with the birth of Jesus (from Luke) and the famous story of the "good tidings of great joy" brought by the angel of the Lord to the shepherds in the fields. This selection ends with the picture of the twelve-year-old Jesus questioning and answering the learned interpreters of the scriptures and the laws. There follows Matthew's account of the Sermon on the Mount, which contains Christ's basic doctrines and also the words of the Lord's Prayer. The next selection (from Luke) contains the famous parables of the lost sheep, the lost piece of silver, and the prodigal son, along with Jesus' account of why he speaks in parables. The rest of the selection, also from Matthew, narrates the Last Supper, the agony in the garden, the betrayal and arrest of Jesus, his denial by Peter, and then the trial before Pontius Pilate and the Crucifixion, ending with the Resurrection and Christ's command to the disciples to "teach all nations."

When Alexander died at Babylon in 323 B.C. after conquering the whole of the immense land empire of the Persians, his generals divided the spoils between them; Ptolemy took Egypt (his descendants ruled it until the last of them, Cleopatra, went down to defeat with Mark Antony in 31 B.C.); and Palestine, together with most of the Middle East, came under the control of Seleucus and his descendants the Seleucids. Over the whole area Greek became the language of administration, and in the cities, at any rate, Greek culture took firm hold; the ruins of its typical buildings—temple, theater, and gymnasium—still testify to its wide dissemination.

In Palestine, however, the attempts to impose Greek culture ran into the stubborn resistance of the Jews, who after a long war succeeded in retaining the right to practice their own religion and observe their own laws. Eventually, in the first century B.C., the area came under Roman control; it was before a Roman official, Pontius Pilate, that Jesus was tried and condemned to death.

While the governing officials conducted their business in Greek or Latin, the Jewish population spoke a Semitic dialect called Aramaic (though the scriptures that their rabbis expounded were written in classical Hebrew). Jesus' native tongue was Aramaic (some of his last words on the cross—*Eli Eli lama sabachthani*—are in that language), but he must have learned classical Hebrew to be able to dispute with the rabbis in the temple, and it is quite likely that he knew enough Greek to speak to and understand Roman and Greek officials. But his preaching to the crowds that came to hear him was in Aramaic, and when he died on the cross in A.D. 30 it must have been in that language that his disciples remembered and perhaps began to record his words.

He had given them the mission, however, to "teach all nations," and if his message was to go outside the narrow confines of Aramaic-speaking Palestine, it would have to be in a Greek version. And it is in that language, the "common" Greek of the Middle East (not the highly wrought literary Greek of the Athenian writers), that the four Gospels were written, probably in the last third of the first century A.D. In that language the message was accessible to anyone in the Middle East and mainland Greece who could read at all; later, as Latin versions were made, the Gospels (the word means "good news") could be read all over the Roman Empire.

The translation in the anthology is the so-called Authorized Version of the Old and New Testaments, which was published in A.D. 1611; it was made on the authorization of King James I of England by the leading scholars of the English Protestant Church. It drew heavily on earlier translations but received its final form in a great age for the English language, the age of Marlowe, Shakespeare, Spenser, and Jonson. It has been a classic of English literature ever since, a text that for many centuries has been the common property of all English speakers and that has enriched the language of all who have written in English since the book first appeared.

Classroom Strategies

One assignment.

One aspect of the Gospel narratives, especially that of Matthew, that may puzzle students is the frequency of reference to the Old Testament, often to cite a prophecy that is being or is about to be fulfilled. Many of these references are made by Jesus himself, as, for example, when he predicts that his disciples will desert him in his hour of need and cites the prophet Zechariah (13.7: "For it is written, I will smite the shepherd and the sheep of the flock shall be scattered abroad"), or by the narrator, as in the case of the potter's field bought with the thirty pieces of silver paid to Judas—a fulfillment, says Matthew, of a prophecy made by Jeremiah (in the text it is in Zechariah 11.13: "And they took the thirty pieces of silver, the price of him that was valued, whom they of the children of Israel did not value, and gave them for the potter's field").

The purpose of these references is to establish Jesus' claim to be the promised Messiah, a Hebrew word that means "anointed" (the Greek word for which is *christos*, hence our word *Christ*). A king was anointed with holy oil (a king or queen still is in the British coronation ceremony), but this king, the Messiah, was to be one appointed by God to deliver his people, the Jews, and establish his kingdom in righteousness. Jesus' claim to be that Messiah was one of the reasons for the hostility of many of the Jews, for they expected the Messiah to deliver them from the Romans, while Jesus, announcing that his kingdom was not of this world, renounced violent action of any kind. It is with reference to this claim to be the Messiah that the Roman magistrate Pilate, not understanding its theological nature, can ask Jesus, "Art thou the King of the Jews?" (Matthew 27.11) and that the mocking legend can be fixed to the cross: "THIS IS JESUS THE KING OF THE JEWS" (27.37).

By the end of the Book of Matthew (the one that is clearly aimed especially at a Jewish, as Luke's is at a Greek, audience), the mission of the Messiah has become worldwide. The resurrected Jesus tells his disciples: "Go ye therefore, and teach all nations" (28.19).

Topic for Discussion

All three of the parables in the selection—the lost sheep, the lost silver piece, and the prodigal son—emphasize the lesson that the redeemed sinner is more precious to God than the righteous person who never sinned. This implies a conception of God unlike that found in the Old Testament (cf. the Genesis stories of the Garden of Eden and the Flood) or in Greek literature and thought (cf. the gods of the *Iliad*, the *Odyssey*, and the *Oresteia*). The parables emphasize the entirely new emphasis that Christian doctrine was to place on human repentance and divine mercy.

Topic for Writing

Compare the recommendations for human conduct offered in the Beatitudes (Matthew 5.3–11) and those that are implied in the Greek texts you have read.

[The contrast is striking in the case of the heroic values of an Achilles or Odysseus; perhaps the only one of Jesus' commands that one can imagine Achilles accepting is "Blessed are the pure in heart" (which he would probably have understood as meaning "Blessed are they who speak the truth and hate a liar," cf. *Iliad* IX.378ff.). With Socrates, on the other hand (who was also put to death), many of the commands of Jesus seem perfectly compatible.]

Comparative Perspectives

1. Although Jesus was a Jew, the religious institutions created in his name proved difficult for Jews to embrace but attractive to Greeks. What elements in the Nativity and the Passion narratives seem particularly acceptable and culturally familiar to a pagan audience? Compare, if appropriate, references in The Koran to "The People of the Book," the Christians and Jews whom Muslims acknowledge as sharing previous prophetic revelations.
2. Teaching in parables, as Jesus explains to His disciples, puts a burden on the audience that straightforward instruction does not. Why does this method of communication particularly suit a religious or spiritual subject?

Further Reading

See also the reading suggestions in the anthology, p. 961.

Barrett, C. K. *The New Testament Background: Selected Documents.* 1961. Documents illustrating the period of the origin and rise of Christianity translated from Greek, Latin, Hebrew, and other languages.

Cook, Stanley. *An Introduction to the Bible.* 1950. Useful chapters are 1, "The English Bible"; 5, "The Books of the Bible: The New Testament"; and 6, "The Messiah and the New Age."

May, H. G., and B. C. Metzger. *The New Oxford Annotated Bible.* 1965; reprinted 1977. Besides presenting an annotated edition of the Old and New Testaments in the Revised Standard Version, this volume contains excellent chapters on modern approaches to biblical study (pp. 1519ff.), literary forms in the Gospels (pp. 1530ff.), and a historical account of Palestine during "the invasion of Hellenism" and the rule of Rome (pp. 1543ff.).

Metzger, B. C. *The New Testament: Its Background, Growth, and Content.* 1965. An up-to-date survey of the historical and doctrinal problems presented by the New Testament, written for the nonspecialist by one of the most prominent biblical scholars of our time. Especially recommended are chapter 4, on the sources of our knowledge of the life and teachings of Jesus, and chapter 6, on his teachings.

LUCIAN

A True Story

Classroom Strategies and Topics for Discussion

A True Story is one of the comic gems of the ancient world: like *The Satyricon*, another comparatively late work that makes fun of the masterpieces of ancient Greek culture, Lucian's self-conscious tour de force provides a wonderful opportunity for you to pause retrospectively at the end of the first major sequence in the anthology. If your students have already read Homer, they are ready to appreciate Lucian's deft allusions to the heroic tradition, a feature of this text that he advertises prominently at the beginning of his second paragraph.

You should make sure your students understand that allusion depends on an audience's ability to "get" references that the author does not flag or explain—you could point out that many of the anthology's footnotes have been provided precisely to elucidate allusions. You may also find it worthwhile to distinguish between the complementary but essentially different literary approaches that we categorize as *satire* or *parody*. Satire, which exposes folly and pretension, can be serious or comic and may inhabit any genre: it is a point of view rather than a static form and its targets are generally social and behavioral. Parody, on the other hand, requires an exquisite sense of form, since it is based on stylistic imitation. The better the parodist's eye, the more successful the parody. It combines affectionate tribute with debunking (broader, less precise imitations that intend mainly ridicule verge into burlesque or travesty). As the headnote makes clear, *A True Story* uses parody to entertain even as it raises fundamental questions about the nature of literature as an art form and as a human enterprise.

Baldly announcing that all writers lie, Lucian then turns on a dime to deploy a full range of technical tricks by which authors feign truth. For example, he highlights the artificiality of a familiar Homeric convention that gives an illusion of verisimilitude by specifying precise details. Your students should be able to recognize that Lucian's "fifty acquaintances" and his telling us that on the eightieth day at sea "the sun broke through" parody Homer's tendency to use fifty to suggest plenitude (as in Priam's fifty sons) and to announce that the ninth, or eleventh, day yields to some decisive action on the tenth, or twelfth. By its very title, of course, *A True Story* skewers a wide range of devices that historians and natural philosophers use to create a semblance of truth.

Fans of science fiction will have a background on which to draw in analyzing why *A True Story* propels its reader to one imaginary setting or another. What impulse prompts writers to depict what they demonstrably cannot have experienced, like life on the moon or some further intergalactic destination? Comic satire abounds in examples that your students will recognize and perhaps go on to read as the year progresses: Voltaire in *Candide* and Swift in *Gulliver's Travels* satirize their own societies by their invention of fictional places that absurdly exaggerate tendencies at home. Fantasy worlds in romances like Ariosto's *Orlando Furioso* tend to be places where wishes that would be denied in the ordinary world can be fulfilled.

With such comparisons in mind, you might ask your students to identify the preoccupations of the traveler in part I: he directly participates in warfare with a variety of grotesque hybrid formations, observes unusual sexual practices, and comments on the local diet (note the ubiquity of beans, a staple of ancient—and many modern—cuisines, and of farce— given their effect on the digestion—in every period as well). Students will have no trouble enumerating the mortal appetites being held up for critique or ridicule here. As much of the first part of *A True Story* has to do with the logistics of waging war, you might have your students look back over the readings they've done elsewhere in the anthology: in how many does the battlefield dominate events? In what ways does Lucian show how ridiculous, rather than heroic, war really is? Even more does Lucian make fun of the tall tales brought back by travelers and historians, particularly through his vivid descriptions of oddly constructed creatures. Travel writers seem always to have reported on the monstrous forms to be found beyond the boundary lines of the civilized world (this is a point you may want to return to when you reach Othello's stories of "men whose heads / Do grow beneath their shoulders" and Gulliver's encounters with the Houyhnhnms). The allegorical implications of centaurs and minotaurs are not hard to discern. What are we to make, however, of Flounderfoots and Lobstertails, of Crabhands and Tunaheads, "bound to each other by a military pact as well as emotional ties"?

It appears that something about our experience of our own bodies leads writers to populate their works with beings who violate the species divide. In some contexts, hybridity is a source of horror—your students will be well versed when it comes to werewolves and vampires, among others. But in *A True Story*, in cartoons and in caricatures, hybridity gives rise to humor. Lucian's method of draining a potentially serious theme of emotive content leaves us with absurdities that require a reexamination of received values and assumptions.

He introduces us to his gallery of monsters early in part I, with the comparison of the grapevine women to Daphne turning into a tree. Although Lucian, who chose Greek over Latin, may not be alluding to Ovid's *Metamorphoses* here, your students are likeliest to recognize the myth from its Ovidian treatment, and a comparison between the two writers is instructive. Even so ironic an artist as Ovid tends to give psychological interest and pathos to the transformations of his tortured human subjects. Lucian's approach is more parodic, turning familiar myths on their heads in the deadpan references to the freaks of nature encountered throughout *A True Story.* Ovid's Daphne is the victim of the predatory Apollo, whereas Lucian's aggressors are the females in the case. The old myth becomes a dirty joke as the hapless men who surrender to these clinging vines undergo an unusual early penile transplant.

It is worth mentioning that Lucian's parallel universes are overwhelmingly male; one productive critical approach to *A True Story* is to examine it in terms of the assumptions about gender that permeate the works of Greek antiquity. Like Zeus, who bears two of his own offspring (Athena and Dionysus), the males on the womanless moon do their own childbearing. Lucian's offhand description of perhaps the most fervent male fantasy, the dream of self-generation, is substantiated by a fabulously specific and wild description of the lunar bodily experience. His disclaimer reiterates the power of his double-sided attitude toward truth: "Any person who doesn't believe that all this is so need only go there himself."

Part II of *A True Story*, set among the "celebrities" of Greek culture, offers particularly rich ground for your students to discover examples of parody. You might take the opportunity to talk here about the kind of humor that fuels American popular culture, which is awash in burlesques like *Naked Gun* or *Get Smart*, and to compare their broad strokes with the minutely observed detail of Lucian's narrative. How does a knowledge of Odysseus's escape from Polyphemus's cave, for example, enrich our appreciation of the carefully laid plans for escaping from the belly of the whale that Lucian describes in the beginning of part II of the narrative?

Getting free of the whale leads us to the Isle of the Blest and to the literary references which your students will most immediately "get." Lucian gives us the inside story on Socrates, who seems to be having a fine time in the afterlife. Ask your students why Lucian makes a point of noting that Plato and the Stoics aren't among the Blest: what is he saying about the importance of a sense of humor? Or consider why he announces that Homer was born in Babylonia: what personal amusement may Lucian, a native of Samosata, situated "on the west bank of the Euphrates River," derive from so settling the vexed question of the origin of the greatest of Greek authors?

Your retrospective exercise could conclude with Lucian's portraits of characters encountered earlier in the semester, while you may point the way ahead by encouraging your students to remember Lucian's treatment of the afterlife when they move on to read Dante or Ariosto later in the term. And if you read *The Trial of Renard* or *The Wife of Bath's Tale*, you will have further opportunity of looking closely again at parody, in these cases of medieval epic and Arthurian romance.

Topics for Writing

1. Survival skills in *A True Story*: how may the dangers that Lucian encounters and the way he addresses them comment on ancient

Greek literature and society? What equivalent dangers and responses could be invented by the writer of as true a story set in the contemporary United States?

2. How does Lucian comment on topics already covered in your syllabus, including perhaps the morality of the Trojan War, the pursuit of academic philosophy, or the governance of nations?

3. Write a letter sent by one of your favorite figures in Greek literature in the style of the one Odysseus smuggles past Penelope to send to Kalypso. Some suggestions: Achilles to Peleus, Helen to Clytemnestra, Sappho to Lucian.

Comparative Perspectives

1. Lucian apologizes for having "nothing true to record—I never had any experiences worth talking about." Does a writer have to write about personal experience? What kinds of "truth" can fiction convey?

2. Why do nations at peace return obsessively to narratives of war? How would you contrast the absurd series of conflicts recounted in a *A True Story* with the significance of war in epic works like the *Iliad* or the *Aeneid* or *The Song of Roland*?

3. In the beginning of *A True Story*, Lucian talks about the "tomfoolery" of travel narratives like the *Odyssey*. Consider the ways in which parody can simultaneously discredit and pay tribute to the works it imitates.

Further Reading

See also the reading suggestions in the anthology, p. 978.

Hall, Jennifer. *Lucian's Satire*. 1981. A monograph that demonstrates that the weird creatures and events described in *A True Story* differ in degree but not in kind from those in the texts (many now lost) that Lucian parodies.

Marsh, David. *Lucian and the Latins: Humor and Humanism in the Early Renaissance*. 1988. Discusses the rediscovery of Lucian in the early 1400s, with comments on the influence of *A True Story* on Rabelais.

AUGUSTINE

Confessions

Backgrounds

Augustine begins with a reconstruction of the first months of his childhood, based on the "word of others," then describes his own earliest memories; they include a fascinating analysis of the process of learning to understand his parents' speech. He continues with an account of his boyhood, his education, and later his adolescence; one incident from this period, his participation in the theft of fruit from a pear tree, remains in his memory as an example of malice—"my soul was depraved" (p. 1010).

At Carthage, where he was a student, he fell victim to the lusts of the flesh; he also frequented the theater and was one of a gang of rowdy and rebellious students at the university where he studied law and rhetoric. He read for the first time the Gospels (in Latin) but found the style inferior to that of Cicero and was "repelled by their simplicity" (p. 1014). He became professor of rhetoric at Milan in the north of Italy, at that time (late fourth century A.D.) the administrative center of the Western Roman Empire.

His mother, Monica, came to live with him and was distressed to find that he was not yet a Christian. He had great worldly ambitions (conversion would have interfered with them) and was also living with a mistress by whom he had a child. He did not wish to give her up and so resisted the force that drew him toward Christianity but was finally converted when a voice he heard in a garden said: "Take and read" (p. 1020).

He took up the Bible that was on his knees, opened it at random, and found the words of Paul that begin, "Not in rioting and drunkenness" (Romans 13.13). He went in and told his mother he had made up his mind; he left his mistress, resigned his professorship at Milan, joined the church there, which was headed by St. Ambrose, and eventually became a priest. His mother died as she was about to return home to Africa; Augustine records what she had told him about her early life and paints an affecting picture of a simple but devoted woman who lived in the Christian faith through all the trials of a hard life and a difficult marriage.

Augustine wrote his *Confessions* around A.D. 397, a few years after he had become bishop of Hippo, a town second in importance only to Carthage, the capital city of the Roman province of Africa. Although no other example of autobiography survives from classical antiquity, we know that he had predecessors; the Roman statesman Sulla, for example, had written his memoirs in the first century B.C. But, judging from the examples of Greek and Latin biography that have survived—the lives of the famous Greeks and Romans by Plutarch, for example, or the lives of the Roman emperors of the first century A.D. by Suetonius—Augustine's book must have been very different from any of its predecessors. The biographers, for example, hardly mention the childhood and youth of their subjects; they are concerned with the public career and, though they may give lurid details of the subject's private life (especially in the case of Suetonius), they do little to explore the psychology behind the virtues and vices they chronicle.

Augustine's work, however, is a spiritual biography, an account of a man's long and troubled journey toward his final conversion to the Christian faith that his mother had lived by and was to die in, an account, furthermore, pervaded by that sense of sin that is the particular contribution of Christianity to the Western mind. Augustine's genuine regret and shame for his part in the robbery of a neighbor's pear tree is something a classical Greek or Roman would have found incomprehensible.

This concentration on the spiritual life, rather than on the life of activity or the intellect, is the real novelty of the work, and from that stem many of its most remarkable innovations. The account of his childhood, for example, the first in all ancient literature, with its remarkable analysis of the process by which babies learn their parents' language, owes its genesis to Augustine's conviction of the basic sinfulness of man, even children. "In your sight," he says to God, "no man is free from sin, not even a child who has lived only one day on earth." This conviction that sin is innate in human nature and that without God's grace human beings cannot hope for salvation is a world away from the Greek anthropocentric vision of humanity's capacity for heroic action, as warrior, inventor, legislator, or poet, with or without and sometimes in defiance of the gods who are like us in shape as well as in their passions, different only in their overwhelming power.

Classroom Strategies

One assignment.

See "Backgrounds" for a discussion of the main difficulty the modern student will encounter—Augustine's sense of sin. You might add to the discussion of this subject the relevance of the form Augustine employs. The work is not presented as an autobiography; the title *Confessions* is accurate, since all through the work Augustine is speaking directly to God, confessing his sins. This, again, is something unparalleled in the ancient world, one more sign of the transition from the ancient to the medieval world that is visible in the pages of Augustine's book. No Greek or Roman would "confess" to a god; prayers, sacrifice, worship by hymns or dance, consultation by oracle—these were the pagan approaches to the gods. The very idea that a god would be interested in an individual's confession of wrongdoing is alien to the ancient mentality; the gods, for one thing, are not so closely concerned with human feeling and conduct. Augustine's sense of sin is oppressive, but, on other hand, his conviction that God is interested in him is a comfort that the pagan could not enjoy.

Topic for Discussion and Writing

Compare Augustine's evaluation of his own conduct with that offered by Socrates in the *Apology* and the complete lack of self-criticism or evaluation by Achilles in the *Iliad* (until, in book XXIV, he does for a moment see himself through the eyes of others).

Comparative Perspectives

1. Augustine is ashamed of having wept for Dido. What does he think is wrong with reading imaginative literature? How would you compare the attitudes of Lucian toward classical epic?
2. Look closely at Augustine's tribute to his mother, Monica. What virtues does he particularly commend in her? Would you want to see her conduct of family life emulated by women today? Compare her view of marriage and a woman's responsibilities to her husband with that of Rebekah in Genesis or Homer's Penelope.

Further Reading

See also the reading suggestions in the anthology, p. 1005.

Marrou, H. *St. Augustine and His Influence through the Ages.* n.d. An introduction to the life and works, lavishly illustrated, with selections (translated) from other works than the *Confessions* and an estimate of his importance for later centuries.

Masterpieces of the Middle Ages

THE KORAN

Backgrounds

About the year A.D. 570 a young man was born into the Quraysh tribe of Mecca. He was given the name Muhammad, and since his father had died before his birth and his mother died while he was about six, he was raised first by his grandfather and then by his uncle, Abu Talib. In his early twenties he was married to the wealthy widow Khadija, who was some years older than him. The marriage was prompted by convenience—he was a poor orphan, she a middle-aged widow—but by all appearances it was a happy and loving one. He had been trained as a merchant by his uncle and had a talent for commerce. Their affairs prospered.

Muhammad had a serious, spiritual bent and often withdrew to meditate. One day in the year 610, while he was meditating in a cave outside Mecca, the Angel Gabriel appeared to him, ordered him to "Recite," and revealed to him the first verses of what became the Koran. Other verses followed, and Muhammad gradually gathered a circle of believers around him. The first was his wife, and the second his nephew, Ali. (Ali was married to Muhammad's daughter, Fatimah; became the fourth caliph, or successor, to him as leader of the community; and through his marriage to the Prophet's only surviving child, was the focus of the legitimist claims of the Shi'ite community.)

Others followed, and the success of this fledgling community threatened the established order of Mecca. Mecca's success as a trading center rested on its importance as a center of pilgrimage. Muhammad's God demanded the destruction of the idols that were the objects of pilgrimage. He also challenged the tribal basis of the society, saying that faith was more important than blood. He even went so far as to say that all the Meccans' ancestors who had not worshiped God were suffering the torments of damnation. Eventually, he was disowned by his own tribe, a virtual sentence of death, because it left him without protection from his enemies since there was no civil government outside of the tribal alliances. He survived by being adopted into another tribe. His situation was perilous, and some of his followers fled to temporary refuge in Ethiopia. Eventually, in 622, he and his community made a flight (Arabic *hijra*) to the oasis center of Medina at the invitation of the local residents. There he established a Muslim community, which he led until his death in 632. During this period, he attracted many converts from all over Arabia. He also forced out the Jewish tribes that had been resident there so that Medina became wholly Muslim.

In 624, Muhammad initiated a war with Mecca that ended with a complete Muslim victory in 630. All the Meccans converted to Islam, and the remaining tribes of Arabia followed their example in short order. Mecca became the center of the new religion, and a few months before his death, Muhammad returned to Mecca to make a pilgrimage to the Ka'ba—now emptied of idols—a journey that established the pilgrimage ritual that is followed to the present day.

Shortly before his death, Muslim expeditions were sent against Islam's neighbors to the north. There was a brief pause after the Prophet's death while the question of his succession was settled, but then the Muslim conquests continued to the north, west, and east with astonishing success. Within a century, Islam stretched from the Atlantic in the west to central Asia in the east, and from northern Syria to the southern shore of Arabia.

Classroom Strategies

One assignment.

Classroom Discussion

For those familiar with the Bible, the Koran is a hard book to get used to. It lacks the narrative thread of the Old Testament and is poor in the vivid stories and the rich variety of characters and incidents that reading the Bible has taught us to expect in a book of revelation. And despite the fact that "the Merciful," (ar-rahmân) and "the Munificent" (ar-rahîm) are the two commonest epithets given to God by Muslims, the revelations that make up the Koran more often speak of God's wrath and the punishments He inflicts on unbelievers than of His mercy and generosity.

While acknowledging where one's personal tastes lie, however, it can be self-defeating to read the Koran simply as an inferior version of the Bible. Whatever else it is, the Koran is a work of revelation that has inspired and continues to inspire Muslims throughout the world. Even today, Islam is the fastest-growing evangelical religion and one that has hundreds of millions of adherents in the Middle East, Asia, and Africa as well as large and increasingly influential communities in Europe, the U.K., and the United States. Indeed, it now seems likely that Muslims will displace Jews as the largest religious minority in the United States sometime early in the twenty-first century. Islam has served as the basis for a world civilization that in its golden age was the equal of any that existed before the modern transformation of Europe. The Koran has also provided the foundation for rich and varied literatures in a great many languages. For these reasons alone it merits careful study.

Examining the differences between the Koran and the Bible obliges us to read the Bible from a new perspective. It illuminates, for example, the extent to which the Bible is embedded in the story of a single nation, the

Jews, and is the product of a lengthy historical process. Although the Koran is deeply linked to the Arabs by reason of its language, it does not explicitly elevate that nation over any other or designate it as chosen by God for special greatness. The Bible evolved over many generations, and many voices contributed to its composition. The revelations that make up the Koran were all mediated by a single personality, Muhammad, and in a single, brief historical moment. Despite differences in tone and emphasis, the Koran has a coherence and singleness of vision that makes it unlike the Bible. However, texts of revelation all seem to have some features in common—the exhortative tone of divine authority, an insistence on the transcendental meaning of human history, an oracular style that invites interpretation while inveighing against it, and the resistance of the heedless human community to the warnings of its prophets.

The most familiar portions of the Koran, and so the most accessible, are probably the prophetic tales. Sura 5 (The Table) indicates an awareness of at least portions of the story of Christ's birth from the Gospels (*anjil*). But Islam rejects the divinity of Jesus and the idea of the Trinity (which seems to have been understood to include God the Father, Jesus, and Mary), as Sura 5 makes clear in its concluding paragraphs. There are few other allusions to the teachings of Jesus Christ and none to indicate an awareness of the other portions of the New Testament. It seems, in short, as though the source was oral, not written, and might have resulted from conversations with Christians that Muhammad met in his travels north to Syria. But having said that, we enter the uncertain ground of speculation about whether or not Muhammad was the "author" of the Koran or simply the agency by which it was revealed. Christians and Jews are obliged by their faiths to assume that he was the author, and Muslims, by theirs to reject any suggestion that words of the Koran are anyone but God's. In the Muslim view, the Koran's revelations were sent to correct and complete all prior revelations.

The Koran's relation to the Old Testament is both more obvious and more problematic. The Koran does not refer to the Old Testament, but it does to the books of the Torah, which are described as a single book of revelation, like the Koran. A revelation that Jesus was sent to confirm. The tales of the prophets that appear in both the Old Testament and the Koran are inevitably the focus of efforts to understand the relation of the two texts. They appear in the Koran as allusions or illustrations in a number of Suras, but are not gathered into independent narratives as they are in the Old Testament. Even when the scattered parts are gathered together, however, the versions are significantly different. Sura 12 (Joseph), which ignores completely Joseph's role as leader of the Jews, illustrates these differences most obviously. This famous Sura, the single long continuous narrative in the Koran, differs from the biblical treatment of this story (which Muhammad almost certainly had never read) by ignoring Joseph's role as leader of the Jews and by stressing the involvement of Allah in every significant human decision. As the headnote points out, much is made of Joseph's extraordinary beauty (p. 1052), which became proverbial in Islam; thus this telling of the story shows a sympathetic understanding of the motives of the Prince's wife. Moreover, Sura 12 tells us that Joseph "would have succumbed to" Potiphar's wife "had he not been shown a sign from his Lord." By contrast, Genesis emphasizes Joseph's resourcefulness and his morally informed refusal to abuse his master's trust.

Other brief vignettes in Sura 5 (The Table) illustrate the same tendency in the Koran to glorify the power of Allah and blunt the struggle of the individual conscience; free will is not so important as the all-embracing protection Allah extends to believers. The abbreviated version of the murder of Abel by Cain (significantly, the names of "Adam's two sons" are not given) does not include the tense dialogues between Cain and Abel and then between Cain and God that readers who know the story from Genesis will remember. Rather, the Koran stresses the swiftness of the murdering son's repentance when he recognizes that Allah has sent him a sign.

Narrative chronology is also unimportant in the Koran. The prophets are connected to each other principally by their prophetic role, and there is little concern to link them by genealogy or much concern for historical sequence. A retelling of the story of Jesus and Mary may immediately precede a brief excerpt from the story of Abraham.

Koranic references to the prophets seem sketchy and incomplete in comparison with the more detailed biblical versions. Early Muslims seem to have been puzzled by these stories, too, and sought information about the prophets from Christian and Jewish converts to Islam. However, this material from outside the Koran was suspect at the same time that it was informative. It is an article of faith for Muslims that the Koran is perfect and self-contained. From the Muslim point of view, the fuller biblical versions of the prophetic tales distort and undermine the original intention of these stories. What appears as allusiveness to us is the divinely sanctioned style of revelation.

Topics for Writing

1. Compare the accounts of Cain and Abel, Joseph, Moses, or Noah in the Koran with those in the Old Testament of the Bible. How do the narrative strategies of these versions alter both their "message" and their relation to the larger discursive fabric in which they appear? Could you write an Islamic critique of the Old Testament versions of the prophetic tales?
2. What is the Koranic attitude toward women as revealed in Sura 12 (Joseph)?
3. How do Islamic perceptions of Heaven and Hell differ from those of Christianity and Judaism?
4. How does the Koran make the case for itself as an immortal work, the actual words of God?

Comparative Perspectives

1. Compare the Koran's many descriptions of paradise and the rewards that the righteous will enjoy there with Dante's vision of

Paradise at the end of *The Divine Comedy*. How much in these per-
fect worlds seem culturally specific?
[Note gardens, carpets, and fountains.]
2. Compare the emphasis on the purity required by pilgrimage in the
   Koran with Chaucer's treatment of pilgrimage in *The Canterbury
   Tales*.

Further Reading

See also the reading suggestions in the anthology, p. 1041.

Arberry, A. J., trans. The Koran. 1955. The most poetic translation.

Esposito, John L. *Islam: The Straight Path*. 1988. Both useful and up to
date.

Fisher, Michael J., and Mehdi Abedi. *Debating Muslims*. 1990. There is a
thoughtful discussion of the dialogic nature of the Koran in part 2.

Gibb, H. A. R. *Islam*, 2nd rev. ed. 1962. This classic is still lucid and
insightful.

Peter, F. E. *Children of Abraham: Judaism, Christianity and Islam*. 1982.
Contains an excellent brief introduction to the comparative study of
these three religions.

Schuon, Frithjof. *Understanding Islam*, 3rd ed. Translated by D. M.
Matheson. 1972. An explication of Islamic beliefs and an impassioned
defense of them. Chapter 2 is especially useful on the logic of the
Koran.

BEOWULF

Backgrounds

No divisions are indicated in the Old English poem, but there is general agreement that it falls naturally into two parts. Part 1 tells the story
of the hero's fight with Grendel and his mother. Part 2 deals with the
fight with the dragon. You may find an outline listing the sequence of
topics (or groups of topics) helpful. Such an outline may be especially
appropriate in view of the poet's fondness for including brief narratives
not actually a part of the main story. These are sometimes called "digres-
sions," but this term is inaccurate as well as unfriendly. The poet never
loses sight of his theme and purpose; rather, a situation or event in the
story of Beowulf often reminds him—by similarity or contrast—of a figure or an incident from Germanic tradition. The "included narratives"
(as we shall call them) are sometimes closely related to the central plot:
thus Beowulf's account of the swimming feat shared with Breca both
refutes Unferth's disparaging remarks and reinforces his fitness to undertake the contest with Grendel. (It is a substantial item of his résumé!)
And near the end of the poem, the gloomy forecast of a Geatish
spokesman—now that the great king Beowulf is gone—is justified by references to earlier wars between the Geats and foreign nations. Neverthe-

less, it may prove helpful to recognize the distinction between Beowulf's
exploits (and their context) and the other topics in the poem. The
included narratives are enclosed in brackets in the following list.

1. Pp. 1062–63: The ship burial of the Danish king Scyld; his royal
    descendants down to Hrothgar, who builds the splendid hall named
    Heorot. (Includes the *Prologue* to the poem.)
2. Pp. 1063–71: Heorot ravaged by the monster Grendel; arrival of
    Beowulf, a Geatish prince; entertainment in Heorot; offer to await
    Grendel in the hall. [Included narrative: the swimming feat of
    young Beowulf and Breca.]
3. Pp. 1071–79: Beowulf's victory over Grendel; celebration with
    speeches and gift giving. [Included narratives: Sigemund, the
    dragon-slayer; the story of Hnaef and Finn.]
4. Pp. 1079–84: Heorot invaded by Grendel's mother, who kills
    Aeschere; Beowulf's fight with her in the underwater room, and
    return to Heorot.
5. Pp. 1084–91: Renewed celebration in Heorot; Beowulf's farewell
    to Hrothgar; return voyage of the Geats to Hygelac's kingdom.
    [Included narratives: Heremod's disastrous career as a warning to
    Beowulf; the taming of Modthryth.] Beowulf's report to King
    Hygelac, his uncle, marks the end of part 1. [Included narrative:
    Ingeld and renewal of a Danish-Heatho-Bard feud—represented as
    a prophecy by Beowulf.]
6. Pp. 1091–95: Beowulf and the dragon. [Included narratives:
    Hygelac's expedition against the Frisians and Franks, in which he
    was killed, his death avenged by Beowulf, who killed Daeghrefn,
    the slayer of Hygelac; Beowulf supports young Eofor and succeeds
    him as king of the Geats when Heardred is killed in a battle with
    Swedes; Beowulf's autobiographical speech recounting earlier
    Geatish wars.]
7. Pp. 1095–1103: With Wiglaf's help, Beowulf finally kills the dragon;
    the hero gives directions for his funeral pyre and memorial mound;
    Beowulf's death. [Included narratives: the herald's prophecy of wars
    between Geats and Swedes, Frisians, and Franks; he recounts
    episodes from times past, notably the deeds of the Swedish king
    Ongentheow.]

Classroom Strategies

Assignments will naturally depend on the length of time devoted to the
poem. The list above may serve as a flexible outline of the possibilities:
the area covered in each item could provide enough material for a single
class period. In the event of time restrictions, combinations of these sections are possible.

The range of emphases in teaching *Beowulf* is wide indeed; each
instructor is free to decide which focus is best suited for the course. The
editor's view is indicated, more or less, in the headnote in the anthology
and in "Topics for Discussion and Writing," below. Judicious use of visual

aids—slides, photographs, etc.—have proved especially valuable in any approach to the poem.

Approaches to Teaching Beowulf, edited by Jess B. Bessinger Jr. and Robert F. Yeager (from the Masterpieces of World Literature series, MLA, 1984) is a rich mine of materials and information. Donald K. Fry (pp. 144–49) offers an extensive list of visual materials. The book also contains, as its primary content, groups of essays by experienced scholars arranged according to particular focus: undergraduate and graduate classes in Old English, in translation, mixed undergraduate and graduate classes, etc. Along with the books mentioned in the anthology, this volume provides abundant guidance in both teaching focus and further reading.

Topics for Discussion and Writing

1. Do you find Beowulf more or less attractive than Homer's Achilles or Odysseus?

   [You should defend your preference by citing acts, situations, and speeches from the poems. Then try to form a comprehensive but concise statement of your view.]

2. Which is the more dangerous antagonist for Beowulf: Grendel or Grendel's mother?

   [Discuss specific features of each contest, for example, the killing of Hondscioh, the escape of Grendel from Heorot, the fearsome head of Grendel, which Beowulf brings back to Heorot; and the fierceness of Grendel's mother's struggle with the hero, the lucky discovery of a sword at the essential moment.]

3. The poem has been described as a portrait of the ideal ruler, "a mirror for princes" of the age. What do you think of this view?

   [Consider the traits of character shown in the narrative—the motives of his acts; his treatment of Unferth, Hrothgar, Wealtheow, Wiglaf, Hygd, and Hrethric; including the similarities and contrasts suggested by reference to other figures of Germanic tradition.]

4. In a speech after the hero's death, Wiglaf expresses regret that his friends could not persuade Beowulf to leave the dragon alone. What do you think of this view?

   [Consider such aspects as these: what the dragon was doing; the apparent absence of anyone else to cope with the dragon; the hero's motives (the glory and the gold); the responsibility of the king for the welfare of his people. (If you have read Sophocles' play *Oedipus the King*—in the anthology—you might compare Oedipus' refusal to follow the advice of others, especially Tiresias.)]

Comparative Perspectives

1. What happens to women in the world of *Beowulf*? Compare gender roles and relations in heroic narratives of other cultures in the middle ages.

2. What does the hero's choice of weapons in this poem tell us about him as a fighter and as a human being? Compare the weapons and the means of dealing with their enemies chosen by other heroes, looking for evidence about them in the same way.
   [Consider Achilles, Odysseus, Roland.]

Further Reading

See the reading suggestions in the anthology, pp. 1060–61.

THE SONG OF ROLAND

Backgrounds

In A.D. 777 Charles, king of the Franks, later known as Emperor Charlemagne, concluded an agreement with a rebel faction of the Saracen rulers of Spain. In return for sending an army in support of that faction, Charlemagne was to be acknowledged sovereign of the entire country. But things did not work out as planned. The great city of Saragossa, which by the agreement was to welcome Charles's entry, kept its gates closed against him, and following a fruitless six-week siege, he decided to withdraw. On August 15, 778, as it made its way home through the Pyrenees, his army was set upon in the manner described in the following passage from a life of Charlemagne, written about fifty years after the event:

> It happened this way: as the army was proceeding, stretched out in a long thin column because of the narrowness of that defile, the Basques [*Wascones*] lay in ambush on top of a mountain—the place is thickly covered with woods and therefore well suited for such covert attacks; and they rushed down upon the end of the baggage train and upon those troops in the rear guard who were protecting the main army ahead, forced them down to the bottom of the valley, engaged them in battle and killed them to the last man; then they looted the baggage, and protected by the gathering night they scattered in every direction with all the speed they had. In what took place the Basques were favored by the lightness of their arms and the terrain in which they fought; and the Franks were put thoroughly at a disadvantage by the great weight of their arms and the unevenness of the ground. In this battle were killed Eggihardus, seneschal of the royal table; Anshelmus, count of the palace; and Hruodlandus [i.e., Roland], prefect of the marches of Brittany, among many others.

It is on this incident, altogether transformed by storytellers' imaginations, that the *Song* is based. As the poem presents it, Charles's withdrawal from Saragossa is brought about by a trick. The Saracen king of Spain, Marsilion, seeing his country laid waste by seven years of French invasion and even Saragossa about to fall, sends Charles a deceitful message promising to surrender sovereignty if he and his forces will return to France. Marsilion and the other Arab leaders will, they promise, speedily follow him there, confess his rule, and convert to Christianity.

To Charles and his barons, worn by years of war, the offer looks attractive and is accepted, though one of their number opposes it: Roland. Now word of their acceptance must be sent to Marsilion, and the question is who shall go? The last time ambassadors were sent to the Arabs, they were executed. Various stalwart heroes volunteer—Roland, Oliver, Turpin, and others—but Charles is unwilling to risk them. At last Roland nominates his stepfather, Ganelon, a choice all immediately approve. All, that is, except Ganelon, who is outraged and plans revenge. Reaching Saragossa as Charles's ambassador, he tells Marsilion and the other Arab leaders that the surest way to be rid of the French forever is to kill their stoutest fighting men—Roland, Oliver, and the Twelve Peers—by a sortie against the forces that will be left behind to protect the army's rear as it makes its way through the mountain passes. He, Ganelon, will see to it that Roland and the rest are in that rear guard.

Returning to the French camp, Ganelon announces that the Arabs will behave as promised. Naturally, a rear guard will have to be established for security's sake, and who so suitable to command it as Roland and his dauntless friends? In the great battle that follows, twenty thousand French soldiers are slain with their leaders until only Roland remains— dying not because any Saracen has bested him but because he has burst his temples by his efforts to recall Charles's armies with mighty blasts upon the oliphant, the ivory horn.

Summoned, too late, by Roland's trumpet, the emperor Charles returns with his main army and destroys Marsilion and his allies. There follows a long episode telling of his later victory over the great Saracen leader Baligant, after which the scene changes to the headquarters at Aix. Ganelon is brought to trial; his claim that his acts against Roland involved no treason against Charles is finally disallowed. There ensues a "judicial combat" between the emperor's champion Tierri and Ganelon's representative Pinabel; victory was left in the hands of God in the traditional view of such affairs. Pinabel is defeated, and Ganelon is executed.

The poem itself offers abundant evidence that it has a background in the "oral" tradition of poetic composition. First, there is a pattern of repetition; for example, the idea that Charles will, or may, or should leave Spain and return to his capital at Aix is stated at lines 36ff., 51ff., 134ff., and 187ff. The scene and the participants vary, of course, but the thought is expressed again and again in very similar phrasing. Entire scenes are often closely parallel: Charles and Marsilion hold assemblies, receive ambassadors, listen to counselors, and render decisions essentially in the same manner. The battles are series of single combats between notable fighters and the action as well as the language describing it is often much the same from one encounter to the next. And since the deeds and the skills remain essentially identical, it is natural that the words and phrases that describe them should do so as well. The result is a large number of more or less uniform phrases or short sentences. In the *Roland* and in the Greek epics and in the Old English *Beowulf* also the result is a body of *formulaic* diction (differing from one language to another) conspicuous in poems deriving from a background of oral tradition. These poems were meant to be listened to by an audience, rather than read by a solitary individual in silence. Hence the recurrence of set phrases, like the repetition of scenes, would reinforce the narrative and reassure (rather than annoy) the public for which the poems were composed.

Roland is by general consent the finest example of a popular genre of narrative poetry known in French as the *chanson de geste*. Poems of this kind dealt typically with great deeds done in war or warlike adventure; normally love is absent or unimportant, and this especially differentiates the *chanson de geste* from the romance (French *roman*). Again typically, *Roland* has a tenuous relation to actual history; the central background figure is Charles, king of the Franks (crowned emperor by the pope in the year 800, the first head of the Holy Roman Empire). But comparison of the historical kernel, given on earlier pages, with the poet's narrative will indicate the extent of the transformation.

As intimated in the headnote in the anthology, the attitude of the poet is emphatically "positive"; the story as he tells it is filled with enthusiasm for king, Charles, whom all his feudal vassals extol with complete sincerity; for country, "sweet France," almost a refrain in many a *laisse*; and for the Christian religion. Indeed, Charles feels an obligation either to annihilate the heathen religion of the Saracens by destroying or by converting its adherents. Neither the poet nor any of his Christian characters expresses the least doubt as to the rightness of this purpose. It may seem a bit strange to us that they know so little about the faith they oppose; the poem makes them polytheists, worshippers, oddly enough, of the Greek god Apollo as well as the Arabic prophet Mahoun (Muhammad). Historically, of course, they have always been strict worshippers of one god, Allah, whose prophet was Muhammad. In short, the poet is an ardent partisan untroubled by qualms of any kind. Once the modern reader understands and accepts this fact, he or she should be free to enjoy the unremitting energy deployed in the narrative, to delight in the brilliant pageantry of its assemblies, to "identify" with Roland and his comrades in the procession of military duels.

But *Roland* is not simply a narrative of straightforward action; the plot is complicated by the treachery of Ganelon and later by the disagreement between Oliver and Roland. The poet carefully shows us how Ganelon sets about his object, the destruction of Roland. This is no easy task. First, he must convince King Marsilion that Roland, not Charles, is an implacable enemy of the Saracens, and he must begin by convincing Blancandrin, the envoy who has come from Marsilion and who will return with Ganelon himself. Then he must persuade Marsilion to send hostages and false promises of submission to Charles and then to attack with overwhelming force the small army that Charles will leave behind as a rear guard under Roland's command. If we dwell for a moment on the several uncertainties in this plan—the number of things that could go wrong—we realize what a skillful diplomat Ganelon must have been. Thus his initial harshness in stating Charles's (alleged) terms is designed to anger Marsilion and his court, to get them in the mood to fight. Once that is done, the anger can be directed against Roland. The poet's lines make it clear that Ganelon took a deliberate risk; there were two moments at which he might have been struck down by an enraged Saracen. (This topic could be a focus of class discussion or written assignments.)

Oliver, whose sister has been promised in marriage to Roland, is also his closest friend and, apparently, second only to him in valor. From the beginning onward the poet calls attention to the difference between these devoted friends. When Roland offers himself as the envoy to Marsilion, it is Oliver who protests at once (lines 255–57):

> "No, no, not you!" said Oliver the Count,
> "that heart in you is wild, spoils for a fight,
> how I would worry—you'd fight with them, I know."

Later, when both see the huge Saracen army approaching the rear guard, Oliver pleads with Roland to blow the trumpet, which will bring Charles to the rescue; Roland is adamant in his refusal. Finally, after the rear guard has suffered total defeat and death stares the survivors in the face, Roland wants to sound the horn; now Oliver objects, and his anger is evident when he breaks off the marriage arrangement between his sister and Roland. His reply to Roland, who asks why Oliver is angry with him, is important for the poet's characterization of Roland: it is judgment, not madness, that makes a good vassal; Roland had rejected (good) judgment when he refused to sound the horn while there was time. The reply occupies an entire *laisse* (no. 131). The relationship between the two men (which need not be further rehearsed here) is one of the major foci of the narrative; it should receive due attention in the classroom. Nowhere else in the poem is there a relationship of friendship, then alienation, then misunderstanding, and finally reconciliation at death. As for the attitude of the poet, it seems clear that he uses the contrast of the two men to point to a flaw in the character of Roland. Immediately after Roland's rejection of Oliver's repeated pleas that the horn be sounded (before the battle), we find the line (1093), "Roland is good, and Oliver is wise." (The word translated *good* is the French *proz*, which may best be rendered "valiant.") The distinction, made incidentally in this passage, is confirmed and developed in *laisse* 131.

But Roland's defect does not lead the author to "prefer" Oliver or to treat him as of comparable importance to Roland. It is clear that Roland is the central figure in the poem as a whole and especially in the first half—until his death. He is the only man who declares that Marsilion does not intend to keep his promise of submission to Charles; now the poet has already told us (readers or listeners) the same thing. This weights our sympathy in advance on Roland's side. Then, while Oliver's deeds in the battle are heroic, like those of all the leaders of the French, Roland's are superheroic (but never treated as incredible or ridiculous). After the death of all the rest—except Turpin, and again after *his* death— Roland and Roland alone holds the stage for many a *laisse*. (A good topic for oral discussion or an essay assignment might be found here.)

The fighting archbishop, Turpin, proves, at least, in the poet's view, that the crusading zeal of Charles and Roland is righteous. He promises paradise to the French warriors; the penance he assigns for their confessed sins is to fight bravely! His prominence in the story is indicated by the fact that he dies last of all—except Roland. In this war, church and state are indeed united.

Classroom Strategies

You will, of course, divide the poem for class assignments according to the time available, but here are a few convenient breaks in the narrative to the death of Roland:

1. *Laisses* 1–27: Charles chooses Ganelon as envoy to Marsilion.
2. *Laisses* 28–53: Ganelon and Marsilion plot treachery.
3. *Laisses* 54–71, 79–95, 104–15, and 125–27: destruction of the rear guard.
4. *Laisses* 128–76: the last great deeds and death of Roland.

Topics for Discussion

1. The poet's attitude toward Roland.
   [Take account of the passages cited in item 3 under "Topics for Writing"; then note that Roland dominates the action of the poem both before and after the disagreement with Oliver; overall as well as piece by piece Roland is paramount; note his well-nigh superhuman exertion after the rest of the French are all dead and the enemy either dead or fled, etc. He is a flawed hero but nonetheless the hero of the poem.]
2. Archbishop Turpin and the Crusaders' attitude.
   [Turpin's prominence as both fighting man and priest; his hearing the confessions of the French and assigning the penance of valor in battle; the final blessing of the slain leaders whose bodies Roland brings to Turpin; the repeated assertion that Christians are right and pagans are wrong (in the course of the poem).]
3. The supernatural and the superhuman elements in the poem.
   [Omens; dreams; the angel Gabriel; the exertions of Roland in the final scenes. Does all this amount to a miscellany of the incredible, tacitly ridiculed by the poet? Or is it so handled that the reader accepts it without demur, with no distress over its improbability in our prosaic, workaday world?]
4. Elements of oral poetry in *Roland*.
   [The frequent pattern of repetition of incidents or situations or items of dialogue—for example, Oliver's three requests that Roland blow the horn (lines 1051–92) and Roland's three refusals, matched by Roland's later declaration that he will now blow it and Oliver's dissent, both stated twice (lines 1702–21). In climactic situations like these such repetition is still effective for the modern

reader, though the partial repetition of identical phrasing shows
that we have here a relic of oral practice.]

Topics for Writing

1. How does Ganelon persuade King Marsilion to plan an attack
   against Roland and the rear guard?

   [Begin with the talk between Ganelon and the Saracen envoy
   Blancandrin during their journey from Charles's headquarters to
   Marsilion's. Then Ganelon states Charles's message in the harshest,
   most offensive terms possible; and, acting as his surrogate, draws
   Marsilion's hot anger on himself. But with Blancandrin's help this
   anger is diverted from Ganelon (and Charles) and directed at
   Roland. They now plan the destruction of Roland by means of the
   attack on the rear guard.]
2. The poet's parallel treatment of the courts and entourage of
   Charles and Marsilion.

   [Each is shown presiding over a group of leaders and advisers of
   the ruler; each has a select group of warriors (the twelve—*douze*—
   peers) distinguished above the mass; and heading these groups are
   Charles's nephew, Roland, and Marsilion's nephew, Aelroth. The
   peers do battle with peers on the opposing side; nearly all are spectacular fighters, though the French are (individually) superior (the
   Saracen victory is due to overwhelming numbers). Students' papers
   should quote or cite specific passages of the poem, usually moving
   from the first assemblies onward.]
3. Oliver's attitude toward Roland.

   [Begin with Oliver's protest when Roland offers to go as Charles's
   envoy to Marsilion (lines 255–57). Go on to Oliver's urging Roland
   to blow the horn that will call Charles to the rescue (lines 1049–92:
   Oliver asks three times and Roland refuses three times); then to
   Roland's wish to blow the horn when it is clear that the French will
   be destroyed, whereupon Oliver dissents—and breaks off the
   betrothal of his sister Aude to Roland (line 1702–21); then to
   Oliver's answer to Roland's question, "Why are you angry at me?"
   (lines 1722–37), "I will tell you what makes a vassal good: / it is
   judgment, it is never madness. . . " Finally there is an implicit reconciliation just before Oliver's death (2010–23).]

Comparative Perspectives

1. Heroic literature shows reverence for kings even while it reveals
   their human limitations. What gesture repeatedly describes Charles
   the Great? How does this link him with *Beowulf*'s Hrothgar?

   [See the opening of *laisse* 15 of *The Song of Roland*, in which
   "The Emperor held his head bowed down with this, / and stroked
   his beard, and smoothed his mustache down, / and speaks no
   word." In these narratives, kings may be ineffectual, malign, or
   wrong, but their right to rule is never challenged.]

2. The attitudes toward Islam in *The Song of Roland* demonstrate how the Saracens threatened medieval Christians. Compare the view of the Christian world in the Koran.
   [Cf. references to "The People of the Book" in the Koran.]

Further Reading

See the reading suggestions in the anthology, p. 1107.

MARIE DE FRANCE

Lanval *and* Laüstic

Classroom Strategies and Topics for Discussion

With Marie de France, a leading figure in the Renaissance of the twelfth century, medieval literature moves decisively from the heroic to the romantic. The headnote's reference to romances as "novelistic narratives" is a good point from which to start a discussion of the *lai,* the genre with which Marie is primarily identified. Much briefer than the romance (variously represented in the anthology by *Sir Gawain and the Green Knight, The Wife of Bath's Tale,* and Malory's *Morte Darthur*), *lais* are distinguished by their intensity, their use of symbols, and their frequent appeal to the supernatural. Although the narratives are pared down, by invoking the symbolic and the supernatural they offer surprisingly acute insights into motive and personality. In their penetration of her human actors and the scenes that surround them, Marie's *lais* do indeed prefigure the novel as we know it today.

In introducing their work, the translators of *Lanval* and *Laüstic* point out that the *"lai . . .* generally starts from a position of lack and crisis" and moves swiftly to a moment of happiness that is then severely tested. The topic is generally love, and in this respect as well Marie sets a pattern that is to define much of the great narrative fiction written by women down to the present day. Looking at the way individuals are revealed by the choices they make in love and marriage, she is a precursor of writers like Jane Austen and George Eliot and the lesser authors of romances that many of your students doubtless cherish. Like these novelists, Marie is an astute recorder of manners. Today's students often think of "good manners" as phony, externalized poses. Reading the fiction of manners should prove otherwise.

Without saying so explicitly, in *Lanval* Marie undercuts the Arthurian court (as Chaucer's Wife of Bath will do from a very different vantage point two centuries later) by emphasizing the good manners of Lanval, which put to shame the unexplained neglect that he suffers at the hands of knights who are supposed to have perfected good behavior. In *Laüstic,* her keen eye for the physical circumstances in which her characters live allows for a different critique of manners and the way they express the truth of human nature.

By beginning the action of *Lanval* in late spring, Marie de France appeals to the same seasonal expectations that set the mood for so many of the love lyrics in the anthology: spring and summer are times when mind and body can flower into romantic radiance along with fields and trees. You might ask your students why Marie specifically mentions Pentecost and St. John's Day—festival days that offer a hiatus from the everyday responsibilities of the workaday world by reminding believers of their ties to another, higher world in touch with the miraculous. The appearance of the otherworldly to the unhappy hero is heralded by a detail your students will probably recognize—Lanval's trembling horse resembles the sensitive animals who populate vampire and werewolf movies and always know well before their human owners that the supernatural has invaded the ordinary world. (According to Malory, Pentecost was also the occasion for an annual oath sworn by the Knights of the Round Table to defend ladies and gentlewomen, "upon pain of death." If Marie was familiar with this tradition, her reference to Pentecost compounds the ironies of Lanval's difficulties, since his impetuous defense of his lady both defies her explicit orders and enrages the queen.)

The generosity and kindness of the extravagantly outfitted and alluringly beautiful ladies show up Arthur's unexplained denial of gifts deserved to a lonely foreigner. Although the lady is clearly supernatural, she is never called a fairy; surprisingly, her attractions are described in highly material terms. Even her clothing seems paradoxical: in warm weather, she wears white ermine that reveals more than it conceals. Likening her to Semiramis and Octavian may be yet another stab at Arthur, who never approaches the imperial sway associated with these famed rulers, but Semiramis in particular, legendary for her incestuous lust, is a curiously compromised figure of comparison. However capricious the lady might turn out to be, Lanval—"neither foolish nor illmannered"—behaves perfectly with his unearthly lover and graciously with those in need. His lavish charity reveals his moral superiority to the court that has withheld its rewards from him.

Marie paints a compelling picture of the society that first snubbed and then tries Lanval: note the introduction of the queen "reclining by a window cut out of the stone" (p. 1172), indolent and watchful at once, and the ferocity with which she strikes out at Lanval when he rejects her. It is typical of medieval narrative that it declines to explicate moments so fraught with drama. Marie's great gift for suggesting interiority comes through in the crisis that this scene between lady and vassal precipitates, with both retreating to their bedchambers, hurt and angry. Poor Arthur, happily returning from a day in the woods to a demanding wife, is faced with a catastrophe at once domestic and political.

The failure of King Arthur's court is carefully delineated; the legendary companionship of the Round Table has been flawed from the start. The emphasis on Gawain and his ever-present entourage and the comment that "a hundred" would have liked to see Lanval acquitted remind us of how estranged the foreign knight has been from the group activities that prevail throughout this tale. Whose fault is it that there is no place for this sensitive, alienated soul in this public realm? At the very end, Marie implies that the martial concerns of the Arthurian world have deformed the good manners for which it has become legendary. Perhaps the heavy marble block that supports armed warriors about to mount their chargers symbolizes the crudity that has infected the chivalric world. The alienated hero has no real choice but to follow his unearthly lover, who bears him away to the mystical land of Avalon rather than to battle. If you plan to move on to read the *Morte Darthur,* you will want to call your students' attention to this moment, for the dying Arthur himself will be gathered to the Vale of Avalon, the only place where he can finally escape the conflicts that brought his kingdom down.

In turning to *Laüstic,* you may want to spend a few moments discussing the authorial self-consciousness that leads Marie to address her audience directly and refer to her own tale-telling. She pays attention to her titles and prides herself on her linguistic range, for words count in her poetry. Although she is a writer, she probably functioned as an oral performer as well, perhaps offering her *lais* to the court as an evening's entertainment. References to her literary situation seem most appropriate as they frame the very brief *Laüstic,* which is, as the headnote points out, much like the jeweled reliquary that contains the nightingale and by extension its song, the essence of poetic art.

It would be rewarding to ask your students to locate the center of narrative consciousness in both *Lanval* and *Laüstic.* Marie de France displays unusual interest in her female characters and the drives that motivate them, matters about which the headnote provides helpful guidance. Yet she is no special pleader for her heroines. Lanval himself is very much the center of his tale, the cynosure of two powerful women. *Laüstic,* on the other hand, begins with the friendship of the two knights of St. Malo, and only focuses on the lady when the love triangle has been established. The suggestion that the bachelor falls in love with his married friend's wife out of a sense of rivalry rather than for any good qualities possessed by the lady herself qualifies our response to this ultimately failed love affair.

The real interest here seems to be in the adjoining houses that create the proximity that brings the lovers together but also rest on the wall that keeps them apart. It is perhaps not too distant a digression to spend some time talking about the importance of architecture in the frequent tales of adulterous passion that distinguish medieval European literature. Ask your students to think back to the mead-hall of *Beowulf,* where Hrothgar's warriors congregate; only the king and queen seem to have private accommodations. Look ahead to a bawdy tale like Boccaccio's Sixth Story of the Ninth Day, which, like many a fabliau, derives its humor from the complex geography of the shared bedroom. Adulterous love is a theme primarily in aristocratic literature because a person needs time and privacy to indulge it. The two knights of St. Malo have up-to-date homes, it would appear, but they are crammed together in limited urban space. Without a luxurious, self-standing castle, adultery on a grand scale appears hard to sustain.

Marie de France can be quite direct about cruelty and pain, as in her depiction of the husband's obsessive pursuit of the nightingale. He correctly understands that the bird represents his wife's personal freedom, whether or not he suspects her of adulterous love. Marie implies that this need to assert her separate being is the real source of the love the wife feels for her neighbor; perhaps she is spared a direct attack because the love never takes a material form. The spatter of blood on her breast is a mild rebuke, hardly a scarlet letter.

Keeping other materials in the anthology again in mind, you may want to assign *Laüstic* in tandem with Boccaccio's Ninth Story of the Fourth Day, which seems to be an elaborate variation on the basic plot of *Laüstic*. The symbolism of the cherished nightingale, an emblem of a love that never really transgressed the bounds of marriage, is transformed to the brutal reality of a lover's heart served up to the unsuspecting lady, who consumes it and then kills herself. The casual horror inflicted by the husband in Boccaccio's story does not belong in the Breton *lai*, a more delicate genre suited to the first great woman writer in England.

Topics for Writing

Detailed observation of the material world in Marie de France's *lais* gives substance to a genre that shows the importance of transcending the material world.

1. Discuss the physical details that describe the regal elegance and sexual attractions of the otherworldly lady in *Lanval*. How is she shown to possess qualities that diminish Arthur's realm and his jealous queen?
2. Show the significance of the adjoining houses and the jeweled casket in *Laüstic*.

Comparative Perspectives

1. Marie de France flavors her poetry with allusions to oral performance. Compare her self-reflective comments on her art form with the traces of oral formulaic in the early epic poems of the medieval period, like *Beowulf* and *The Song of Roland*.
2. Compare and contrast the response of Lanval to the queen's advances and accusation with those of Joseph to Potiphar's wife in Genesis and /or the Koran. Why in each case does the man refuse the lady's offer of herself? How is the lady treated by the narrator?

THORSTEIN THE STAFF-STRUCK

Backgrounds

The events of the story take place in northeastern Iceland, near the coast and mostly at Thorarin's farm in Sunnudale or at Hof, the home stead of Bjarni, the head of a household including his wife, Rannveig; his brothers, Thorhall and Thorvald, who are his dependents or subordinates; and his chief servant, Thord. Our story is a pendant to a longer saga (*Vopnfirdinga saga*) in which Bjarni is the principal figure; hence the allusions to his acts at Bodvarsdale, as well as the account of his descendants at the end of the story. The protagonists in *Thorstein the Staff-Struck* are old Thorarin and his son, Thorstein, on one side and Bjarni, with his family and household, on the other. But it is important to note the mixture—sometimes amounting to conflict—of motives *within* the several characters. Thus Thorstein, who surely knows that Thord's blow was intentional, would prefer to avoid further violence; one motive, implied rather than spelled out, is his aged father's precarious physical and economic condition. If Thorstein should be killed or forced to go into exile, old Thorarin would be left destitute and helpless. Knowing the old man's bellicose disposition, Thorstein tries to keep him from hearing of Thord's act; but he does learn about it and hence goads Thorstein to action by accusing him of cowardice. Now note the contrast between Thorstein and Thord. Thord, who surely knew that he had been the unjustifiable aggressor, is offered a way out: he can declare the injury unintentional and pay a fee. According to the code of that age and country, this would be an honorable settlement for both men. But it does not appeal to Thord, whose foolish arrogance costs him his life.

In this situation, Bjarni, the master and necessarily the protector of Thord, has no easy alternative to the step he takes, namely prosecution of Thorstein for homicide, ending in a sentence of exile. We must remember that Iceland in the tenth century had no public means of enforcing judicial decisions; the plaintiff when victorious had to step in and see that the verdict was carried out. When Bjarni does nothing in this direction, malicious gossip, shared by the brothers Thorhall and Thorwald in his own household, ridicules him as a coward. It is a nice touch on the author's part to have Bjarni *overhear* this kind of talk; and the reader will think it a fit response when Bjarni sends Thorhall and Thorvald to kill Thorstein—if they can! When he kills them instead, Bjarni is once again forced into the position of reluctant avenger. But now the major protagonists, Bjarni and Thorstein, must face each other. You should point out the abundant detail with which their encounter is narrated—with time out for shoe-tying and a word with old Thorarin back in the house. All this enables us to understand the characters of the two men better; and a near-final surprise comes with the hopeless attempt of Thorarin to beat Bjarni (who has told him that he has killed Thorstein). Then the final reconciliation satisfies protagonists and reader alike.

Topics for Discussion

1. The authors of Icelandic sagas do not overtly declare their attitudes toward the characters. Usually much can be inferred, though sometimes a measure of doubt may remain. Students might be asked to attack or defend such a conclusion as this: "The author approves of Thorstein, admires Bjarni, holds Thorhall and Thorvald in contempt, enjoys Thorarin with reservations, is amiably amused by Rannveig and the other (unnamed) female character."

2. The role of Rannveig, wife of Bjarni.

   [She goads Bjarni into going after Thorstein and then seems to discourage him from the act, at any rate without her help. Their two conversations dramatize the conflict in Bjarni's own mind (although in the sagas women traditionally incite their kinsman to vengeance).]

Topic for Writing

The reluctant avengers.

[Thorstein would prefer to treat Thord's blow as an accident both because he is "even-tempered" and because he fears for his aged father's welfare if he (Thorstein) should be killed. Bjarni is not eager to avenge Thord because he believes that Thorstein never attacks anyone without good reason. Yet both Thorstein and Bjarni ultimately feel compelled to fight in order to maintain their reputation as men of courage (essential to a satisfactory life in that civilization). Their final confrontation provides a happy solution in the form of reconciliation.]

Comparatives Perspectives

1. Compare this story's treatment of shifting attitudes toward the need for vengeance (embodied in the contrast between Thorarin and Thorstein) to the treatment of the same theme in the *Oresteia*. How important is Bjarni's conversion to Christianity to the development of the theme? What spiritual change plays a similar role in the end of *The Eumenides?*
2. Compare and contrast the portrait of a marriage in this short narrative with that in *The Tale of the Merchant and His Wife* in *The Thousand and One Nights*. What view of women do these texts seem to share?

Further Reading

See also the reading suggestions in the anthology, p. 1179.

Byock, Jesse L. *Feud in the Icelandic Saga*. 1982.

MEDIEVAL LYRICS: A SELECTION

Classroom Strategies and Topics for Discussion

This rich trove of chronologically organized lyric poems offers a variety of teaching opportunities. One mode of organizing your materials is to select lyrics according to the categories enumerated in the headnote. You could have your students read an apparently homogeneous group of poems that explore seasonal celebrations, with their embroidery of birds and flowers, say, or several of the spiritual effusions representative of the three great monotheistic traditions that shaped the European medieval sensibility. Close study of a sequence of such thematically related poems will reveal, of course, that they are not genuinely homogeneous at all but reflective of very different authorial sensibilities, as the discussion below will suggest.

If you have not yet concentrated on the short lyric as a distinct genre, you could choose a few of the more complex poems in this selection and work through them with your students in great detail, examining the way idiosyncratic speaking voices capture the play of mind as they twist and turn through their subjects. You might also consider using a single poem to complement another work you are studying, either to indicate how widespread certain conventional assumptions were within medieval culture itself, or to juxtapose works from different periods with each other, to show your students how certain thematic preoccupations may be treated differently in different times and places. Many of these themes will recur in the second volume, most obviously in Continental Romantic Lyrics: A Selection, but elsewhere as well, and some notable foreshadowings are mentioned here, so that you can alert your students and take advantage of echoes and connections that can help you shape a year-long course.

Here are a few suggestions for each of these approaches. It is hard to overstress the constant revisiting of nature as a dominant lyric concern in century after century and culture after culture. At some point in your discussion you may want to ask your students to write a few lines of verse themselves, to articulate a personal response to the turn of the seasons, the song of a bird, the color of flowers, the patterns of clouds in the sky— one has to be hardened indeed not to have felt a sense of wonder in the presence of great natural beauty. Models may be found in a grouping of spring and summer poems that might include any or all of the following: *Song of Summer*; *The Singing Lute*; *Spring Song*; Judah Halevi's *Summer*; Jaufré Rudel's *Love Song*, Hadewijch of Brabant's *The Cult of Love*, Guido Cavalcanti's *An Encounter*. You might ask your students to single out the details typical of this subgenre. Keenly observed pictures of flora and fauna express the intimacy with which human beings lived in the natural world until very recently; at the same time, such references quickly became conventional tropes, expressing a sense of literary community as much as any genuine encounter with the natural world. The catalog, a literary device students may remember from classical epic, unites both the natural and the artificial by simultaneously evoking a sense of nature's plenitude and literature's variety.

The anonymous *Song of Summer*, a virtuosic accounting of Western poetry's favorite birds and their attributes, is a good point at which to begin. Here, as so often with these medieval lyrics, there is no strict dividing line between secular and sacred (indeed, perhaps the hallmark of the period is the effortless interweaving of the two, an acknowledgement of the divine in every aspect of created life). Here, the catalog of birds yields to the poet's initially surprising elevation of the diligent, unglamorous bee. You may wish to explain that bees became symbolic of the Virgin Mary because it was thought that they did not physically reproduce their young but instead gathered them up—immaculately, as it were—from the flowers they visited.

Ibn Arfa' Ra'suh's *The Singing Lute* illustrated the special role of the garden trope in Islamic poetry. The Koran, as the penultimate verse of *The Table* (p. 1051 in the anthology) demonstrates, abounds in references to the gardens of paradise. Here, too, an apparently secular poem interweaves sacred motifs—neither world is intelligible without the other. Wine (forbidden, of course, to Muslims in this world) promotes the inebriation sought by the Sufis as the mystical means to know the divine. (You may want to make a note about returning to *The Singing Lute* if you plan to teach Naguib Mahfouz's wonderful short story *Zaabalawi* in the second semester of your course.) As the headnote suggests, the garden here is also a place of high culture: the fragile gazelle, covered in elegant embroidered silks, is almost an advertisement for a sophisticated union of nature and commerce. A connection may be made here to the garden imagery in The Song of Songs. (Note that Hildegard of Bingen in *A Hymn to St. Maximus* and Judah Halevi in *Summer* explicitly refer to the biblical poem; without being specifically indebted to the same source, *The Singing Lute*'s use of garden imagery indicates how profoundly these paradisal images are embedded in the shared inheritance of the Middle East.) The gazelle then gives way to a tribute to the patron, the great ruler of the East (the source of silks) and the West (the place of the poet). Finally, the poem doubles back around itself to become a song of unrequited love (again, a familiar equation of God and the beloved is available to the interpreter). The powerful ruler deigns to greet his servants; the disdainful beloved, by contrast, ignores the poet-suitor.

One might conclude this grouping with the *Spring Song* of William IX, duke of Aquitaine. Here, the little birds are themselves poets, "each in their own language" knowing participants in what is clearly a well established genre. This sense of emotions both fresh and time-tested recurs in the delicate early spring setting of a real human relationship, fragile but already rooted. Not for this poet the "strange talk," the vaunting that turns into gossip and destroys new love. The bold final image proclaims the solidity of love, food into which the poet and his lady have cut with a knife, not a tremulous emotion that might melt with the frost on the leaves.

The ever-changing interplay of society, religion, psychology, and natural imagery to be observed in this trio of early poems emerges in almost all the selections in this unit. These concerns similarly color every one of the more extended narratives available among *Masterpieces of the Middle Ages*, making for another valuable way of using these poems in the classroom. Rather than devote an entire session to lyric poetry per se, consider using individual poems as an establishing point for discussion of a major text: from Judah Halevi's *Summer*, for example, one may jump directly into the opening lines of *The Canterbury Tales*, in which April's sweet showers penetrate dry March. From Christine de Pizan's *Alone in Martyrdom,* an autobiographical poem that uses familiar pastoral imagery (the young widow resembles "the turtledove without her mate" and "the ewe that the wolf seeks to kill"), one might move ahead in the anthology to the work of Marguerite de Navarre and consider the opportunities open to women who wished to write in the early modern period, or to Petrarch, whom Christine acknowledged as her master. All three incor-

porated and transmuted personal experience into their art, raising again
the question of the relationship of nature to art. Most obviously, perhaps,
one may want to teach Dante the lyric poet as a way of introducing Dante
the poet of *The Divine Comedy*. Recall the imagined literary symposium
among lovers and friends in *Love and Poetry* in relation to canto IV of the
Inferno, where Dante and Virgil join the great poets of classical antiquity
for a short seminar, a kind of busman's holiday on the way down to hell.

Less capacious than Dante's great work, the religious lyrics in this
selection tend to concentrate on heaven, and they show the influence of
liturgical forms. Students familiar with biblical poetry and antiphonal
church music will appreciate the reason why Notker's *Hymn to Holy
Women* is laid out in parallel stanzas on the page. For a precise reading of
this intricate poem, you may want to consult Peter Dronke's magisterial
survey, *The Medieval Lyric,* in which he explains the genesis of Notker's
poem in a pair of dream visions. It is not necessary to go into such detail,
however, to appreciate the vivid visual imagination at work in this text
and to grasp the familiar tribute to women, who, through Mary, as the
headnote points out, were empowered to redeem the Edenic fall. The
address to the serpent and the embrace of feminine bravery (on the part
even of courtesans) could lead to a discussion of other strong women in
fictional medieval texts you will discuss.

Or it could lead equally to an account of the remarkable Hildegard of
Bingen, whose genius has recently been celebrated on the nine hun-
dredth anniversary of her birth. One of the great medieval visionary
artists and writers, a scientist and a memoirist, author of one of the first
medieval dramas (*Ordo virtutem*) and composer of liturgical songs in
honor of the Virgin Mary (*Symphonia*), Hildegard (like her work) is now
accessible as she has not been for hundreds of years. In *A Hymn to St.
Maximus*, as in Notker's *Hymn*, we are in the presence of an imagination
deeply influenced by the visual arts. The ladder of Notker's poem, based
ultimately on Jacob's ladder, describes an avenue linking human and
divine as do the vertical images used to describe St. Maximus. Note the
word "Lucent" that begins stanza 3B. Behind both poems is the tradition
of illuminated manuscripts and stained-glass windows. Hildegard begins
her visionary prose work *Scivias* with these words: "It happened that, in
the eleven hundred and forty-first year of the Incarnation of the Son of
God, Jesus Christ, when I was forty-two years and seven months old,
Heaven was opened and a fiery light of exceeding brilliance came and
permeated my whole brain, and inflamed my whole breast." This brilliance infuses Hildegard's hymn, subject of another one of Dronke's
learned analyses, with its helpful synthesis: "the saint is masterpiece of
both nature and art," captured in the Latin pun on the word *gemma* (line
8), "both bud and jewel."

To the rich sensory trappings of Catholic worship captured in both of
these remarkable poems, one might contrast the tragic Hebrew poem
here called *The Sacrifice of Isaac,* another masterpiece of liturgical style.
At the age of thirteen, Ephraim ben Jacob, a native of Bonn, lived
through the massacre of the Jews in the Second Crusade (1146). Years

later, he commemorated that event in this poem and various learned biblical commentaries. As the headnote points out, the stanza that begins with line 61 takes as its point of departure a tradition that Abraham—"the alert one" (line 29)—responded to God's command so swiftly that he did actually did sacrifice Isaac once. The source of this tradition is unclear; in *The Last Trial*, Shalom Spiegel speculates that it would have received terrible confirmation in the massacres of the Jews of Germany during the First and Second Crusades. One Hebrew chronicle describes the pile of corpses that greeted the Crusaders after the townspeople had committed suicide rather than endure forced conversion. Sifting through the bodies, the Crusaders came upon still-breathing bodies and offered to save these survivors if they would convert. When these half-dead Jews refused, the text says "they proceeded to torture them some more, until *they killed then a second time.*"

Literally, the poem's title means *The Binding of Isaac*: lest he squirm involuntarily from the knife, becoming a blemished and thus unacceptable sacrifice, Isaac (the legend teaches) requested to be tightly bound. Notice that the poem ends with a sequence of references to binding and prayer that the bonds separating God from His people be broken. Indirectly, though its learned allusion, Ephraim's poem asks, How long oh Lord?

Despite their differing subjects, these three religious lyrics share some characteristics that students may ponder: in their ease of biblical reference, the complexity of their emotional range, and their recognition of the sublimity of struggle that informs true faith, they are hallmarks of the deep and serious spirituality of an era that is, as the headnote reminds us, "an age of faith"—but not only an age of faith.

The suffering but obedient father who is called upon to bring his child to the point of the knife may raise parallels with the Virgin Mary, brought into new prominence by medieval Christianity. Alluded to in several poems already mentioned, she is directly the subject of two more poems in this selection, each of which might profitably be read in tandem and in conjunction with Notker's *Hymn*. The four lines of *Calvary* express the intense pity of the speaker for the mother whose child is on the cross; the *Lament of the Virgin* speaks for Mary, evoking in graphic physical detail the bodily pain that so many of the great Northern painters of the era made palpable to view.

If the writers of these powerful religions poems tend to submerge themselves in their visions, others among these selected lyrics bristle with the restless intelligence of strong individual personalities. It would be interesting to teach as a group some of the poems in which the speakers are physically in motion, like those of Walahfrid Strabo or The Archpoet, whose journeys both provide the organizing scheme for the poems discussed below and embody the quest motif that gives shape to so many medieval narratives.

It helps students new to lyric to think of each poem as a small, self-contained drama. You might examine Walahfrid Strabo's poem of exile, asking students to identify the speaker's motives for leaving the "happy island" that he cannot put out of his mind. Driven out by "Shameful penury," lonely and cold, this traveler seeks "heart-felt wisdom" that seems to elude him. The headnote gives important biographical information about Walahfrid; college students on a bad day may recognize themselves in this sad portrait of a homesick wanderer and take courage from the ultimate success that he seems to have made of his life.

To Walahfrid's Penseroso one might juxtapose the dashing Archpoet, an Allegro who prefers not "to sit firm upon a rock." This portrait of a questing vagabond (line 23) who comes to rest in a tavern presents a type in which college students taking off on spring break might wish to recognize themselves. It appears that readers through the centuries have identified with this wanderer, for Peter Dronke call the *Confession* "perhaps the best-known poem in Medieval Latin." Dronke cautions against reading it as sincere autobiography, however. Certainly it seems to be uttered outside the confessional. Taking the opportunity to remind students that not all lyrics unlock the poet's heart, you might ask them to trace the progressive lightening of this poem, which starts with "fierce indignation" in which the speaker compares himself to a "withered leaf," and explain why so many writer like to pose as free spirits even if, as Dronke suggests, they are actually dutiful civil servants.

Motion, both physical and mental, is at the core of Walther von der Vogelweide's *Dancing Girl*, which begins with the troubadour offering a garland to a pretty girl, turns into a dream, and ends with him looking at another group of dancers, trying to find that girl again. The circular image of the garland opens and closes the poem, but the speaker's quest is open-ended. In Guido Cavalcanti's sophisticated version of a similar encounter, the poet makes a definitive foray into the woods for an idyllic embrace with the god of love looking on; the minnesinger's artless dancing girl becomes a glamorous shepherdess. Dronke calls this *pastorela* "perhaps the highest expression of the Arcadian ideal in medieval lyric."

Another kaleidoscopic poem, Alexander the Wild's *Strawberry Picking*, begins with a memory of children racing across the meadows and of a group of dancers, like Walther's, crowning the prettiest girl with a garland. Shifting patterns of movement adumbrate the loss of childhood and the fall into adult experience that this poem seems to trace. By the fifth stanza, genial reminiscence has yielded to monitory allegory: in the enigmatic cry "Children, right here there was a snake! / he has bitten our pony" (lines 31–32), Dronke hears an allusion to the prophetic vision of Dan, one of the twelve tribes of Israel:

> Dan shall be a serpent in the way,
> An adder in the path,
> That biteth the horse heels
> So that his rider shall fall backward.
> (Genesis 49.17)

The children have been ambushed; they must "make haste" now to exit the forest. The aimless freedom of the opening gives way in the last stanza to uncertain "loitering" and unexpected violation. Childhood is forever gone.

Repeated scenes of everyday life like the garland dance are worth noting, especially if one can reinforce them with period illustrations from some of the wonderful facsimile Books of Hours easily available in libraries these days (or digitized images increasingly accessible from different museum sites on the Internet). With the writings of the Middle Ages, we have access to the sights and sounds that gave them being. The melody for *Strawberry Picking* can be found on p. 245 of *The Medieval Lyric* and sung today; Hildegard of Bingen's music can be heard on numerous recordings. Almost a thousand years after real people left their mark on the material world, we can make contact with the vibrancy of their experience through their art and their music.

Asking your students to look at the sources of the metaphors in the poetry they read gives them a window into the concerns of a time and a place as well as a reference point by which to judge what we mean by the timelessness of great literature. You might conclude a discussion of the medieval lyric by noting that several of these poems mirror the increasing mercantilization of the material world. In *The Scorpions*, for example, Alfonso X finds no comfort on the traditional pastoral images with which so many of the earlier lyrics concern themselves. The earth on which this monarch works seems scorched; he is beset by traitors, symbolized by the scorpions of his title. Being a king is not as satisfying as being the pilot of a merchant ship, "selling vinegar and flour."

To contrast Alfonso's imagery with the use of commercial terms in the charming *Balade* of Charles d'Orleans or with the netherworld of the decaying shopkeepers in Villon's *Testament* underscores how complex the medieval period was (and how complex, by extension, is all human experience). The wonder of lyric poetry is that it manages to make the Helmet-seller's pitiless catalog of her physical features as compelling as the lover's catalog of birds.

The chronological organization of this section makes it possible to trace a world in flux. Despite the stereotyped notion of the poet removed from earthly concerns in some isolated ivory tower, to which some of your students may initially subscribe, these lyrics (like all the poems in the anthology) demonstrate the tangibility of their subject matter. Part of the pleasure of reading poetry is to imagine what private impulses and public experiences spurred the poet to write. Poetry reaches out into the world, and yet it is ultimately more than the sum of its contents, even in translation, as any survey of the selections included here can immediately show.

Topics for Writing

1. Link one of the poems in this selection to a longer work that offers a contrasting perspective on its subject matter:

   a. Compare the complicated vision of the fox in Dafydd ap Gwilym's *The Fox* to the portrait of the animal as trickster in *The*

Trial of Renard; or to the hunting of the fox as victim in *Sir Gawain and the Green Knight*.

b. Compare the tenor of the conversation between Gawain and Sir Bercilak's lady with the tone of *A Lover's Prize* by Beatrice, countess of Dia.

c. Compare the dancing girl who captures Walther von der Vogelweide's imagination or the shepherdess who entrances Guido Cavalcanti in *An Encounter* with Griselda in Boccaccio's Tenth Story of the Tenth Day. How important is the social status of the girl who attracts the male admirer? In what ways does the girl stand for qualities beyond herself?

d. Compare the admiring tone of *The Ruin* with the speech of the Last Survivor in *Beowulf* (p. 1092).

e. Compare the conflation of sex and war in *In Battle* with Othello's greeting to Desdemona in Act II of Shakespeare's play or with the alternation of episodes in Ariosto's *Orlando Furioso*.

f. Evaluate the terms offered by Charles d'Orleans's *Balade*, in which the speaker proposes buying kisses at a discount and giving his heart on deposit in return, and investigate the tonal difference between Charles's use of commercial imagery and the investigation of the economics of marriage elucidated by Chaucer's Wife of Bath in her *Prologue*.

2. Link one of the poems in this selection to a later work that alludes to the poet:

a. What qualities expressed in Bertrand de Born's *In Praise of War* seem consistent with Dante's consigning him to the Inferno (p. 1389)?

b. Dante called Arnaut Daniel "il miglior fabbro" (a term that means "the better craftsman" and was later appropriated by T. S. Eliot in gratitude to Ezra Pound for his editorial assistance with *The Waste Land*). Daniel's *The Art of Love* begins with the image of the poet as craftsman. Describe the hard labor he devotes to this "usurious" lover's demand. What is there especially to admire in Daniel's facility with metaphor (as, for example, in the melodramatic last stanza)?

c. In *The Wife of Bath's Tale*, how does Chaucer dramatize the debate on "gentilesse" launched by Guido Guinizelli in *Love and Nobility* and taken up by Dante?

3. Link one of the poems in this selection to a prior work that influenced it:

a. How does Rabbi Ephraim ben Jacob's poem *The Sacrifice of Isaac* give tragic currency to the biblical story that is its source (pp. 58–59)?

b. Christine de Pizan and Petrarch.

4. Medieval literature can be brutally detailed. Choose a poem that confronts the reality of physical suffering and decay and discuss the degree to which rhetorical devices can turn cruelty into art. (Good choices includes Villon's well-known and unsparing *Testament,* for the

sheer virtuosity with which it shapes ugliness into elegant stanzas; *The Sacrifice of Isaac*, for reiterating a determination to trust the divine will through its constant reference to biblical verses; *Lament of the Virgin*, for underscoring the redemptive purpose of Christ's Passion.)

5. The language of poetry can help transmute grief so that it becomes bearable. Discuss the voice in Meir Halevi Abulafia's *A Letter from the Grave*, in which Abulafia offers comfort to his father, and compare the success of his efforts with those of Hadewijch of Brabant in *The Cult of Love*, in which the speaker contrasts herself with the birds, whose laments are short-lived, and finds no use for telling about her pain.

6. Assign a variety of readings in conjunction with an Internet assignment, a museum visit, or listening to or attending a musical or theatrical performance, and ask students to imagine life in the medieval world and to draw specific examples of everyday experience from the music, art and literature of the period.

Further Reading

See also the reading suggestions in the anthology, p. 1189.

Wilson, Katherine M. *Medieval Women Writers.* 1984. A useful compilation of short biographies, with discussions of Hildegard of Bingen and Christine de Pizan.

MEDIEVAL TALES: A SELECTION

Classroom Strategies and Topics for Discussion

These lively short narratives provide an extraordinary variety of opportunities for classroom discussion, but one unifying theme they seem to share is a concern for the proper relationship between the individual and the community. A good starting point, then, would be in every case to ask students to reconstruct the social assumptions that these tales take for granted and frequently subvert. The following comments will treat each sequence individually, since all of the tales can stand on their own. At the same time, since you most likely will want to draw connections among them and other assignments, attention will be paid to some of the many possible combinations that work well in the classroom.

An overview of the eight separate tales contained in this unit suggests that they move from simplicity to complexity. Yet even the shortest of them is far from simple-minded; all of these tales can challenge students even as they are almost guaranteed to amuse and surprise them. You may wish to raise at once the question of community in introducing the two brief exempla by Petrus Alfonsi that begin the selection. Why are we going to Mecca in a short Latin piece written for Christian readers by a converted Jew? How do we account for its praise of an exemplary camel? Many of the great European medieval romances demonize the Saracen infidel, yet these selections from *The Scholar's Guide*, like a number of the medieval lyrics in the anthology, bespeak the often comfortable and intimate relations of the three monotheistic cultures, especially as they came together in al-Andalus.

Should your students read selections from *The Thousand and One Nights*, Boccaccio's *Decameron*, or Chaucer's *Canterbury Tales*, they will recognize evidence of the stockpile shared by medieval storytellers. *The Two City Dwellers and the Country Man* appears to be a distant and rudimentary analogue of the narrative at the core of *The Pardoner's Tale*, for example. Setting it within the context of a Meccan destination, which hints of pilgrimage (the experience that continues to unify the far-flung adherents of Islam), presupposes a community that puts a premium on hospitality.

Both of Petrus Alfonsi's exempla revolve around the refusal to distribute food fairly. We also see in the two city dwellers themselves a mistaken notion of their own urban superiority; outwitted by the country man, they are the first characters in this selection of tales to see a reversal of the expected social order. In *The King's Tailor's Apprentice*, with the apprentice called Nedui and the supervising eunuch, we are again in an essentially Islamic cultural milieu, but the universal application of the story transcends any one creed. These benign celebrations of a swift intellect, told within a frame that emphasizes the orderly transmission of values from parent to child, conclude on one more ecumenical note, with the father implicitly chastening his son for the pleasure he seems to feel in seeing others punished. In citing the teaching of Moses (more commonly attributed to Rabbi Hillel), Petrus Alfonsi honors his own origins and complicates the revenge motif that lies on the surface of these two small exempla.

With the four thirteenth-century fabliaux, we move on to another country and another sensibility. Revenge is simply the nature of the world in these old French tales; nevertheless, hospitality continues to be an important virtue, and cleverness to earn its just rewards. Although it would be delusory to read fabliaux in quest of moral improvement, you may certainly ask your students to investigate the moral universe that motivates the genre. The eponymous butcher of Abbeville, for example, as Thomas C. Cooke points out in the study cited below, seems "almost the ideal man" on the evidence of the poem's second stanza. Like so many of these stories, his begins with a need to spend the night in somebody else's house. If the butcher eventually sleeps with his host's women and sells him his own sheep, the tale has made it clear that the priest (not coincidentally, of course, the deserving victim of such depredations in many fabliaux) has richly earned his comeuppance.

The tellers of these tales, with their keen eye for domestic detail and disdain for snobbish pretension, appreciate competence (in butchery as in bed and many another place) and skewer hypocrisy. Many fabliaux are inhabited by exceedingly well-dressed women who don't quite protest enough. (Note the detailed description of the deacon's lady's pleated green gown and her halfhearted objection to the butcher's proposition, good points to raise if you plan to read *The Miller's Tale*, whose teenage village heroine boasts a smart black-and white ensemble and succumbs remarkably quickly to the handy Nicholas's approach.) The real hypocrites, however, tend to be the selfish priests, whose way of life betrays their absolute indifference to their churchly duties, and the victims are often ill-advised old husbands, like the hunchback in the selection in the anthology or the rather more pathetic John of *The Miller's Tale*. (These character types are staples of comic satire, of course—you may want to recall them if you go on to teach *Tartuffe* in the second semester of your course.)

Although *The Butcher of Abbeville* has a far more pleasant tone than does *The Three Hunchbacks*, both stories offer fascinating windows on daily life in the real world. One of the delights of teaching these tales is to train your students to read with an archeologist's attention to minutiae. Without neglecting the many rural scenes typical of the genre, Charles Muscatine notes that "the flourishing of the fabliaux, the rise of the cities, and the emergence of an urban middle class are equally visible symptoms of the same social and spiritual climate." Ask your students to characterize the standard of living in the fabliaux' world. The delicate cuisine (peas with bacon are a feature of many a medieval tale, to judge from the selections in the anthology) and the rich interiors of the priest's "manse" in Abbeville and the hunchback's townhouse in Douay bear witness to an atmosphere of such wealth that we happily excuse the efforts of those who are less well-off to take advantage of this plenty.

Discuss with your students the importance of furniture and real estate location in *The Three Hunchbacks*: were it not for an intricate three-drawered bed and its two-story situation on a canal, the hunchback's house would not be the scene of this remarkable story. You will not be able to avoid the question of cruelty in many of these medieval works; in this case, it's important to notice the improvisatory nature of events that are the product of chance, not careful plotting (again, a contrast with *The Miller's Tale* would be instructive). The situation of the hunchback's beautiful young wife is deftly sketched. From one angle, she seems a sympathetic figure: starved for entertainment, she invites the three hunchbacked minstrels to return to their house in her husband's absence (and gives us a glimpse of the life of the strolling players who sang and told stories in private homes, illustrating the point made in the headnote about the performative nature of much medieval literature). Still, it's important to note, rather more cynically, that she is quite happy to exploit the porter and sheds not a tear on account of the accident that frees her.

Adding to the macabre humor of the story is the casual use of disability as a comic trait in itself. The weird disposal of the three dead hunchbacks is almost a textbook illustration of Henri Bergson's famous definition of comedy as a defense against the dehumanizing effects of standardization and regimentation: when one is reduced to a body that looks exactly like another's, can one be an individual deserving of sympathy? The shock comes with the fourth hunchback, the man of property who presumably has an individualized identity, but who is doomed by the porter's mechanized response to yet one more misshapen body. In farce, where dehumanization is the rule, one rarely feels sorry for flat characters caught in automatic routines. Indeed, in the cheerfully amoral climate of the fabliau, the offered lesson of the story seems misplaced, as the narrator appears to acknowledge. While he dutifully quotes Durant's conclusion, "everything on earth's for sale," this has little to do with the husband's death. Prefiguring Alison's fate in *The Miller's Tale*, the wife here escapes unscathed. And despite disposing of a few inconvenient corpses at a good price, she does seem relatively blameless.

If Bergson seems the tutelary genius of *The Three Hunchbacks*, perhaps Freud would smile on the efficacious work accomplished by *The Wild Dream*. Both here and in *The Ring That Controlled Erections*, the fullblown bawdiness for which the fabliaux are famed takes center stage. Students are generally amazed by the explicit detail of such stories, and it is appropriate to ask why these obscene anecdotes should have been such a staple of popular culture. One route is to inquire what, if anything, is wrong with describing genitalia and their propensities? (If your students have read the selections from Genesis in the anthology, you might ask them to recall the first result of eating the fruit of the tree of knowledge of good and evil: what attitudes make nakedness shameful?) Another profitable avenue is to explore the coexistence during the Middle Ages of bawdy fabliaux and romantic tales of chivalry, classic examples of the way popular and elite forms "correct" and feed off each other.

You might also point out that these particular tales show none of the mean-spirited pleasure in other persons' pain or discomfort that many fabliaux and *The Trial of Renard* do demonstrate. Instead, in this quartet of stories, there is a satisfied sense of bargains well struck, of getting what one pays for—and paying for what one gets.

That equilibrium is missing from the wild lawlessness at the heart of *The Trial of Renard*, a genuinely subversive narrative. Though the Renard stories owe their form to the animal fable, they are emphatically not themselves such fables, since they have no uplifting moral lessons to teach. You may want to spend some time talking through the interpretive possibilities created by the employment of animals as characters. Your students may be familiar with some of Aesop's fables, and it will be helpful to discuss how the Renard stories differ from them; you may also ask them to react to the headnote's citing of cartoon characters like the Road Runner and Wile E. Coyote. In fact, a brief investigation of the humor in cartoons is a very good way to talk about comedy in general: if your class deplores the cruelty of some of these tales, as noted above, ask them why we laugh at people who slip on banana peels. The speaking animals in the twelfth-century Renard sequence mock the heroic pretensions of chivalric culture, another example of a "low" form deriving its power from the existence of a "higher," idealized genre. The late twentieth century has seen cartoons that mock contemporary genres that define another kind of honor, like the detective story. *The Trial of Renard*, however, finds humor but little that seems heroic or admirable in its central character's amoral predation.

That the collective title for the group of stories to which it belongs is the *Romance of Renard* attests to their parodic power. There may be something noble about King Noble, who shows flashes of the grand beneficence of both Charlemagne and King Arthur. Little in the behavior of the feral aristocrats who inhabit his court, however, seems humane; deplorably, perhaps, a great deal of it is human. Although you will want to be sure that your students understand the historical specifics of the political burlesque in *The Trial of Renard*, the eternal relevance of its mordant depiction of government in action should not be missed. If King Noble the Lion represents in some ways the twelfth-century monarch, Louis VII, who, as the headnote indicates, imposed a truce upon the fractious nobility, the poem's generally disenchanted view of hypocrisy among the powerful also deserves careful consideration in the classroom.

As the poem starts, Noble recommends that Ysengrin give up his vendetta against Renard, since "nowadays one sees all sorts / Of cuckolds, even ruling courts!" How timeless and timely this worldly-wise counsel seems (some commentators believe that medieval audiences would have recognized this as a swipe at the scandalous Eleanor of Aquitaine, whose marriage to the pious Louis was annulled in 1152). Bruin the bear, not the brightest member of Noble's court, says out loud what many a favor-currying politician less publicly puts into practice: "We will hate anyone you say." While the guardians of absolute morality, led by Clamor the bull, seems obsessed by the sexual misconduct of which Renard is accused (this in itself is a joke, of course, since bulls traditionally embody virility rather than *pudeur*), Grinbert the badger, Renard's cousin, undercuts their righteous objections. In the animal as in the human world, rape cases are always notoriously hard to win; with marvelous deftness, the author reminds us that Hersent is, after all, a wolf, whose "fur stood on end" when she hears her innocence questioned. Her offer to undergo trial by ordeal seems heroic, but to rich ironic effect; for Hersent here echoes Iseult, one of the great heroines of tragic romance, to be sure, but also compromised, adulterous, and untrustworthy. Only by cheating did Iseult pass her trial; for his part, Ysengrin is wise enough to know that testing his wife's honor can lead only to his humiliation.

In this story, Renard is the center of attention for many reasons. The narrative begins with a murder charge leveled against the fox by the bereaved hen Pinte. Given the occasion by this rather unsurprising event (as the headnote should remind your students, all this means is that a fox has eaten a chicken), *The Trial of Renard* finds targets for satiric commentary on every side. The body of Pinte's tragically deceased sister turns out to have miracle-working properties, like the relics of so many medieval saints. The author's knowing glance at the conspiracy of the wolf and the dog, who falsely testify to having been cured of earaches on the martyr's grave, takes aim at the religious establishment that profited from such testimony, much as his allusions to Charlemagne and Iseult parody the world of chivalric romance. Nowhere, according to the translator, Patricia Terry, is the voice of the author more prominent than in Renard's explanation of his failure to answer the king's summons (lines 498–537): the poor are badly treated at table when they venture into the courts of the mighty, who let themselves be robbed by their cooks and stewards. Through this falsely pious comment, of course, Renard segues into his masterstroke, an apparently casual reference to the fresh honey that he just consumed to complete his delicious meal of peas and bacon.

Bruin, who has happily ventured to Renard's den, is now "on the hook." With feigned reluctance, the fox shows the bear an enormous tree that purportedly houses a store of honey. Trapped in the oak, the credulous, greedy Bruin must run for his life, leaving much of his muzzle behind, to escape from the enraged villagers who "swarm through the trees," human beings who intrude on the animal world and act like animals in the process. It is a mark of the author's skill that he can move easily between the two realms, satirizing all manner of human foibles by looking at animals and at people, without losing his bearings.

As in *The Butcher of Abbeville*, the corruption of the priesthood is simply a given. The parish priest, "Father of Martin de la Tour," wounds the suffering bear in the side (one wonders just how sacrilegiously this reference was intended, especially since at the sight of the mangled bear, King Noble vows to avenge his wrongs "by the death of Christ"). Of the young Martin, himself destined for Holy Orders, we shortly hear when Renard tricks Tibert the cat, another rogue who would have been ready to collaborate with the fox, into tripping the noose set to catch Renard when he next tries to raid the henhouse. The dizzying pace of the narrative reaches an apogee as one event triggers another. Awakened by the commotion, Martin's parents race from their bed to catch the predator, whom they assume to be the fox; but the cat manages to defend himself by unmanning the priest, who has run outdoors *en deshabille,* to the horror of his concubine.

Neither the animal nor the human community can take much more of Renard's anarchic will. When Grinbert summons his cousin to court, Renard manages a confession of sorts before leaving his family. Prostrating himself in what looks at first like a gesture of humility (soon revealed by the author to be merely the posture required to exit from his lair), Renard goes before the court and delivers a proud speech to King Noble (now called the "emperor," presumably to remind the well-read audience of Charlemagne listening to Roland). Self-serving and arrogant, Renard nevertheless raises some troubling questions; this remarkable comic parody seems deeply serious as well when Renard asks whether his victims share no responsibility for their own fates. Even Noble, however, whose predisposition to favor Renard is clear in the earlier parts of the poem, is outraged as the fox appeals for sympathy: "It's a sin to drag me here to speak, / Old as I am, before this court." Taken out to the gallows, Renard escapes again. He will expiate by sailing to the Holy Land, a promise that is accepted, although Noble remarks that pilgrims usually return more corrupt than when they set out. Incorrigible, impenitent, and free, Renard escapes his pursuers, managing to grab the cowardly rabbit for dinner along the way (although the hare himself escapes when Renard stops to boast—see lines 1525–32). As the poem ends, we know that his story is not over: miraculously rejuvenated after a good meal and a bath, Renard lives on in the bosom of his loving family.

Renard, a ruthless rogue, lives on in other guises too, not all of them in the Saturday morning cartoons. How many movies make us complicit with ruthless gangsters who have happy homes? You will want to ask your students why we take pleasure in the gratuitous cruelty and outrageous duplicity of outlaws like Renard. Do we all wish we had the courage to express the contempt he so gleefully displays for social pieties? Why do we laugh at his obscene gestures?

Finally, the selection returns to the exemplum, but, as the headnote says, a very mysterious one. What is the lesson that we are to learn from *The Cursed Dancers of Colbeck*? Ambiguities abound in this short narrative, beginning with the title of the handbook in which it appears, *Handling Sin*. As Mark Miller suggests in the excellent article listed at the end of the headnote, we are always handling sin—we cannot escape it; and so we must learn to deal with it. Robert Mannyng's manual addresses the seven deadly sins and a host of others. This selection begins on a seemingly puritanical note, warning against "carols, wrestling, or summer games," but quickly limits their potential for sacrilege to the venue in which they are performed. While at first glance one is hard pressed to understand why dancing and singing carols at Christmas time should be considered sacrilegious, we soon see that, by pursuing such activities in the church or churchyard, the participants are competing with the holy services conducted by the priest, putting their own pleasures before God.

The conflict between the individual and society that underlies all of these medieval tales is heightened here by the nature of the offending carolers, who are called "fools" in the text but should be understood, in Miller's words, as "a group of wandering madmen." Somehow these alien beings, whose names Mannyng carefully lists (as if to assure us that this all really happened, although he has already hedged by noting that "most of" what he says is "the gospel truth"), have made contact with the priest's daughter and recruit her to join in their rivalry with her father's Mass. (That a priest should have a family is here again taken for granted. It is not the occasion for satire, as in the fabliaux or *The Trial of Renard*, but seems just one more troublesome sign of the difficulty that the Church had in enforcing its dictates, in this case, clerical celibacy.)

When Robert the priest curses the dancers, the focus of the story changes. The priest becomes the principal offender, and his son his accuser. His daughter Ave (presumably a form of "Eve," another disobedient female) has paid the price for her father's wrath. The dancers have been frozen into robotic motion, a parody of a parody, and the unholy nature of their unauthorized dancing is forgotten in the general horror at their loss of humanity. Even the Emperor tries to ameliorate the situation, to no avail.

When the term of the curse expires, the dancers resume their activities, although no longer in solidarity. The loss of Ave's arm reenacts the fragmentation that has divided the mad dancers of Colbeck from themselves and from the Christian community. Ironically, her severed arm is treated like a holy relic, confusing the moral of the story even more; Robert the priest dies too, while nothing else seems to have changed. At the end, Mannyng almost admits he doesn't know what to make of this exemplum: "some hold it an idle story." The tale ends with too many statements of its moral lesson for us to know which one to follow. The article by Miller provides a sophisticated summation: "Their ossification in a parody or perversion of Christian community is replaced, not by their incorporation into the body of the faithful, but by their fragmentation into solitary versions of the dance." Your students' reactions will likely not be so elegant, but you can profitably work with whatever lingering confusion they may feel. The deepest value of these assorted medieval tales is that they demonstrate the diversity and inventiveness of an era that too many think of as hidebound and moralistic.

Topics for Writing

1. What do we, can we, or should we learn from fiction?
    [The focus of this assignment may shift according to the works you ask your students to discuss. Like the novel, which was a vehicle for "news," many of these short medieval tales provide pleasure by giving us information about how people live; others, especially the exempla, teach lessons, although the lessons are not always clear. And sometimes, what we learn is simply to admire the keen eye and fertile imagination of authors, both high and low. As always, the challenge for student writers is to present textual evidence that will persuade the reader of the truth of their claims.]
2. Consider the attitudes toward the body in medieval narrative: the hedonistic celebrations of pleasure in the fabliaux, where the body and its needs and self-expression reign supreme; or the graphic descriptions of punishment in *The Trial of Renard*, where the natural cruelty of the animal world seeps into the sense of what is normal in human affairs as well; or the dismembered arm of Ave in *The Cursed Dancers of Colbeck*, perhaps a sign of the perverse difficulty we have in coordinating our actions in harmony with those of others and the expectations of the community.
    [This topic will link well with the work of Boccaccio and Chaucer, too, particularly perhaps the Ninth Story of the Fourth Day and the Eighth Story of the Fifth Day of the *Decameron*, *The Wife of Bath's Prologue*, and *The Pardoner's Tale*.]
3. Consider the question of human agency and responsibility: What is the source of the greed seen in the tales of Petrus Alfonsi or the fabliaux? Can Renard stop himself? Should he? Why do those mad dancers dance? Why does the priest curse them?

Comparative Perspectives

Discuss the techniques by which farce encourages us to laugh at situations that would not be so funny in "real life," using literary examples from the three time periods covered in Volume 1 of the anthology: from the ancient world, *Lysistrata*, *Pseudolus*, *The Satyricon*, and *A True Story*; from the medieval world, the fabliaux, *The Trial of Renard*, and *The Miller's Tale*; from the Renaissance, *Gargantua and Pantagruel*.

Further Reading

See also the reading suggestions in the anthology, pp. 1231–32.

Cooke, Thomas D. *The Old French and Chaucerian Fabliaux: A Study of Their Comic Climax.* 1978. Some helpful comments about a few of the fabliaux in the anthology.

DANTE ALIGHIERI

The Divine Comedy

Backgrounds

The headnote provides a general view of *The Divine Comedy* as a whole as well as a more detailed account of the *Inferno* and the parts of the *Purgatorio* and the *Paradiso* included in the anthology. The headnotes and footnotes to the individual cantos offer ample guidance and abundant information about the persons, places, and thoughts encountered along the way.

Many people know—or know of—the *Inferno* but not the *Purgatorio* or *Paradiso* and hence infer that Dante was exclusively or at least unduly preoccupied with evil. We should point out that only one-third of *The Divine Comedy* is focused on the bad, one-third shows people in pursuit of the good (*Purgatorio*), and one-third describes the enjoyment of the good (*Paradiso*).

Some people in our time are alienated by the doctrine of eternal punishment; why not redeem everybody, after suitable reformation? The first answer, of course, is that Dante was following orthodox Christian teaching. But there are other answers philosophically and aesthetically more satisfactory to our age. Do we want to see every villain in every serious film reformed? Could we believe in the repentance of Iago in Shakespeare's *Othello* or of Goneril and Regan in *King Lear*? The (psychological) truth about such men and women—and innumerable others who have actually lived in this world—is that they do not want to reform. They would be unhappy in Heaven. What the *Inferno* reveals to us is the final state or consummation of the people who have chosen one of the various kinds of wrong conduct. The range is from the illicit lovers of the fifth canto to the figures enclosed in ice at the center of the Earth in the final canto. Lawless passion was the lovers' choice—rather than reasonable restraint; now they are blown about by the winds; they have no hope of *peace*. The people in the ice endure the cold—the lack of feeling that enabled them to betray and kill their kindred on the Earth.

It is worth noting that moral criteria may have changed since Dante wrote his poem. Homosexuality is apparently the only reason why Brunetto Latini is in Hell, and the Florentine usurers also on the burning sands might now be regarded as respectable bankers. Dante was a conservative in economics.

The *Purgatorio* has been called the most *human* of the three parts of the poem—the part that comes closest to the experience and attitudes of most of us. For we are not hopelessly sunk in evil or infallibly committed to good, but we should like to avoid the one and attain the other—if only we knew how to do it. The *Purgatorio* dramatizes and exemplifies the Christian teaching about the way. The front page of a newspaper or the daily telecast of news indicates that things are far from all right in our world today. The same was true in Dante's time. Conflict, violence, cruelty within and between families and nations are evidence that the human situation is not satisfactory. According to Christian teaching, the ultimate source (on Earth) of these bad things is the uncontrolled passions and appetites of the individual human being. Long before Dante, the Church had described these excesses as the Seven Cardinal (or Deadly) Sins: illicit love, gluttony (any undue concern about food), avarice (and its opposite, reckless spending), sloth (idleness as a way of life), selfish and unjustified anger, envy (the wish for another person's loss or failure), and pride (not proper self-esteem but haughtiness and aggression). Each of these stems from a vice or fault, a flaw in the moral character of the man or woman. In Roman Catholic practice—modern as well as medieval—he or she should confess to a priest, ask God's forgiveness, repent sincerely, and promise to mend. The priest might also assign a penance, which, especially in medieval times, might be painful or burdensome. It was assumed that most people would not have completed the process of purgation before death; hence the doctrine of Purgatory as an interval of purification (for a true Christian) between the end of earthly life and entry into Heaven.

Dante's *Purgatorio* is based quite clearly and directly on Church doctrine and practice. But he is careful to assign self-discipline—or discipline gladly accepted—in a rationally appropriate manner. Thus his penitents exert themselves to the utmost in practicing the virtue opposite to the vice under correction at the time; so the proud behave humbly (symbolized by the heavy weights they carry on their backs—in a canto not included in the selections); and Pope Adrian, who had been too fond of material wealth, is literally brought down to bare earth. The suffering of the soul in Purgatory would be meaningless if it were permanent, if it served no purpose. It is important to remember that Purgatory is an interlude, a preparation for Heaven. Moreover, Dante intended his readers to apply the example of his poem to the amendment of their lives while still in this world.

It is worth remarking that there are no terraces on the mountain of Purgatory for such specific crimes as murder or robbery. The reason is that all crimes are motivated by one or more of the Seven Cardinal Sins; when the man or woman has got rid of the inclination to evil, there will be no temptation to kill or steal. On the other hand, murderers and robbers are classified as such in the *Inferno*—because a vice, or flaw of character, may have variable consequences. It may amount only to self-indulgence without direct harm to another person; or it may lead to the worst imaginable crimes.

Classroom Strategies

The reader's immediate experience of the poem should come first; then that experience can be integrated in an increasingly wide range of events, ideas, and horizons. As to class assignments, obviously they must depend on the amount of time available for the segment (Dante) as a whole; two or three cantos might be average.

In our time it cannot be taken for granted that most students will be familiar with the basic doctrine and belief of organized Christianity, that is, the Church. But Dante, like Chaucer and every other medieval and Renaissance writer, could assume this knowledge and hence allude to it with confidence that he would be understood. Indeed, it was condensed in capsule form in the Creed regularly recited in many services of worship. The following is one version, known as the Apostles' Creed:

> I believe in God, the Father almighty, creator of Heaven and earth. I believe in Jesus Christ, his only Son, our Lord. He was conceived by the power of the Holy Spirit and born of the Virgin Mary. He suffered under Pontius Pilate, was crucified, died and was buried. He descended to the dead. On the third day he rose again. He ascended into Heaven, and is seated at the right hand of the Father. He will come again to judge the living and the dead. I believe in the Holy Spirit, the holy Catholic Church, the communion of saints, the forgiveness of sins, the resurrection of the body, and the life everlasting.

Of course, it is not suggested that the Creed be taught systematically, but an occasional reference to one or another of the statements in it may clear up many a passage in the anthology.

The teacher should take full advantage of the episode of the grafters in cantos XXI and XXII. Students who are turned on by nothing else will enjoy this crude, malicious, sly, malevolent cartoon comedy once it becomes clear to them. The milieu of low-level corrupt office holders has not changed much since Dante's time; we still talk about "sticky" fingers, and cartoonists often wield the tar brush or its equivalent. Furthermore, the poignance of Virgil's rescue of Dante at the end of this sequence provides a good opportunity to discuss the relationship between the two: how it changes and deepens in the course of the journey. The conclusion of the topic must await the *Purgatorio:* Virgil's farewell and Dante's sudden awareness that Virgil is no longer at his side.

Topics for Discussion

1. The suitability of the penalties to the sins in the *Inferno.*
    [This is relevant throughout, including the area outside the nine circles; thus those in the ante-Hell—those sometimes called the moral neutrals—are plagued by annoying *little* things, unpleasant insects, etc. The "virtuous pagans" in the first circle are not actively punished; they live without the good of participating in God, as Christians must do by definition. The poet does not usually explain why the various conditions in Hell are appropriate; hence we can

profitably think about the matter. Fire, in sundry form, is familiar to us as a punishment; ice, which Dante makes the ultimate penalty, may seem strange to us at first. Reflection may well change our view.]

2. The differences between upper and lower Hell.

[Basically, the people in the upper Hell were guilty of (excessive) self-indulgence. They loved not wisely but too well—other persons, material goods (thus either as misers or spendthrifts), food and drink, or their own aggressive impulses (anger). Primarily, they did not deliberately seek to injure other persons. Those in the lower regions (violence and fraud) did precisely that—in a great variety of ways.]

3. Possible differences between Dante's perspective and ours.

[It has been suggested that one category of the angry in the *Inferno*—the incorrigibly morose—might now be treated as patients in a mental hospital. Similarly, modern views of homosexuality do not regard it as either a sin or a crime, and the same can be said of suicide. Dante's view depended on the idea that we belong to God as our Creator; He has prescribed the manner and set the limits of our lives in definite ways; we dare not interfere.]

4. Mini-tragedies in the *Inferno*.

[It has been said that Dante's portrayal of a number of the most notable figures in the *Inferno* amounts to a series of microscopic tragedies: Paolo and Francesca in canto V, Pier della Vigne in XIII, and Ulysses in XXVI are notable examples. These are people very attractive in personality, intellect, or even character; but they knowingly made the wrong decisions and so decided their own fate.]

Topics for Writing

1. For some of the major figures of the poem, personality and character are indicated by the speeches that Dante puts in their mouths.

[Thus in canto V of the *Inferno,* Francesca's good manners are indicated by her courteous greeting of Dante; her "romantic" temperament by the tercet in which she tells of her homeland; her adherence to the "doctrine" of courtly love by the three tercets each beginning with the word *love;* her habit of blaming something besides herself shows through in the reference to the book about Lancelot; and perhaps her vindictiveness in the single verse in which she foretells the punishment of her slayer (lines 106–7).

In canto XIII the lawyer-poet Pier delle Vigne may seem to play— seriously—with words as he contrasts and pairs "locking and unlocking," "inflamed" (verb, then past participle, then verb again), all in a severely logical and antithetical account of his unfortunate experience (lines 58–78).

2. The method of contrasting pairs of persons.

[In *Inferno* X the Florentine aristocrats Farinata and Cavalcante (the elder) rise to talk with Dante from their shared tomb among the unbelievers. Farinata is proud, haughty, disdainful of unknown characters like the present visitor (Dante)—"he glanced at me, and as if in disdain / he asked of me: 'Who were your ancestors?' " (lines 41–42). Their ensuing dialogue is interrupted by Cavalcante, who asks about his son, Dante's closest friend at one time. Distressed at Dante's uncertain answer, he is overcome by grief and sinks down into the tomb. Thereupon Farinata resumes his remarks just as if there had been no interruption.

In the Circle of Evil Counselors (*Inferno* XXVI–XXVII), we come to the Greek Ulysses, deviser of the Trojan horse, and to an Italian politician of the thirteenth century. Virgil conjures the flame that is Ulysses to utterance remote, detached, impersonal (so far as its auditors are concerned), but in itself lofty and splendid. After a bit the flame that the soul of the politician has now become (Guido da Montefeltro) addresses Dante, asks for news of Italy, and telling Dante he is sure the story won't get out, indulges his urge to tell how he was tricked into a final sin that accounted for his present situation. Thus this garrulous old gossip is juxtaposed to the sublime Homeric hero.]

3. The grafters and the demons of popular lore (*Inferno* XXI, XXII, and XXIII.1–54).

[The more or less grotesque and comical names of the demons who have charge of the grafters in their ditches and pools of pitch; the tricks they play on sinners trying to escape momentarily; their readiness to deceive the travelers with barefaced lies, solemnly spoken; the rough handling of the sinners, like bags of stuff, carried on a demon's shoulder. The crouching, fearful, utterly undignified figure of Dante the traveler in this episode; its biographical counterpart in his being charged with misuse of funds while an office holder in Florence.]

Comparative Perspective

Discuss the imagery invoked in Dante's vision of the punishment of "Mahomet" in canto XXVIII of the *Inferno*. How does it reflect the medieval Christian fear of Islam? What other Western works have you read in which this fear is echoed? Do you find similar preoccupations with rival religions in the Koran?

Further Reading

See also the reading suggestions in the anthology, p. 1300.

Clements, R. J., ed. *American Critical Essays on Dante*. 1969.

Slade, Carole, ed. *Approaches to Teaching Dante's* Divine Comedy. 1982.

GIOVANNI BOCCACCIO

The Decameron

Backgrounds

Boccaccio's introduction (not in the anthology) is the counterpart, with some differences, of Chaucer's *General Prologue*. Each provides the setting for a long sequence of tales. There is a measure of chance or coincidence in both groups of storytellers. Boccaccio's seven young ladies, happening to meet in a church (though they are already friends or acquaintances), decide to leave plague-ridden Florence and live with more safety on their country estates; they invite three young gentlemen, also well known to them, to share their plans. Chaucer's twenty-nine pilgrims—traveling alone or in twos or threes or even more—all happen to have come for a night's lodging to an inn or tavern in Southwark, across the Thames from London, on the route to Canterbury. Boccaccio's company decide to spend part of each day in telling stories and agree that on the first day each of the ten is to tell a tale on a topic of his or her own choosing. In Chaucer's account the innkeeper takes charge of proceedings; he plans four tales to be told by each traveler; the order is to be determined by lot, and he says the Knight is due to tell the first tale.

Chaucer has no real equivalent of Boccaccio's extended and vivid account of the plague in Florence (not in the anthology). Boccaccio knew the Italian plague of 1348 from his own experience. His description of the mode of life of the company of young folk in the country, though idealized, is perhaps not too far from actuality. The physical comforts, the apparent abundance of food and other necessities, the ease with which the people move from place to place, all these reflect what was possible or even usual among the wealthy class of Italians in the fourteenth century. They also have the pleasing manners of gentlefolk; they treat one another with courtesy and consideration—from which good-natured jest and humor are not excluded. It may seem idyllic to us, but it was probably nonetheless realistic.

[THE FIRST STORY OF THE FIRST DAY]

The storytelling proper begins with Panfilo's announcement that God's infinite grace descends upon people not "through any merit of their own" and that God attends to "the purity of the supplicant's motives." These general truths will take on interpretive significance at the conclusion of this story of a bad man who becomes a kind of saint. The First Story of the First Day, then, might be treated as a parody of a Saint's Life; certainly, the elaborate introductory strategies suggest that the audience is being prepared for a weighty and important narrative.

After telling us that God works in mysterious ways, Panfilo moves to an account of the network of financial and political relationships that bind Ser Cepperello and Musciatto, for one of the mysteries of this story is why so bad a man should honor those obligations "in a gentle and amiable fashion that ran contrary to his nature." How evil that nature is has been abundantly documented with great rhetorical flourish, with Panfilo devoting considerable energy in the long paragraph on p. 1433 to explain what a great sinner Ciappelletto is (ask your students to note every use of *great* here), at the point where hagiographers establish the credentials of their subjects.

Even the name Ciappelletto is a lie, since the French among whom this Florentine notary spends much of his time mistake *Cepperello,* which means, as the footnote indicates, "little stump," for the far more elegant *Ciappelletto,* "little garland." This substitution of a flattering name for an ignoble one prefigures the plot of the story. And yet this evil man does a great favor for his hosts and then for the multitudes who visit and profit by their visits to his tomb.

The power of words attested to in the aside on naming suggests that Boccaccio has decided to begin the *Decameron's* narratives with a tribute to language and its power. Ser Ciappelletto, after all, reinvents himself through his words in the course of the brilliant false confession he makes to the credulous friar, who will see to it that he is entombed in a holy chapel (and not thrown into a "moat like a dog," as his perturbed hosts had feared). The ruse is undertaken because of words overheard (Ser Ciappelletto engages to save the honor of the Italian bankers in whose home he is lodging when he hears their agitated discussion of the effects his death might have on their reputation and safety). The brothers station themselves "behind a wooden partition"—almost a false confessional in itself—to eavesdrop on Ser Ciappelletto and the friar, in order to satisfy themselves that their reputations will be safe when their guest dies. And, it might be noted, the "sin" that this master liar saves for his final challenge to God's mercy is that once, when he was a little boy, he cursed his mother. In sum, Ser Ciappelletto is a great storyteller; but God puts this greatness to unintended uses.

The narrative concludes with Panfilo reiterating his hymn to God's powers, which can find the good in the bad, and with a recognition of the ways in which speaking and hearing and telling stories can promote the divine purpose: "let us praise [a verbal counteraction of the curse] the name of Him with whom we began our storytelling, let us hold Him in reverence, and let us commend ourselves to Him in the hour of our need, in the certain knowledge that we shall be heard." Boccaccio has the last word: "And there the narrator fell silent."

THE NINTH STORY OF THE FOURTH DAY

The Fourth Day's topic is love stories with unhappy endings. As the footnote indicates, the story of the eaten heart was well-known in medieval Europe; this macabre incident is based on the life of the troubadour Guillem de Cabestaing, and Marie de France tells an analogous *lai* in *Laüstic.* Although so different in plot from the story of Ser Ciappelletto, this tale too pays tribute to verbal art. In appropriating his source material, it appears, Boccaccio suppresses the poetic identity of the tragic male protagonist, but he also brusquely turns away from the fate of the butchering husband, whose punishment is an important part of the Provençal original. Instead, the story (again, the comparison to *Laüstic* is suggestive) reaches its highpoint with the magnificent pronouncement and suicide of the lady and the verses commemorating the lovers in their shared tomb (a theme to pursue in relation to Ser Ciappelletto's).

[THE EIGHTH STORY OF THE FIFTH DAY]

The Fifth Day is devoted to love stories that end in happiness after a period of misfortune. The strange story of Nastagio degli Onesti, a critique of obsessive love, echoes two of the other tales in the anthology, which have been selected in part to demonstrate how Boccaccio orchestrates his one hundred stories as variations on a series of themes. We have already noted the repeated motif of the tomb. Here, we find another use of the heart torn from the body. The horrific vision that Nastagio sees has this brutal act at its center; the gruesome spectacle of which it is the climax alludes to the depiction of such punishments in Dante's *Inferno*, perhaps to prod the audience into reflection on the harshness of Dante's unsparing view of crime and punishment.

The theatricality of presentation in this story is worth pondering: to satisfy his friends' urging that he abandon his fruitless and expensive quest of the haughty lady who refuses him, Nastagio makes a show of setting out on a long journey. He instead organizes a lavish camping expedition just three miles out of town, and there he finds himself witness to another deceptive show, on a far grander scale, enacting a routine even more obsessive than his own unrewarded pursuit of love. The Sisyphean horrors that he witnesses and then turns to his own advantage are the sort of forest nightmare that will in turn be taken up by Ariosto in his *Orlando Furioso*, a comparison that you may want to exploit later on, to aid your students' understanding of the aura of tinsel about this entire episode and throughout Ariosto's great poem.

Staying with Boccaccio, you should be able to convince your students that the Eighth Story of the Fifth Day is another self-conscious comment on the power of storytelling. Nastagio's lady is smart enough to "read" the *grand guignol* she has witnessed correctly, as if it were a moral exemplum that works its desired end. Interestingly, this tale is told by Filomena, one of the seven women who decide to flee plague-ridden Florence in the introduction to the book. She is described as "prudent," or "discerning," when she deprecates their ability to take care of themselves in such difficult circumstances and initiates the decision then taken collectively to include men in their retreat. While the *Decameron* is notable for its sensitivity to women's concerns, Filomena's story emphatically does not approve of Messer Paolo Traversari's high-handed daughter, who clearly lacks prudence and makes her own decisions without parental or manly guidance throughout. Perhaps Filomena wishes to correct the excessive cruelty of the lady celebrated in the courtly love tradition. Watching the punishment of the hard-hearted naked fugitive is enough to make the ladies of Ravenna "much more tractable to men's pleasures than they had ever been in the past." Your students, perhaps especially the women among them, may wish to debate whether the story fits the day's agenda: how happily does it end?

[THE SIXTH STORY OF THE NINTH DAY]

The topic for the ninth day, as for the first, is open. If you have read *The Butcher of Abbeville,* your students will recognize the tale of Pinuccio as a *fabliau.* If you are limited to situating it within the *Decameron* selections, you can point to it as another example of the way Boccaccio's narratives revise each other as the days go on. Pinuccio may be viewed as a less exalted cousin of Nastagio degli Onesti, as the maiden he goes in quest of is frankly lower-class (and therefore more malleable than the daughter of the Traversari family). Like Nastagio, Pinuccio sets out on a phony voyage. Where the nobleman "mustered an enormous baggage-train" to make his three-mile foray into the forest, the Florentine gentleman feigns a voyage by loading a pair of saddlebags "probably with straw" and reversing direction so that he can plausibly ask the genial host to give him—and his indispensable sidekick—overnight lodgings.

The headnote explicates the significance of the cradle within the mercantile world in which the story is set; you may also want to note the prominence given to the surprised wife, who is so much more intelligent than Pinuccio the schemer but no more resourceful than her daughter, Niccolosa, who—unlike the Traversari lady—does not end up with a husband, but seems satisfied nevertheless.

[THE TENTH STORY OF THE TENTH DAY]

The final story in the *Decameron* culminates a day dedicated to examples of "magnificence," or the performance of generous deeds that have won fame for the doers. The famous tale of Gualtieri and Griselda matches the First Story of the First Day for its complexity and for the controversy it has generated. Another Saint's Life, it features a heroine who may be as problematic a subject as Ser Ciappelletto. Dioneo's irony, however, is reserved for Gualtieri (what, for example, does the reference in the opening paragraph to the Marquis's intelligence actually mean?).

One fruitful approach to this story is to view it as a fairy tale; Griselda reacts to the attendant instructed to take her first child from her with a request that the little girl not be left "to be devoured by the beasts and the birds" (p. 1453) unless he has been expressly told to do so. Your students will probably recognize this as a motif from *Snow White,* among other such folktales, and it is worth exploring the fears of abandonment in a cruel world that such stories exploit. But the *Decameron* version of the story of Griselda, which was recast by Petrarch as an allegory of the love between God (as represented by Gualtieri) and the Church (Griselda) insists on establishing a biblical frame of reference as well. Have your students identify the biblical allusions in Boccaccio's version, and then ask them how these allusions should be interpreted. Note details of Gualtieri's selection of his bride (he had "been casting an

appreciative eye on the manners of a poor girl from a neighboring village," not unlike Pinuccio in the Sixth Story of the Ninth Day, whose
"eye" had been caught by the honest host's daughter). Having made
preparations for a wedding without nominating the bride, Gualtieri meets
Griselda "as she was returning with water from the fountain" (p. 1452).
This is a repeated motif in Genesis; it is how Isaac, for one, meets
Rebekah and decides to marry her (and in Christian typology, this union
represented the love of Christ for the Church).

More striking and upsetting are the allusions that make Griselda a figure of Job, whose beautiful response to God's trial she embodies: "Naked
came I out of my mothers' womb and naked shall I return thither: the
Lord gave and the Lord hath taken away; blessed be the name of the
Lord" (p. 73). This is footnoted in the anthology, and you might inform
your class that the suffering of Job was frequently invoked during the
time of plague in which the *Decameron* is set. Why is Griselda being
tested? Why are human beings subjected to such cruel trials by a divinity
who is supposed to love his creatures?

The footnotes also cite an echo of Mary's answer to Gabriel in the
Annunciation. What mysterious purpose is Griselda serving here? The
allusions suggest that Griselda in her imperturbable acceptance exemplifies the generosity that is the day's theme. But the community within the
story views Gualtieri in theses terms as well, regarding him "as the wisest
and most discerning man on earth" (p. 1452). In the concluding paragraph of the story, Dioneo unequivocally judges Gualtieri as a tyrant,
remarking on his good luck to have found a "celestial spirit" to dwell in
his house, while he "would be better employed as [a swineherd]."

Some critics see a political motive in the republican Boccaccio's
description of a despotic Marquis. Whether this is true or not, it can be
said with certainty that, like the First Story of the First Day, this final
story turns expectations inside out. Although the story is set up as the last
in a sequence of celebrations of the magnificence of the ruler, Dioneo
explicitly announces that the Marquis disproves the theme. Instead he
celebrates the magnificence of the ruler's victim. Or does this story really
warn us against the kind of martyrdom that the faithful Griselda seems
ready to accept? "Who but Griselda" would be so masochistic as to
endure the public humiliation that her husband visits upon her?

In asking questions such as these, today's readers join the interpretive
community that Boccaccio's ten fictional storytellers form as a refuge
against death and disease. The most perfectly shaped of the framed tales
in the anthology (*The Thousand and One Nights*, *The Canterbury Tales*,
and the *Heptameron* are all unfinished), the *Decameron* continues to be
an inexhaustible source of inspiration.

Topics for Writing

1. Discuss the internal narratives contained in the First Tale of the
   First Day or the Eighth Story of the Fifth Day: how does Ser Ciappelletto's confession or the spectacle of horror that Nastagio degli

Onesti comes upon embody the power of fiction?

2. Among Boccaccio's ten storytellers are seven women, and the *Decameron* as a whole is addressed to women. Comment on the depiction of gender relations in the stories you have read. Are the female narrators more sympathetic to women's concerns than the males? Do you think women are favored in the way they are portrayed? Give examples to support your argument.

Comparative Perspectives

1. Does the repeated scene in the forest that Nastagio degli Onesti witnesses fit the theory of the *contrapasso* that governs punishment in Dante's *Inferno*?

2. Compare the frame tales in the *Decameron, The Thousand and One Nights, The Canterbury Tales,* and/or the *Heptameron*. In each case, what is the reason for telling stories? Do the stories accomplish the purpose for which they are intended? How important is the relationship between the tale and the teller in the selections you choose to discuss?

3. Is Griselda the ideal woman? Explain your answer and compare her behavior with that of other highly praised literary wives, to be selected from possibilities that include Rebekah in Genesis, Penelope in the *Odyssey*, Shahrazad in *The Thousand and One Nights*, Desdemona in *Othello*.

Further Reading

See also the reading suggestions in the anthology, p. 1431.

Potter, Joy Hambueden. *Five Frames for the* Decameron: *Communication and Social Systems in the* Cornice. 1982. Helpful review of the social situation behind the tellers, who are described as on "a retreat . . . during which they both learn and reassess the value of their society."

Seung, T. K. *Cultural Thematics: The Formation of the Faustian Ethos.* 1976. Contains interesting analyses of the "sovereign will" displayed in the first and the last stories of the *Decameron*.

SIR GAWAIN AND THE GREEN KNIGHT

Backgrounds

[PART I]

The poet quickly tells how, after the fall of Troy, various of the surviving Trojan warriors migrated to the west and founded new nations; among them Brutus came to Britain; later Arthur ruled as king in Camelot. This will be a wondrous tale of events during a Christmas–New Year's holiday there. Arthur; his queen, Guinevere; and Gawain, his nephew, are at a high table or dais; many other knights sit at other tables; all await the feast; but Arthur has vowed not to begin until someone comes to tell him of a "wonder." Suddenly a huge horse and rider, both covered in green, dash into the hall and approach the dais; the visitor has neither spear nor shield but carries a branch of green holly in one hand and a large ax in the other. He asks who is in charge here; Arthur answers and invites him to dismount and be treated as a guest. He declines, saying he has heard of the prowess and courtesy of Arthur's knights; he comes in peace to propose a Christmas game. Arthur assents, and the Green Knight offers his head to be stricken off with the ax—on condition that a return blow be accepted a year and a day hence. When all the company remain silent, he taunts them harshly, whereupon Arthur in anger and shame steps forward to accept the challenge. But now Gawain intervenes, asking that he be allowed to take over in place of the king; Gawain modestly says he is the weakest of all in body and mind and of no consequence except for his kinship to the king. This folly, he says, fits not a king. His request is granted, and now the Green Knight, repeating the conditions of the challenge, dismounts, lies down, uncovers his neck, and is neatly beheaded by Gawain's blow with the ax. But the Green Knight rises, catches his head up from the floor, mounts his horse, and tells Gawain to come next year and look for the Knight of the Green Chapel, who will be ready with the return blow. He then rides rapidly out of the hall; the company resume their feasting.

[PART II]

The seasons pass in due course until All Hallows Day (November 1), when Gawain is ready to start on his journey in search of the Knight of the Green Chapel. He bids king and friends farewell; he is richly armed, as his horse, Gringolet, is handsomely caparisoned; the pentangle (five-pointed star figure) on Gawain's shield includes in its symbolism his devotion to Mary, queen of Heaven and all his moral virtues. As Gawain departs, some of the court regret that the affair was not better handled: it is a shame that he is likely to lose his life, "Beheaded by an elf-man, for empty pride" (line 681). In the course of Gawain's solitary journey, he is threatened by wild animals and wild men and hampered by winter cold and sleet; he prays to Mary for guidance. Presently, he catches sight of a splendid castle and surrounding grounds, approaches, and is greeted by the porter, who lets down the drawbridge. The lord of the castle welcomes Gawain, and he is finely entertained, wined, and dined. There are two ladies in the host's family, one comely and beautiful, the other ugly and graceless. After the visit has lasted from Christmas Eve till St. John's day (December 27), Gawain says he must continue his search for the Green Chapel; his host assures him that it is close by, and so Gawain can stay on as a guest for three more days. The host then proposes a game: he will go hunting each day, while Gawain rests (after his tiring journey) in the castle; each evening the host will give Gawain whatever he has got on the hunt and Gawain will give him whatever he has received in the castle.

[Part III]

As noted in the headnote, the same narrative sequence is maintained for all three days: first, the start of the hunt; then the visit of the lady, the host's wife, to Gawain's bedchamber; then the conclusion of the hunt, the evening meal, and the exchange of gifts. On the first day the host and his company hunt deer and bring home many carcasses, duly presented to Gawain; he duly gives the host a single kiss. On the second day comes the boar hunt; and Gawain correctly gives the host two kisses. The third day the quarry is a fox; and Gawain correctly bestows three kisses on the host but silently withholds the silk belt that the lady had given him, with the promise that it would ensure the wearer against death.

[Part IV]

Early on New Year's morning Gawain sets out to keep his rendezvous; the young guide whom the host assigned to him warns him of the great danger facing him at the hands of the savage Knight of the Green Chapel and says he (the guide) will keep silent if Gawain avoids a meeting; Gawain says he must keep faith, and trusts to God. Proceeding, Gawain soon comes to a sort of mound; he hears nearby, but out of sight, someone sharpening a blade on a grindstone. Gawain calls out, giving his name, and the Green Knight comes over the crest of a hill carrying a huge Danish ax. Gawain duly prepares to receive the blow, but twice the Green Knight feints, bringing the ax down but not touching Gawain; the third time he lets the blade graze Gawain's neck, drawing a few drops of blood. Thereupon Gawain leaps up and offers to resist any further blows. But the Green Knight now explains that he was the host in the castle (of Bercilak); the two feints correspond to the two days on which Gawain carried out the exchange faithfully and in full; the slight scratch made by the third blow was Gawain's due because he kept back the silk belt—but only because it might save his life. Gawain quickly gives back the belt and reproaches himself bitterly for cowardice and covetousness. But the Green Knight declares Gawain, who has confessed the fault and suffered the penance (of the third stroke), as pure as the day he was born; and invites him to return to the castle, where his wife (the lady who had visited Gawain in his bedchamber) will be glad to see him. The host also gives the belt once more to Gawain, who must keep it as a reminder of the event; Gawain says he will keep it as a warning of his spiritual weakness and peril. In answer to Gawain's question, the Green Knight says that the old, ugly lady in the castle is Morgan le Faye, King Arthur's half-sister; she is an enchantress and an enemy of Guinevere, and hence was responsible for the visit of the Green Knight to Camelot. Gawain makes his way back to Arthur's court, where he tells the whole story; the belt is used as a model of a baldric to be worn by knights of the court.

The earliest extant literary treatment of the "beheading game" is in the Irish prose narrative *The Feast of Bricriu* (*Fled Bricrend*), dated approximately in the eighth century. Cuchulainn, the great warrior of the Ulster cycle of tales, is engaged in a contest with other fighters for the right to the "hero's portion" at a feast. A rough-looking figure of magical powers invites each of them in turn to an exchange of blows in the manner of Gawain and the Green Knight, but the time interval is one day instead of a year. The others fail to keep the appointment for the return blow, Cuchulain alone is faithful, and he receives an entirely harmless blow and is declared the winner of the contest. (The Irish episode is translated in Kittredge, *A Study of Sir Gawain and the Green Knight*.) The Irish plot was taken over by French and perhaps other medieval storytellers; the anonymous author of the selection probably knew it in *The Book* (*Le Livre*) *de Caradoc*, which appears among the "continuations" of the Old French Percival romance. (For discussion and summaries, see Larry D. Benson, *Art and Tradition in Sir Gawain and the Green Knight*, 1965.) The temptation plot was also familiar from various romances (see Benson); of course, it has an ancient history, e.g., the story of Joseph and Potiphar's wife in Genesis 39.7–20 as well as the deeply tragic Greek tale of Hippolytus and Phaedra. The author of the English romance may have been the first to combine the two plots.

In his descriptions and characterizations he also makes abundant use of tradition. Thus the knight in green costume, carrying a bough of holly, was a familiar figure representing the verdure of spring in the new year. Not combined with this but rather juxtaposed is the green color of his skin; this, along with the enormous shock of hair covering his shoulders, may well have reminded medieval listeners or readers of the figure of the Wild Man, the uncouth stranger who often erupts in royal courts (in romances). Both traditions are doubtless related to prototypes of ultimate (pre-Christian) ritual significance; one thinks of spring festivals and sacrifices, the renewal of the waste land at the end of winter—though it is unlikely that the fourteenth-century audience made conscious connections of this kind.

In the portrayal of Gawain, the poet makes an independent use of tradition. In this poem Gawain is a brave, spotless Christian knight, imbued with the five chivalric virtues and devoted to the Virgin Mary, his heavenly patroness; he is, of course, keenly sensitive in any matter of truth or honor. But, while making him also peerless in courtesy (conduct as a cultivated gentleman), the poet definitely does not attach to Gawain the habits of a medieval Casanova. But that is just the reputation that Gawain had acquired in romance tradition by the late fourteenth century. What the poet does is to have the temptress—the wife of the Green

Knight—pretend to believe that Gawain had well earned this latter reputation and ought to have no hesitation about living up to it. She is playing
a game, of course; with the resources of a magic household and
entourage and a shape-shifter for a husband, she incurs no risk, however
Gawain may respond to her overtures. Thus she is free to deploy the
whole gamut of invitation, including praise, entreaty, pretended unhappi-
ness at his rejection, disbelief that he can really be Gawain—no holds
need be barred and none are. This is a hilariously comic situation, and
the author takes full advantage of it.

Gawain, on the other hand, is deterred by his situation as a guest of
the lord of the castle and the agreement to exchange winnings at the end
of each day; by the fact that such an intrigue is a sin; and by his preoccupation with the approaching rendezvous with the Green Knight. Yet we
can see that he feels deeply the obligation to behave always with courtesy
(good manners and consideration of the lady's emotions). Nevertheless,
the poet indicates that Gawain was genuinely moved, at least on the third
day; we are told at the beginning of the visit that he delights in the lady's
company—and there is a reminder that Mary had better look after her
knight.

The parallel patterning of the hunts and the lady's visits has been
noted. Probably it is significant that the third hunt, of the fox—regarded
in that age as vermin—is paired with Gawain's breach of faith in not giving the belt to his host, a reprehensible act even if extenuated by the circumstances.

The humor of the situation after the Green Knight has delivered the
final stroke must not be missed. Gawain instantly springs up ready to
defend himself (against further attack, beyond the terms of the agreement); and the Green Knight quietly stands there, doubtless laughing to
·himself. Presently he explains the whole design. But the amused reader
can sympathize with Gawain in his chagrin at the deception that has
been practiced on him; he has been under such pressure for so long!
Even the most ardent feminist should forgive his outburst against the
wiles of women. Indeed, the art and skill of the poet maintain the
reader's sympathy with and esteem for Gawain through the many scenes
in which he inevitably becomes a figure of comedy.

Classroom Strategies

You must see to it that students discover the many and various delights
of the romance. Once they get into it, they will see how much fun it can
be—as well as being a serious treatment of important issues. Early on,
some of the vivid descriptive and "action" passages might well be read
aloud in class. Later, some of the dialogue between Gawain and the lady
should receive oral dramatization, with parts appropriately assigned to
members of the class.

Topics for Discussion

1. Reasons for Gawain's chagrin and self-disgust.

[When he throws the girdle at the Green Knight, he realizes that he has been made a fool of, but that it is his own fault; but it is also true that he has been obliged to play a game without knowing the rules, and he has shown a flaw by not returning the girdle earlier (as promised by the terms of the agreement)—a fault that he *need* not have committed—as he has just discovered. In his view—at the moment, at least—the flaw cancels out his persevering resistance of the other temptations that the lady had pressed on him.]

2. What is the verdict of others (than Gawain) on his conduct?

[Sir Bercilak (the Green Knight himself) lets the ax barely scratch the skin of Gawain's neck and afterward declares him wholly absolved and invites him to return to the castle for more festivity. Arthur's court adopts the girdle as a badge of honor— rather than shame or disgrace. The reader is likely to see the narrative as a series of extreme tests imposed (without his full knowledge) on a superlative knight, courtier, and man of scrupulous honor. He passes them all with flying colors—with one slight exception, and there he believed his life was at stake. Since the author leads the reader to this conclusion, it must have been his also.]

3. Does the author indulge in too much descriptive detail?

[There is certainly a rich abundance: the festivity at Arthur's court, the elaborate clothing and arming of Gawain for the journey, the details of the three hunts, etc. But is the description static? Or is something happening all the time within the descriptions? And could there be a difference between the spontaneous interest of the fourteenth-century listener and the twentieth-century reader?]

Topics for Writing

1. Characterization of the Green Knight.

[To some extent a dual personality: the outlandish visitor at Arthur's feast and Sir Bercilak, Gawain's host at the castle. How are these necessarily somewhat different? Is there an underlying unity?]

2. The story as a Christmas "game"—in two parts.

[The initial setting at Arthur's court; the wait for a wonder; the Green Knight's challenge (which is noted as a "folly" but nevertheless must be taken seriously); the Christmas season a year later at Bercilak's castle; the triple exchange of gifts; the happy conclusion of both plots on New Year's morning.]

3. Gawain as a graceful naysayer.

[A close look at Gawain's part in the dialogue with the lady on the three mornings; how he maintains his (attributed) reputation for courtesy but still remains modest about himself; how he avoids involvement without giving offense; the details of his acceptance of the girdle.]

Comparative Perspectives

1. Gawain's quest for the Green Knight is accompanied by detailed descriptions of the changing seasons of the year. How does this attention to weather and landscape complement the figure of the giant knight, who appears both in green and, as Sir Bercilak, with a beard "of a beaver's hue"—that is, a deep brown? How would you compare the role played by seasonal change in the characters' lives here with that in other poems and narratives you have read?
2. Gawain is introduced as a nephew of King Arthur. What features of feudal and aristocratic societies make this an important relationship? How do similar family ties put subtle pressures on the young heroes of other heroic tales you have read?

Further Reading

See the reading suggestions in the anthology, p. 1459.

GEOFFREY CHAUCER

The Canterbury Tales

Backgrounds

GENERAL PROLOGUE

The Knight, his son the Squire, and their servant the Yeoman make up a group of three traveling together. The account of the Knight is representative and typical, rather than based on any individual actual person. He is a professional soldier of notable experience and exemplary character. It has been shown that various English knights took part in most or all of the campaigns mentioned. Such a young soldier as the Squire might well have served with English armies in France in one or more campaigns of the Hundred Years' War.

Next comes another group of three: the Prioress, another nun who serves as her secretary, and an accompanying priest; neither the secretary nor the priest is described in the *General Prologue*. Chaucer's attitude toward the Prioress has been much discussed among scholars. It has been pointed out that she has many of the qualities expected in a fashionable lady of the period but not necessarily in a nun: meticulous table manners, graceful costume, the use of (insular!) French. The "love" emblematic on her brooch may be ambivalent—religious or ordinary earthly; her tenderness about the pet dogs—not monastic—seems to be an individual trait. Chaucer seems amused by the various items *not* generally approved for nuns, yet fully appreciative of an exquisite person.

Chaucer's treatment of the Monk is rather different. He does not merely tell us that the Monk is an ardent hunter and that he is often away from his monastery, etc.; he repeatedly notes that these things were contrary to monastic "rule" and precedent. Consequently, when Chaucer declares his approval of the Monk's way of life, some kind of irony must be involved. One view is that, in *The Canterbury Tales*, there are two

Chaucers—one is the sophisticated author, the other is the simple, suggestible pilgrim—and that sometimes we hear the voice of one, sometimes of the other. Thus Chaucer the author painted the portrait of the Monk, but Chaucer the pilgrim liked and approved of his way of life. Without making so sharp a division as this, we can at least agree that Chaucer occasionally pretends to say what would contradict other clear positions or attitudes; he enjoys a moment of make-believe.

Unlike monks, friars were expected to leave their "house," to go out into the world and serve, especially, the poor and helpless—after the example of St. Francis and other founders. But Chaucer makes it evident that this Friar had all the traits of an expert salesman and used them assiduously for his own enrichment and enjoyment—leaving the poor to themselves.

The next several pilgrims require no comment here; then we come to the Parson, who, like the Knight, receives a full and entirely favorable treatment. Later still, there is the Summoner, a thoroughly unsavory and corrupt but also comic figure. He is not a member of the clergy; instead, he is a kind of policeman or constable attached to the Church court presided over by an archdeacon. The Summoner is apparently an associate of the Pardoner, who comes next in Chaucer's list. The latter's occupation is discussed in the headnote. Here it may be added that the Pardoner has often been regarded as a eunuch *ex nativitate* (by birth, congenitally); it has also been shown that Chaucer's description and language might apply to homosexual characters. There may thus be innuendo in the mention of the association between the Summoner and the Pardoner. And the present account should be kept in mind when the reader comes to the bitter altercation between the Pardoner and the Host at the end of *The Pardoner's Tale*.

THE MILLER'S PROLOGUE AND TALE

The Prologue: When the Knight has told his tale—a romance of chivalry and of courtly love (not included in the anthology)—the Host invites the Monk (next in social rank to the Knight) to continue with the storytelling. But the Miller, partly drunk, insists on telling his tale at once. It is in some ways a parody of high romance, but primarily it is a very fully developed *fabliau*.

The Tale: John, a comparatively rich old carpenter of Oxford, has a pretty young wife, Alison; and there are two young servants, male and female. They have a boarder living in the house, Nicholas, who is a student at the university and a semiprofessional astrologer. He and Alison plan an (uncourtly!) intrigue, but they will have to be cautious—the husband is jealous. Meanwhile the parish clerk, Absolom, is infatuated with Alison (who has no interest in him) and likes to serenade her under the window at night.

Nicholas shuts himself up in his room for a time; John, who likes the young man, comes to his room to inquire. Nicholas explains that he knows from his astrology that a flood greater than Noah's is in the offing;

but they can save themselves if they keep the news a secret. The carpenter must hang huge baskets from the ceiling or loft and he, Alison, and Nicholas will climb up and bed down, each in one of the baskets. (The servants have been sent out of town.) Then Nicholas and Alison—the weary John has gone to sleep—climb out, go downstairs and so to bed. Presently Absolom comes singing and pleading for at least a kiss from Alison. She sits on the windowsill, her rear projecting outward; Absolom's kiss chills all his amorous itch and inspires him with a plan for revenge.

Obtaining a colter or plowshare well heated at one end from a late-working blacksmith, Absolom returns and asks Alison for another kiss. This time Nicholas projects over the window; Absolom is ready with the hot iron. When Nicholas yells "Water! Water!" the carpenter wakes up and instantly cuts the rope holding his basket (expecting that form of navigation during the flood), falls to the floor, and breaks his arm. In the aftermath Nicholas and Alison insist that only the foolish John believed a flood was imminent.

THE WIFE OF BATH'S PROLOGUE AND TALE

The Prologue: The Wife of Bath has the longest prologue in *The Canterbury Tales,* an apology for her life that threatens to overwhelm her (slightly) more succinct tale. Apparently rambling, the *Prologue* is in fact quite well organized, according to the principles of medieval argumentation. From her opening announcement, she contrasts the claims of experience with those of authority. In her *Prologue,* she draws amply on both as evidence for her views on sexuality and marriage. She manipulates her frequent biblical references and quotations to bring objective authority to justify her many marriages (Solomon is a favorite) and to demonstrate that virginity is a self-limiting ideal not to be universally imposed (Paul is undercut).

When the Pardoner interrupts her well-argued defense of heterosexual activity, the Wife of Bath turns to personal experience (which, as the headnote suggests, is actually as much rooted in the misogynist texts of literary authority as in any authentic life experience that this fictional character can claim). Her first three husbands were "good," inasmuch as they were old and she could control them, and she shows off the aggressive ways in which she attacked before they could chastise her.

At the midway point in her *Prologue,* when Alison comes to her fourth husband, she momentarily falters (note the repeated effort, at lines 454 and 483, to explain her life with the first man to have cheated on her). Rather than inquire too deeply into this humiliating experience, she launches into the great defense of her own charms and the poignant recognition that they are fading.

Boasting of the pain she dealt the man who had pained her, she moves on quickly to the story of her life with husband number five, the young clerk who made this eager conversationalist deaf in one ear and over whom she eventually triumphed. Here again, she becomes the mouthpiece for the antifeminine tirades of her clerkly husband, a technique aptly captured in a telling detail: to stop him from reading at night when she wanted to go to bed, she tore three pages out of his book (line 787). Shortly after losing that final battle with a wife twice his age, Jenkin died (one might well ask what killed him), and the Wife of Bath is on pilgrimage, as we learn in the *General Prologue*, to see if she can find her sixth husband.

The Tale: Interrupted again by the Friar, a nefarious charmer who preys on widows, the Wife of Bath pays him back in the brilliant prelude to her Tale. In her story about one of King Arthur's knights, a singularly ignoble rapist, she takes us back to the world of fairies and elves, stopping to compare the dull contemporary world to this charmed past, maliciously noting that the incubi of the old (pre-Christian) world who impregnated innocent women have been replaced by the friars of the new dispensation, who may try to force themselves on women but to no avail—they are, she implies, an impotent bunch (line 23).

In the *Tale* itself, she seems to identify more with the questing knight than with his victim, for the question the queen and her ladies put to the knight is the Wife's own question as well (not to mention Sigmund Freud's): "what is the thing that most of all / Women desire" (lines 39–40)? Searching for the answer provides another opportunity for a literary-historical review; notably, Dante is cited as the authority on the importance of true gentility, as opposed to mere family inheritance. The knight answers correctly because listening to his unattractive old wife has led him (and the Wife herself, we feel) to see that every human being must understand how little we actually can control. To gain sovereignty is to give it up; typically, Alison disclaims this moral truth almost as soon as it is affirmed, returning in her concluding lines to her aggressive, self-protective stance.

THE PARDONER'S PROLOGUE AND TALE

The Prologue: In this exuberant address to his fellow pilgrims the Pardoner boasts about his skill in getting money from the simple, rustic people who listen to his preaching. His text, "The root of evil is greed," serves to loosen their wallets and fill his own. His fake relics, he assures them, will cure ills of domestic animals, prevent suspicion of wives by husbands, increase the yield of crops—if a suitable offering is made. But note this: it won't work if the person making the offering is guilty of any really serious unconfessed sin. (Thus he intimidates anyone who did not come forward with an offering.)

The Tale: The Pardoner offers this tale as a specimen of his preaching. First, he briefly sets a scene: three young men are in a tavern; they eat and drink to excess, indulge in much profanity, and roll dice. Here the Pardoner inserts a long denunciation of gluttony, drunkenness, profanity, and gambling, with allusions to the Bible, examples from secular history, and a lively imitation of the snoring of a person who has taken too much alcohol—"Samson, Samson"—yet Samson never drank wine! Resuming the story, the revelers hear a bell outside the tavern. Learning from the waiter that it is rung for a man recently slain by this thief Death, they (are just intoxicated enough to) resolve to go immediately in search of this Death, intending to kill him.

Before long they meet a mysterious old man whom they question roughly. Without saying who he is, he describes himself as a hopeless wanderer who would welcome Death; but Death won't have him. The revelers then demand, with threats, that he tell them where Death can be found. He directs them to follow a crooked road to a grove nearby; they will find Death waiting under a tree. They do as he says, but what they find is almost eight bushels of fine gold coins.

After this they forget all about Death and set about ways of guarding the money for themselves. It is decided by lot that two will stay with the gold while the third goes into town to buy food for the (overnight?) wait that they must count on for safety. While one is away, the other two plan to kill him as soon as he returns; and he buys poison to put in one of the jugs of wine that he carries back to the grove. Both designs succeed, and soon all three are dead.

Apparently carried away by his own eloquence, the Pardoner, having quickly concluded his sermon, invites his fellow pilgrims to come forward and make offerings; that is, he tries to treat them like his rural congregations. When he suggests—playfully or not—that the Host should begin, being the most involved in sin, the latter answers him angrily and abusively; finally the Knight insists on a reconciliation, and the incident passes.

Topics for Discussion

1. Of the Lawyer, the Franklin, and the Physician in the *General Prologue,* what remarks by Chaucer might indicate something less than total approval of each? Try to relate the qualifications to the portrait as a whole; bear in mind that these men are neither scoundrels nor saints.

2. In *The Miller's Tale,* how does the overall characterization of John, Alison, Nicholas, and Absolom make it plausible that each would act in the way the story tells it? Take into account such things as John's credulity and (qualified) respect for Nicholas's learning, Alison's youth and beauty, and Absolom's naive taste in love songs.

3. Is *The Miller's Tale* pornography?

   [This would involve an effort to define pornography or at least to decide its essential feature(s). Is Chaucer's story ever suggestive or prurient? Or is it instead honest and forthright? The same questions might be asked in the discussion of Boccaccio's tale of Brother Alberto and Lisetta.]

4. The variety of aspects and settings in which death is referred to in *The Pardoner's Tale.*

   [Consider: the bell heard by the three young men in the tavern (line 182), the waiter's talk about "a sly thief" (line 193), the resolution of the young men (lines 210ff.), the talk of the mysterious old man (lines 238ff.), his directing them to a grove (line 280), the pile of gold (lines 288ff.), the apothecary's drug (lines 362ff.), and the (pretended) bit of friendly wrestling. When and where is there personification? (The use of a capital *D* is a clue.)]

Topics for Writing

1. Men and women of the Church.

   [The Prioress, the Monk, the Friar, the Oxford student, the Parson, and the Pardoner are described in the *General Prologue*. The Priest accompanying the nuns is characterized in the *Prologue* to his tale. The Oxford student is a devoted cleric and serious scholar; the Parson is a diligent and faultless servant and moral guardian of his parish. Chaucer's account of the Prioress is ambivalent: is it basically sympathetic? He admires the skill of the Friar and the Pardoner, but what is his judgment of them otherwise? After noting all these, come back to the Monk and try to assess Chaucer's estimate. Finally, dispose of the question, Was Chaucer in favor of the Church or opposed to it?]

2. Chaucer's pilgrims in Dante's *Inferno*.

   [The headnote to Chaucer suggests that some of the rascals among them might have found a place in one or another of the subdivisions of the Eighth Circle, devoted to Fraud, or dishonesty. Choose several characters and discuss their fitness for such a category. Use both plain statements and indirect indications of both poets.]

Comparative Perspectives

1. As in much Western medieval literature—including Dante's *Inferno* and *Sir Gawain and the Green Knight*—and in the Chaucerian selections in the anthology, punishment for transgression is a concern. Compare Dante's formulation of apt punishments with, as appropriate, the punishments inflicted—or not inflicted—on the characters in *The Miller's Tale* and *The Pardoner's Prologue and Tale*. How does the prevailing vision of punishment here measure up against the punishments suffered by characters in non-Christian narratives of roughly the same period?
   [Cf. *The Thousand and One Nights*.]

2. From the way even the least educated of Chaucer's characters speak, it is clear that the rhetorical traditions of the Middle Ages were available to listeners as much as to readers. Select a passage that shows evidence of popular styles of argumentation and discuss their effect on the tone of Chaucer's tales. Compare the tone of voice in works like *The Book of the Courtier* and the *Heptameron*, which reproduce the conversational style of a highly literate aristocratic culture.

3. How does Chaucer, in *The Wife of Bath's Tale*, take up the debate on "gentilesse" launched by Guido Guinizelli in *Love and Nobility* and continued by Dante in his lyric poems?

Further Reading

See also the reading suggestions in the anthology, p. 1517.

Gibaldi, Joseph, ed. *Approaches to Teaching Chaucer's* Canterbury Tales. 1980.

THE THOUSAND AND ONE NIGHTS

Prologue *and* The Story of the Merchant and the Demon

Background

The Thousand and One Nights begins with a lengthy prologue. Two brothers have ruled their respective kingdoms in equity and peace for ten years. The elder, Shahrayar, desires to see the younger, Shahzaman, and sends for him. Shahzaman appoints a deputy to rule in his stead and sets out. Returning unexpectedly before he has traveled far, he discovers his wife committing adultery with a kitchen boy and executes them both summarily. He arrives in Shahrayar's court depressed but unwilling to tell his brother why. By chance, Shahzaman witnesses the extraordinary infidelity of Shahrayar's wife and attendants with black male slaves from her husband's court. His depression lifts on seeing that even so powerful a monarch as his brother can be wounded as he is. His brother notices the improvement in his spirits and asks the reasons. Eventually Shahzaman must tell him, with the result that Shahrayar secretly witnesses a repetition of his wife's carnival of infidelity. Now he becomes depressed. He and his brother resolve to abandon the court and wander the world seeking someone who is even more afflicted than they are. They discover such an unfortunate in an enormous black demon who stands as much above Shahrayar in power and authority as he does the slave who has cuckolded him. Moreover, this demon has protected his woman by means that should even be more secure than the walls of Shahrayar's palace. Yet she has managed to betray him with a hundred men, including Shahrayar and Shahzaman. Now convinced of the impossibility of finding a virtuous woman, Shahrayar returns to court, slays his wife and her maids and begins an insane and murderous policy designed to ensure that he will never be betrayed again. He marries a new wife each evening and murders her the following morning. Shahzaman returns to Samarkand and is heard from no further.

The people of his realm are outraged and pray to God for deliverance. Shahrayar's vizier is incapable of finding a solution, but the elder of his two daughters, Shahrazad, is uncommonly wise, well read, and exceptionally brave. She plans to save the people, but it requires that she be married to Shahrayar. Her father tries to dissuade her by telling her two stories. He is unsuccessful, and, indeed, his stories seem irrelevant to his purpose. Shahrazad's plan is to use her skill as a storyteller to manipulate Shahrayar into deferring her death endlessly. That is, each night she tells him stories to while away the long hours of the might, and stopping each sunrise just before some crisis. As she expected, Shahrayar's eagerness to hear the end of the story is stronger than his desire to have her executed. She continues this way until he at last pardons her, marries her, and abandons his policy. This lengthy prologue is the frame in which all the tales are set. In the various manuscripts and many printed editions of *The Thousand and One Nights*, the formulaic interruptions at dawn are usually retained. In the translations they usually are not.

Classroom Strategies

The whole section is not too long for a single assignment; however, it can be divided after the *Prologue* and before *The Story of the Merchant and the Demon*.

Topics for Discussion

The theme of justice or the relation of crime to punishment is a central one in this portion of the *Nights*. The young women whom Shahrayar married and murders are innocent of any crime against Shahrayar whatsoever, and by punishing the innocent Shahrayar changes himself from a just ruler into a monster of indifference, a ruler who makes war on his own people. The merchant is equally innocent of evil intent toward the *jinn* or his son. There is, to our eyes at least, an absurd or comical element to this encounter that undermines any inclination to sympathize with the *jinn* in his loss. As pointed out in the headnote, the tales the three travelers tell offer further variations on this theme; moreover, they provide very attractive examples of women who are virtuous and obedient to their fathers or husbands—the herdsman's daughter, the merchant's magical wife, and the butcher's daughter.

The most provocative question raised by the *Prologue* are those of the morality of women and racial discrimination. All too often the story is read through Shahrayar's eyes, and he, his brother, and the demon are seen simply as victims of evil and designing women. The key to a reading that does more justice to the woman's point of view is in the relation of the demon to his captured bride. He is the villain here, not the young woman whom he has stolen away from her husband and home on her wedding night and kept imprisoned at the bottom of the sea solely for his own pleasure. That Shahrayar and Shahzaman don't see this suggests that they are insensitive husbands although they may be just rulers. Shahrayar's assault on the young women of the realm is the height of insanity since by it he, the king, is making warfare on his own people. It suggests that he is angry with them, not just the young women, perhaps because he feels they have shared in his wife's secret and not told him. After all such astonishing performances, which involved so many of the palace staff, can hardly have been a secret to anybody in the palace but Shahrayar.

The selection of black partners for Shahrayar's queen and her attendants may reflect Muslim stereotypes about black male potency, but it is not necessarily invidious for that reason. Islam was not completely color blind, but there have been eminent and distinguished Muslims of African origin in every profession since the time of Muhammad. The demon who is the most powerful figure in the story, and whose misfortune is seen by Shahrayar and Shahzaman as greater than their own, is also black.

Topics for Writing

1. Shahrazad is a better storyteller that her father. She convinces her audience; he doesn't. Is the fault in the tales or the tellers?
2. How are we to understand Shahrayar's madness? Does it make sense to you? That is, are male egos in macho societies that frail or is his a special case?
3. How are women portrayed in these stories? Does "good daughters bad wives" about cover it? What are we to make of that?
4. Shahrayar and Shahzaman are appalled by the actions of their wives. Should we be as well? Can you write a revisionist interpretation that lifts some of the blame off the wives' shoulders?
5. Both the vizier and his daughter, Shahrazad, tell tales that surround their human characters without important animals, but the animals play different roles in the imaginative worlds of father and daughter. Compare and contrast the powers attributed to the animal world in *The Tale of the Ox and the Donkey* and *The Tale of the Merchant and His Wife* with those described in *The Story of the Merchant and the Demon.* How may these differences reflect the contrasting visions of gender relations so central to *The Thousand and One Nights*?

Comparative Perspective

Like Ovid's *Metamorphoses,* Shahrazad's tales feature metamorphosed human beings who are mute in animal form. Compare Ovid's depiction of Io, a maiden turned into a heifer, with Shahrazad's description of circumstances in which family members become deer and dogs. What details does Ovid stress that Shahrazad overlooks? How do the outcomes of their narratives differ? What is the connection between those differences and the details each prefers to emphasize?

[For all the violence that they contain, the basic optimism of Shahrazad's tales contrasts strikingly with Ovid's witty, urbane despair. Students might be asked to reflect on the essentially amoral Ovidian cosmos and the ultimately just and merciful world that the brave and buoyant Shahrazad shows to Shahrayar.]

Further Reading

See also the reading suggestions in the anthology, p. 1588.

Hamori, Andras. *On the Art of Medieval Arabic Literature.* 1974. Several chapters are devoted to the *Nights.*

Malti-Douglas, Fedwa. *Woman's Body, Woman's World.* 1991. See the first chapter.

SIR THOMAS MALORY

Morte Darthur

Classroom Strategies and Topics for Discussion

At the start of the selections in Masterpieces of the Middle Ages, the *Beowulf* poet defines one knightly ideal, in which heroism and loyalty reign supreme; at the end of these selections, and of the Middle Ages themselves, Malory defines a related but broader ideal, which adds Christian faith, romantic love, and personal beauty to round out the notion of chivalric excellence. The warrior culture of northern Europe has been softened by the more cultivated world of the south, and the result is the Matter of Britain, the Arthurian legends that give native Britons a sense of hereditary right on their own island. As described by Geoffrey of Monmouth's *History of the Kings of Britain* (written around 1135), Arthur was supposed to have descended from Brut, himself a descendant of Aeneas, thus giving Britain a history parallel to that of Rome. Almost immediately adopted by Norman-French poets, Arthur is simultaneously the idealistic patron of the Round Table and the betrayed husband brought down by his own illegitimate child. The paradoxes inherent in his situation are already evident to Marie de France in *Lanval*, which offers a good starting point for a review of the Arthurian texts in the anthology, discussed at more length below.

Malory's position at the end of the medieval period is worth comment because one might expect that the final stages of an era would spawn parody rather than celebration. You will want to be sure that your students understand that tone is as much a matter of authorial temperament as it is of chronology; yet they should also understand that the Arthurian matter that is the butt of so many parodic and critical forays in the anthology is of much older vintage than Malory's summative review of a long tradition and that *Morte Darthur* is simultaneously nostalgic and contemporary, a farewell to a dated cultural cliché even as it is an up-to-date reflection of the political and social reality of fifteenth-century England.

Among Malory's sources are the twelfth-century French romances that are subjected to cynical scrutiny by writers as diverse as Dante (Francesca and Paolo initiate their scandalous affair by emulating the behavior of Lancelot and Guinevere as described in the popular *Lancelot du Lac*, one of the best-sellers of the medieval era), the poet(s) of the *Romance of Renard*, Chaucer (in the opening lines of *The Wife of Bath's Tale*), and the Gawain poet. The idealization of Arthur's Round Table being parodied in these masterpieces antedates Malory's reinvigoration and integration of the Matter of Britain.

You will want to propose to your students, then, what is new in Malory's treatment of familiar themes and figures. His *Morte Darthur* is, to begin with, perhaps the first great narrative achievement in "modern" English prose. Fast-moving and episodic, it covers a great deal of territory in a short space in a language of remarkable grace, marked by many devices that students will think of as "poetic": alliteration, repetition, parallelism. A good way to focus this discussion would be to compare the opening paragraph of the selection with the opening of Chaucer's *Canterbury Tales*. Malory invokes the lyric tradition on which Chaucer drew in establishing his springtime setting, but more explicitly shapes it to prepare the reader for the tragic story he is about to tell. Where Chaucer's verse alludes to the plenitude of new life in springtime, Malory's prose transmutes the flower of May into the flower of chivalry. The Edenic echoes of the opening lines are confirmed by the closing reference in the paragraph to the sibling rivalries that are to destroy the created order (as did the hatred of Cain for Abel). Deeper in the narrative lurks the fatal adder that emulates the serpent in Genesis (cf. pp. 54 and 1621).

The economy with which Malory establishes character and suggests psychological motivation also deserves mention. Why has Arthur preferred to ignore the rumors about Lancelot and Guinevere? Why does Lancelot insist on visiting Guinevere, unarmed, although he has been warned that a trap is being set for them? What happens to transform Gawain from Lancelot's staunchest defender to his bitterest enemy? These are the perennial questions that we ask about tragedy and that students love to consider: to what extent are the protagonists doomed by fate, to what extent are they responsible for the events that destroy them?

An excellent anchor for this discussion is Malory's description of Arthur's first premonitory dream. What is the wheel to which the king's chair is tied? Why is it turned upside down? The allusion to the Wheel of Fortune is palpable, and yet it is not sufficient to account for the hideous black water, filled with serpents, into which he is plunged—a pool that seems to invite sexual interpretation. For this is a narrative with incest and lechery at its heart: Mordred is, after all, Arthur's child, the expression of some dark part of the great king's self that will strike at his brain as parent and child destroy each other.

Malory has altered his sources at several points to emphasize the essential goodness of these flawed heroes, opening the way for redemption to them all, so that the end of the *Morte Darthur* is uplifting though sad. One of the most poignant of his repeated phrases, "a man living," on which Lancelot and Gawain both take their stands, leaves the way open for repentance by the man dead. Thus Gawain's spirit comes surrounded by the ladies for whom he had fought as a "man living" to warn Arthur of Mordred (p. 1620), perhaps as atonement for having so fiercely and uncharacteristically pursued Lancelot for unknowingly dispatching Gareth and Gaheris.

Both of the adulterous lovers so typical of medieval romance are ennobled by taking Holy Orders. Modern students may suspect the sincerity of these belated conversions, but Christian literature always holds out the hope of God's mercy to the repentant. (You may want to tell your students the story of the twelfth-century lovers Heloise and Abelard, whose affair was brutally ended when Heloise's uncle had Abelard, one of the great scholars of his time, castrated for having married Heloise, his pupil, in secret. Subsequently, Abelard founded an oratory, The Paraclete, where he taught, and of which the penitent Heloise eventually became Abbess.) Guinevere, whose primary concern in these excerpts seems to be her own survival, and Lancelot, who has abrogated so many sacred vows but exudes "the sweetest savor" (the odor of sanctity) as he expires, die parallel exemplary deaths. (Note the repeated details: on their deathbeds, each is surrounded by a hundred torches, and Lancelot is drawn "in the same horse-bier that Queen Guinevere was laid in.")

Matching this final rededication to spiritual concerns, a constant theme of medieval literature, is Malory's affirmation of the continuance of earthly duty. The book ends not with any of the many beautifully described death scenes (notably the famous ambiguous rendition of the passing of Arthur, the once and future king, which is another of Malory's inventions), but with a catalog of the noble knights who lived on to fight the Turk. *Morte Darthur* concludes with Malory's signature, as it were, writing in "the ninth year of the reign of King Edward the Fourth."

If you have time and your class finds historical references of interest, the relation of *Morte Darthur* to the "real world" merits some consideration. As the headnote in the anthology reminds us, Malory had ample experience of the factionalism that was tearing England apart during the fifteenth century, and his portrait of the disintegration of Arthur's Round Table probably was understood by his original audience to refract, however glancingly, the shifting political fortunes to be observed in their own time.

It is telling that the name Arthur was in vogue as a choice for a noble child in this very period. Modern audiences, whose information about the War of the Roses is usually filtered through Shakespeare's first tetralogy, will link Edward IV (if they know about him at all) with his two legitimate children, the little princes in the Tower. Malory's contemporaries, however, would have been equally aware of Edward's illegitimate but recognized son, Arthur Plantagenet. This Arthur was brought up in the household of Henry VII, founder of the Tudor dynasty, who had married Elizabeth of York, Edward's daughter. Henry and Elizabeth had two sons; the first of them, named Arthur, died before he could reign. His younger brother, Henry VIII, like his daughter Elizabeth, favored a coat of arms that included the legendary once and future king as part of its heraldry.

Topics for Writing

1. Dreams and warnings in *Morte Darthur*.
2. The struggle to live up to the ideals of the Round Table: a study of Lancelot or Gawain or Arthur.

Comparative Perspectives

1. Attitudes toward sexuality in the romance tradition—adultery as the source of passion in Arthurian legend and the *Decameron*.
2. Renunciation and redemption in *Morte Darthur* and the First Story of the First Day of the *Decameron*, or *Everyman*, or the Parable of the Prodigal Son.
3. Ideal and parody: comparing Malory's version of Arthurian materials with other medieval views of the tradition (*Lanval*, *Sir Gawain and the Green Knight*, *The Wife of Bath's Tale*).

Further Reading

See also the reading suggestions in the anthology, p. 1611.

Braswell, Mary Flowers and John Bugge. *The Arthurian Tradition*. 1988. Caroline D. Eckhardt's article, "Prophecy and Nostalgia: Arthurian Symbolism at the Close of the English Middle Ages," pp. 109–26, provides the historical information drawn on above.

Fries, Maureen and Jeanie Watson, eds. *Approaches to Teaching the Arthurian Tradition*. 1992. This volume in the MLA series has a good bibliography and includes a helpful article on teaching Malory by George R. Keiser, who describes his approach in a graduate course, pp. 131–34.

Taylor, Beverly and Elisabeth Brewer. *The Return of Arthur*. 1983. Although this book primarily examines nineteenth- and twentieth-century adaptations of Arthurian materials, it begins with an excellent prologue that discusses the particular importance of Malory to the tradition.

EVERYMAN

Backgrounds

The longer form of the title is given early in the speech of the first character, the Messenger: "The Summoning of Everyman" to a final reckoning with God. The play is not divided into acts and scenes, but lines 1–183 serve as a framework and may be considered the equivalent of a first act. After the Messenger's announcement, God in a speech of sixty-two lines declares his disappointment with humankind: his redemptive sacrifice on the Cross is generally ignored, and the human situation seems to grow steadily worse. Hence He calls on Death to summon humankind to judgment. Everyman comes on stage and is given the summons by Death, who cannot be begged or bribed to delay Everyman's answer; instead, Everyman must prepare at once to go. Here Death leaves the stage and does not return.

Now Everyman asks a long series of his companions for their help; they begin with ready promises, only to renege when they learn where Everyman must go—so much for Fellowship, Kindred, and Goods (riches, wealth). Now (Everyman's) Good Deeds is willing to go with him but has been bound to the Earth by Everyman's sins; she calls on Knowledge, who directs Everyman to Confession, who recommends Penance; after Everyman's earnest prayer of repentance and acceptance of Penance, Good Deeds is released and now free to accompany Everyman. (That is, Everyman is now absolved of his sinful condition.) Strength, Discretion, Beauty, and the Five-Wits will now assist Everyman (as long as he lives on Earth)—that is, the natural endowments of human nature can now be directed rightly instead of sinfully. Five-Wits lectures Everyman on the importance of the priesthood; it is the priest who dispenses the seven holy sacraments of the Christian life. Everyman goes briefly

offstage to receive Holy Communion and extreme unction. Soon Everyman grows weak; he learns that Strength, Discretion, Beauty, and the
Five-Wits (our familiar five senses, touch, sight, etc.) will not go with
him into the cave of death; only Good Deeds will do so and thereby
ensure his acceptance in Heaven—which is announced by an Angel
(probably a voice offstage).

Everyman is a supreme example of a literary work with allegorical
characters, that is, not individual men and women but personified
abstractions or genetic groups such as Fellowship or Kindred or Goods
or Good Deeds. As we have seen in other pieces, allegory was a favorite
pattern of literature in the Middle Ages. The headnote shows that the
abstract characters of *Everyman* may speak on stage very brisk, crisp,
sharp dialogue. The action also moves rapidly and purposefully. It is
clear, on reflection, that the play dramatizes the central moral or spiritual situation of the Christian believer, or at any rate, the medieval
Christian. Absorbed by the business and pleasures of earthly life, he (or
she) may not often remember the inevitability of death and the certainty
of divine judgment. A sudden reminder may alarm and presently disillu-
sion; there follows a genuine realization that "you can't take it"—or
"them" (other persons with whom your own life seems inseparably
involved)—with you. The desertion of Everyman by one after another of
his cherished companions is a poignant experience shared by the reader
or spectator.

Topics for Discussion and Writing

1. The role of Strength, Discretion, Beauty, and Five-Wits.
    [It is noted immediately after Everyman's reorientation that they
    will now direct and assist him on his journey. But when he
    approaches the cave of Death, they too, like his earlier companions,
    depart and leave him. What realities of human life do the two stages
    of their relationship represent? In what sense can it be said that
    Good Deeds, alone, goes with Everyman into the grave?]
2. Why are Fellowship, Kindred, and Goods effective figures in the
    play?
    [They at first cheerfully promise to go with Everyman on his pro-
    jected journey—without bothering to ask where he must go. When
    they learn his destination (Death and the Judgment of God), they
    promptly renege, one after the other. This desertion is a poignant
    experience for Everyman—and for the reader or spectator as well.]
3. Compare *Everyman* with the twentieth-century play (or film) *You
    Can't Take It with You.*
    [In both there is a withdrawal from the usual pattern of life in
    the world. The cause or motivation is different, but the result is a
    readjustment in both cases, and the two are not entirely dissimi-
    lar. The defense of the new perspective in the dialogue of the
    modern piece might correspond to the (religious) reordering in
    Everyman.]

Comparative Perspectives

1. The bracketed stage directions and much of the dialogue in this text hint at a strong pictorial style of presentation aimed at an audience used to interpreting stained-glass windows (for example, the first lines spoken by Goods, which imply that the personified figure may be represented by a money sack, or the gradual strengthening of Good Deeds, who can hardly move until Everyman undergoes penance). Discuss one or two of these moments and compare the dramatic means employed here with those in Greek or Renaissance drama.

2. God appears on stage as a character in medieval morality and mystery plays. In what other cultures do gods take roles on the stage? In what religions would this be impossible, and how does that impossibility inhibit the development of a dramatic tradition?

   [There are no ancient Jewish and Islamic plays, for example, perhaps because both religions prohibit pictorial representation of the unseeable God—cf. Moses and the burning bush, and the power of the voice of God in the Old Testament of the Bible and in the Koran.]

Further Reading

See the reading suggestions in the anthology, pp. 1629–30.

Masterpieces of the Renaissance

FRANCIS PETRARCH

Backgrounds

Petrarch's collection of lyric poetry is known as the *Canzoniere* ("Song Book") and sometimes also as the *Rime sparse* ("Scattered Rhymes"), a title taken from line 1 of the introductory sonnet. Neither of the two is Petrarch's title; his own had been, significantly, in Latin—*Rerum Vulgarium Fragmenta*, "fragments" written in the "vulgar" tongue, i.e., current poetic Italian as opposed to Latin.

The main image of Petrarch, as it has been through the centuries and justifiably remains, is that of the author of sonnets written in honor of his beloved Laura or somehow related to that central experience. The selections in the anthology belong mainly to that category. It should be noted, however, that the *Canzoniere* comprises in all 366 poems numbered by the poet himself; and though an overwhelming majority of these are sonnets (317), many are written in other forms, notably the much longer and the metrically varied *canzone*, of which there are 29. Still other forms represented in the collection are the sestina (9), the ballad (7), and the madrigal (4). Excellence in the poetic art was closely identified in Petrarch's day with technical skill in handling a number of verse patterns and in achieving variety within strict metrical norms. It was also closely identified with music. "Lyric" poetry is named for "lyre," a musical instrument; *canzone* is the Italian for "song"; and the root of the word "sonnet" is in the Latin *sonus*, "sound." Musical accompaniment was regularly seen as part of the "performance" of a poem; in fact, sonnets by Petrarch have been set to music up to our own century.

The ordering of the *Canzoniere* was made by the poet himself; to see it exclusively as a poetic diary of his love for Laura from its inception through its countless modulations to her death and to the continuing celebration of her image is to forget that not all of the *Canzoniere* is devoted to Laura. Sonnets 136–38, to give a particularly extravagant example, are invectives against the papal court at Avignon; and the *canzone* numbered 78 (not to be confused with Sonnet 78, printed in the anthology)—one of the most famous poems in the Italian language—is a lament on politically divided Italy, with an exhortation to peace, in what we may call the mode of "cultural patriotism." (A significant quotation from this poem will be found in the Machiavelli selections in the anthology, at the very close of *The Prince.*) These exceptions allowed for, however, it is fair to say that poems in praise of Laura alive make up the larger part of the collection, and poems commemorating her after death most of the rest.

During his life Petrarch was in contact, professionally and otherwise, with courts, the most memorable being that of the pope at Avignon, in Provence. That region also provides the physical landscape against which Petrarch's love for Laura is imagined. His sonnets can be partly described as courtly love poetry in the sense that they originated in an aristocratic milieu.

Love poetry has, of course, a long tradition from remotest antiquity on. Petrarch's immediate and obvious antecedents are Dante and poets such as Guido Cavalcanti (cf. Dante, *Inferno* X.52–72, and *Purgatorio* XXIV.19ff. [not included in the anthology]), Guido Guinizzelli, and the Provençal "troubadours" (see their poems in Medieval Lyrics: A Selection, pp. 1209–10, 1215–18). Apart from quotations in Latin, the only non-Italian lines in *The Divine Comedy* are spoken by the poet Arnaut Daniel in his native Provençal tongue (*Purgatorio* XXVI.140–47). Petrarch was also steeped, of course, in the culture of antiquity; and the major Latin love poets—Ovid, Tibullus—figure prominently among his sources.

Equally evident in his work are manifestations of the Christian tradition. One is the insistent connection that he makes between his love and the Passion of Christ, as shown in Sonnets 3 and 62. Another is his sense of love as guilt, in the expression of which he initiates the now-familiar Romantic image of the poet as lamenting sufferer. Closely related to both of these is his framework of repentance and confession as if after a sinful life. This, as found in the *Canzoniere,* has its chief source in the *Confessions* of St. Augustine, probably the most important influence in Petrarch's intellectual life. It would not be amiss, in fact, to think of the *Canzoniere* as Petrarch's own Confessions.

The prose selection in the anthology, the letter to Dionisio on the ascent of Mount Ventoux, is an allegory of the sinner's repentance and contrition under the decisive Augustinian influence.

Classroom Strategies

Undoubtedly the least useful strategy is to take the selections from the *Canzoniere* as parts of a poetic diary and follow the many failed attempts to reconstruct the work as an autobiographical love story. Petrarch had practical experience in matters of love—had, in fact, some illegitimate children by a mistress. But it is equally clear that his poems are not only a purification of love in its usual terrestrial senses but are also conscious models of literary convention. The persons of the speaker and his beloved have almost as little historical identity as those of the author and the object of any popular love song. A practical way to cope with this problem, if the Dante selections in the anthology have been previously studied, is to attempt a comparison and contrast between the strictly unearthly view of

Beatrice and whatever is earthly in the image of Laura. Also, as already mentioned, a complete "execution" of a Petrarchan sonnet is probably best imagined with musical accompaniment. At the very least, emphasis should be placed on the musicality of Petrarch's language; and it would be a good idea to have some of the poems read out loud in the original, vowel-rich Italian. (Italian pronunciation is easy to learn; and a colleague conversant with Italian may be available on campus.)

Topics for Discussion and Writing

1. The figure of the speaker of the poem and his varied attitudes between elation and despair.
2. The Petrarchan sonnet and its structure in comparison with the Shakespearean pattern. In particular, compare the endings of the sonnets and the relative effectiveness of Petrarch's closing lines, in Sonnet 90 for example, and that of the closing couplet in the Shakespearean form of the sonnet.
3. Choosing an appropriate passage from the *Paradiso* selections and one of the sonnets on Laura in death, indicate specific differences in the handling of the two feminine images.
4. Petrarch was a public man, a diplomat, and an extremely influential poet. So was, for example, Sir Thomas Wyatt, who introduced the Petrarchan sonnet to England. (Of Wyatt's thirty sonnets, published in *Tottel's Miscellany*—the anthology of English poems published by Richard Tottel in 1557—ten are translations from Petrarch, including the famous *My Galley*, based on #189.) Would such a multidimensional individual be conceivable today?
5. Although we read Petrarch in translation, there is no reason why a topic for discussion shouldn't be (with possible comparisons to the situation in other national literatures) the part that a literary language may have in establishing or indeed creating the identity of a country.

Comparative Perspectives

1. The *Letter to Dionisio da Borgo san Sepolcro* describes an experience that surprises Petrarch, who had begun the ascent of Mount Ventoux "eager to see what so great an elevation had to offer." Unlike the Romantic poets of the nineteenth century, who also were assiduous ascenders of mountains, Petrarch brings his copy of Augustine's *Confessions* with him on his journey, and reading it convinces him that it is more important to look within than (to put it crudely) to go sightseeing. Describe the tension between nature and belief that both Petrarch and Augustine reflect on in their writings. Compare it, if appropriate, to the view of nature in the poems of Bécquer, Leopardi, or Wordsworth, in Vol. 2 of the anthology.
2. Discuss Petrarch's facility in appropriating classical and biblical imagery in comparison with the treatment of such references in his

sources or in earlier poems, in any of the examples listed below. How does Petrarch's way of combining his sources justify considering him a Renaissance writer, although he was a contemporary of Boccaccio's?

    a. The use of The Song of Songs in Canzone #126.

    b. The treatment of Calvary in the medieval lyric on p. 1218 and in Sonnet #62.

    c. Ovid's description of Apollo's pursuit of Daphne and her subsequent metamorphosis and the quasi-metamorphosis in the vision of Laura in the last line of Sonnet #34.

    d. The meaning of Scylla and Charybdis in Virgil and their transformation in Petrarch's Sonnet #189 (see the helpful guidance in the footnote).

    e. The use of classical allusion in Sonnets #34 and 78.

3. Looking forward to one of the many ways that later poets used Petrarch, discuss the creation of the pastoral scene surrounding Laura in #126 and compare the treatment of pastoral in canto I of *Orlando Furioso* or in book IX of *Paradise Lost* (see especially lines 385–454).

Further Reading

See also the reading suggestions in the anthology, p. 1667.

Bergin, Thomas G. *Petrarch*. 1970. A useful study by the Yale Italian scholar and translator of Dante, Petrarch, and other authors.

Bergin, Thomas G., ed. *Selected Sonnets, Odes and Letters*. 1966. With introduction, principal dates in the life of Petrarch, and selected bibliography. A good source for further readings from Petrarch's works.

Bloom, Harold, ed. *Petrarch: Modern Critical Views*. 1989. An excellent collection that includes the essay by John Freccero mentioned in the headnote, as well as an intricate analysis by Robert M. Durling, "The Ascent of Mount Ventoux and The Crisis of Allegory."

Donadoni, Eugenio. *A History of Italian Literature*. 1969. See the chapters on Petrarch's life and on his Italian works. A standard, reliable account of the history of Italian literature, widely used as a textbook in Italian schools.

Harrison, Robert Pogue. *The Body of Beatrice*. 1988. Chapter 5 is "The Death of Dante's Beatrice and the Petrarchan Alternative."

Trinkaus, Charles Edward. *The Poet as Philosopher: Petrarch and the Formation of Renaissance Consciousness*. 1979. Examines how Petrarch's "poetic mentality penetrated and shaped his thought."

Wilkins, Ernest Hatch. *History of Italian Literature*. Revised by Thomas G. Bergin. 1974. Chapter 10 is dedicated to Petrarch. One of the best among the few histories of Italian literature written in English. Professor Wilkins is also a renowned Petrarch scholar.

DESIDERIUS ERASMUS

The Praise of Folly

Backgrounds

The Praise of Folly is divided into four sections; the selections in the anthology are from the first, second, and fourth parts. The work, originally written in Latin, is a satire for which the author has adopted, with tongue in cheek, the structure and manner of a public oration. The "goddess" Folly, after giving her own jocose genealogy as the illegitimate daughter of the god of wealth and plenty (part 1), describes the manner of her birth and identifies the symbolic persons who attend her as she appears before a varied assembly of listeners. She proceeds to declare herself (part 2) the true life-giving goddess on the ground that every man in the act of procreation inevitably makes a fool of himself—hence the very conception of life is Folly's doing. From this premise follows the conclusion that all truly human activity must necessarily contain the life-giving element of folly/foolishness. Folly conducts this argument colorfully, relying on such classic devices of oratory as rhetorical questions, apt quotations, and, above all, vivid anecdotes. Prominent among the targets of her satire are the Stoic philosophers, whose attempt to "eliminate from their wiseman all emotional perturbations" (p. 1686) she naturally scorns. What could such a regimen result in but a "marble statue of a man" unfit for any responsible position ("What army would select him for their general? Indeed, what woman would consent to marry him or put up with him as a husband?")?

Not unaware of life's pains and disappointments, Folly prescribes as remedy a good measure of "foolish" self-love and self-deception. Here again, in a sequence of quick satirical strokes she celebrates the foolish and happy victims of deceit along with their deceivers. Among physicians, for instance, "the more ignorant, bold, and thoughtless one of them is, the more he is valued by these high and mighty princes. Besides, medicine . . . is nothing but a subdivision of flattery, just like rhetoric." As deceivers, lawyers rank next to doctors:

> In fact, I wonder if they don't hold the highest rank of all, since their profession—not to speak of it myself—is universally ridiculed as asinine by the philosophers. Still, all business transactions, from the smallest to the greatest, are absolutely controlled by these asses. They acquire large estates, while a theologian who has carefully read through whole bookcases of divinity nibbles on dried peas, waging continual war with bedbugs and lice. (p. 1690)

Asses, in other words, wait upon other asses, and "everyone is all the happier the more ways he is deluded" (p. 1694). Other categories of foolish but happy maniacs are listed and illustrated in as many brilliant little sketches—hunters, gamblers, nobility buffs, the superstitious.

At this point the speaker—quite transparently a mouthpiece for Erasmus the Christian humanist—shifts to religious "superstitions," to

"absurdities . . . so foolish that even I am almost ashamed of them," such
as the belief in the specific powers of particular saints: "One offers relief
from a toothache, another helps women in labor, another restores stolen
goods. . . . Some saints have a variety of powers, especially the virgin
mother of God, to whom the ordinary run of men attribute more almost
than to her son" (p. 1696). Further on, in the same vein: "Likewise, if any
saint is more legendary or poetic—for example, think of George or
Christopher or Barbara—you will see that such a saint is worshiped with
far more devotion than Peter or Paul or Christ himself" (p. 1699).

The culminating association between religious piety and Folly occurs
in the final section, where the character of the "Christian Fool" is
depicted. Showing in familiar scriptural quotations Christ's preference
for the meek and simple-minded, Folly claims among her followers the
Savior himself, who, "though he was the wisdom of the Father, became
somehow foolish in order to relieve the folly of mortals" (p. 1702).
Along this line, in the grand finale of her oration, Folly vividly describes
the experience of the mystic and defines it as that portion of folly that
will not be taken away by death and as "something very like madness," a
"madness" that is only "a faint taste, as it were, of that future happiness." She realizes at this point, however, that she has forgotten who
she is and has "'gone beyond the pale,'" and comes to the gracefully
ironical and self-deprecating conclusion of her "torrent of jumbled
words" (p. 1705).

The Praise of Folly, though it is far and away Erasmus's most popular
work, occupies a very small place within the wide range of his activity as
a writer, scholar, translator, editor, theologian, and polemicist. He is said
to have completed it in a week (citing the quotations from memory)
while he was the guest of Thomas More at Bucklersbury in the autumn
of 1509 and possibly for this reason is also said to have ascribed little
value to it. Whatever the truth may be in this regard, the piece is as
impressive in its learning and as sober in its implications as anything he
ever wrote. There is no doubt either about its literary merits, the elegance and liveliness of its language, the gusto of its author's droll inventions. Behind the humorous façade, Erasmus's familiarity with the great
texts of the ancient and the medieval worlds—with the Greco-Roman as
well as the Judeo-Christian traditions—is fully visible. More particular
models may also be cited. From the ancient world, the Greek satirist
Lucian, some of whose work Erasmus had translated into Latin, and
from Erasmus's own time, Sebastian Brant's *Ship of Fools* (*Narrenschiff,*
1497), of which there was a Latin translation in 1500, an English one in
1509.

Classroom Strategies

Our selection can be managed in one assignment. As with Petrarch
and most other authors in this section, it may be advisable to explore
first the degree to which the class is acquainted with the main elements
of the Greco-Roman and the Judeo-Christian traditions. Questions on

mythological concepts and themes, such as "Zeus/Jove, father of the gods," or on the historical conflicts between Roman Catholic and Protestant churches in the period of the Reformation will yield information on how to proceed. A basic point to be stressed is that at the time Christianity was also politics, religious divisions and doctrinal controversy being everywhere rampant. Discussions of the meaning of the Reformation and Counter-Reformation may need to be elicited together with class views of the function of satire—both in that era and in our own. Ensuing discussion should bring out the point that Erasmus favored direct contact with Scripture and a return to a simpler purified ritual. In examining the passages about "superstitious" Christian practices, it will be clear that he had particularly the Roman Catholic Church in mind. Unlike the extreme reformers, however, he wished to preserve the unity of the Church and to improve it from within, so he was also well received in papal circles. Under the polemical, flippant surface, it is important to detect the wise and conciliatory nature of Erasmus's piety. At the same time, beneath that surface, it is important to note the home thrusts at absurdities still very much with us today.

Topics for Discussion and Writing

1. Take what seem to be the most memorable objects of Folly's mockery (the Stoics, the Roman Catholic Church, various categories of fools and maniacs, etc.) and ask the class to explain by what means the satirical effects are obtained.
2. Satire may work in two opposite directions at the same time—that is to say, both criticize and undercut the criticism; both praise and undercut the praise. Work on specific passages to see how this happens. Give special attention to the handling of wisdom versus foolishness.
3. The presence of the author is sometimes more, sometimes less detectable under the mask of Folly. With particular emphasis on the selection from part 4, identify passages where the author's presence shows clearly.
4. Satire has been described as presupposing, in the object satirized, some sort of deviation from an accepted or even ideal norm. Discuss what norms can be inferred from a reading of *The Praise of Folly*—what kinds of acts and attitudes, in other words, does the author value?

Comparative Perspective

Folly distinguishes between two different kinds of madness. Explain what she means. From your reading this semester, give examples of both sorts. Given the evidence you cite, do you agree that some forms of madness are to be desired?

[The figure of the vengeful cuckold or Orlando are examples of the first kind; the duped husband of the fabliaux exemplifies the second.]

Further Reading

See also the reading suggestions in the anthology, p. 1682.

Bainton, Roland H. *Erasmus of Christendom.* 1969. An illustrated biography, with emphasis on Erasmus as a Christian philosopher. With notes and bibliography.

Huizinga, Johan. *Erasmus and the Age of Reformation.* Trans. F. Hopman. 1957. A thorough, illustrated study, originally published in 1924, of Erasmus's life and career by the famous author of *The Waning of the Middle Ages.* Chapter IX deals with *The Praise of Folly.*

Olin, John C. *Six Essays on Erasmus.* 1979. Essay 4 is on *The Praise of Folly.*

Thompson, Geraldine. *Under Pretext of Praise: Satiric Mode in Erasmus' Fiction.* 1973. A study of Erasmus's fiction with emphasis on Erasmus as an educator and on his use of irony. Chapter II deals with *The Praise of Folly* as a parody as well as a moral indictment of European society in Erasmus' time.

Tracy, James D. *The Politics of Erasmus: A Pacifist Intellectual and His Political Milieu.* 1978. Erasmus's place in European intellectual history as a political philosopher, with emphasis on the "national matrix" of his political opinions.

Zweig, Stefan. *Erasmus of Rotterdam.* 1934. By an eminent novelist and biographer.

NICCOLÒ MACHIAVELLI

The Prince

Backgrounds

The Prince in a very general sense belongs to the same category as *The Book of the Courtier,* presenting sets of instructions and ultimately the description of an ideal type (the "employer" of the courtier, as it were). Yet from the very first brief chapter (not in the anthology), a briskly didactic tone differentiates it unmistakably from Castiglione's work:

> All the states and governments that ever had or now have power over men were and are of two sorts: either republics or princely states. And princely states also are of two sorts: either hereditary . . . or else new. And the new ones are either brand-new . . . or they are like grafts freshly joined to the hereditary states of a prince. . . . New acquisitions of this sort are either accustomed to living under a prince, or used to being free; they may be acquired either by force of other people's arms or with one's own, either by fortune or by strength [*virtù*].

To each of the twenty-six chapters of *The Prince,* Machiavelli gave a strictly undecorative explanatory title, originally in Latin, then the standard language of scholarly communication. The style of the work makes it one of the supreme examples of vigor and originality in the history of Italian prose. The general distribution of the material is announced in chapter 1. Chapter 2 takes up hereditary princedoms. Chapters 2 and 3 deal with the conquest and maintenance of new provinces by a state already possessing its own structure and form of government. Chapters 4 and 5 concentrate on how best to annex cities or princedoms that had previously lived in freedom under their own laws. Chapters 6 through 9 handle newly formed princedoms acquired by the force of arms (6–7), by crime (8), or by the choice of fellow citizens (9). Chapter 10, as a kind of corollary, discusses the military defense of such newly formed states. Chapter 11 moves to "ecclesiastical states," i.e., the dominions of the pope, their unusual nature, and the vast current power of the papacy. Chapters 12 through 14 examine what to Machiavelli and to most modern statesmen is the major problem in the government of a state—the organization of its armed forces. According to Machiavelli, the prince must not enlist mercenaries but rather have his own armies, the art of war being the only one that pertains to a sovereign. Chapters 15 through 23, in turn, concentrate on the qualities and codes of behavior that should characterize an efficient ruler and inspire his conduct. The uses of praise and blame, of liberality and stinginess, of cruelty and clemency, and finally of keeping or not keeping promises are expressed in a form so definitive and lucid they can hardly be summarized. For a specimen, see the second paragraph of chapter 18, which is possibly the most famous and controversial passage in the history of political writing.

Criteria of efficiency and political expediency pervade the advice given to the prince in chapters 19 through 24. These treat such diverse matters as how to avoid contempt and hatred (19); the utility of protecting the city-state with fortresses (20); the means to acquire a prestigious reputation, the dangers of neutrality, and the recognition to be granted artists and men of talent (21); the way to select and judge private counselors (22), with a corollary on avoiding flatterers (23). Chapter 24 concentrates on the present situation of Italian princedoms and prepares for the last two chapters, where, as indicated more elaborately in the headnote (see pp. 1706–07), the "realistic" and the "poetic" methods are mingled.

The origin of *The Prince* is best described in Machiavelli's letter to Francesco Vettori (pp. 1708–09). Vettori, a prominent public figure under the Medici, was a friend and frequent correspondent of Machiavelli's, in spite of political divergencies; he had been instrumental in obtaining from Pope Leo X (Giovanni de' Medici) Machiavelli's release from imprisonment (cf. the headnote, p. 1706), followed by his confinement to the small estate he owned near Florence, where he wrote *The Prince*. From early in 1513, Machiavelli had begun the writings that were eventually to become his *Discourses on the First Ten Chapters of Livy*, the culminating result of his meditations on Roman history and of his passionate interest in its teachings. In Machiavelli's case, as we know, the strict meaning of Renaissance as the "rebirth" of ancient culture has a particularly concrete validity; for him, the Romans offered supreme models in all areas of human endeavor, most particularly as examples of that political and military competence that in the princes of contemporary Italy he found wanting.

The reasons generally given for Machiavelli's interruption of the *Discourses* to write *The Prince* between July and December of 1513 are highly speculative. Possibly, once launched on the task of political analysis, he felt an understandable urge to draw on his own experiences as a political man and observer of political events in his own time and place. Possibly, too, he hoped that his political sagacity as shown in *The Prince* would capture the attention of the dominant Medici family and bring him a new employment with them.

Machiavelli's sources are mainly his readings in ancient history and his own political experience. Though *The Prince* has resemblances, as noticed earlier, to the established genre of the manual of instruction, its matter, manner, and impact put it beyond easy classification. In Castiglione, our other instance of this kind of literature, apparent similarities of content and conception only put the differences in sharper focus. Castiglione was not unaware of the uses of power, and his courtier's highest manifestation of loyalty is the service of his prince on the battlefield. But his accent falls on the esthetic aspect of human actions, on "style" in performance, and on government of the inner man rather than government of other men. In Machiavelli, on the other hand, even the final "Roman dream" has its roots in his practical notion of Roman political competence, efficiency, and military preparedness.

Classroom Strategies

The Prince offers no special textual difficulties. Its statements, however startling, are as cuttingly clear as anything in political writing. The examples drawn from history may be puzzling inasmuch as they refer to particular and often obscure episodes; yet the contexts in which they are presented, plus the footnotes provided in the anthology, should suffice to suggest the type of situations and the themes they illustrate. Maps may be helpful, not to teach geography or history, but to create in the student's mind some concrete idea of the location and respective sizes of such political entities of the day as the Kingdom of France, the Papal States, and the larger Italian city-states. As for the "moral" aspects of Machiavelli's teachings, a look forward to the "devilish" Machiavelli image through the centuries and particularly to the Elizabethan stage "Machiavel" may be in order. Finally, here as always, reading significant passages aloud will help bring out the dramatic aspect of Machiavelli's prose.

Topics for Discussion and Writing

1. Granted that Machiavelli's own historical context is remote, how far does his pattern of contrasts between political ideals and concrete realities apply today? What do modern rulers of states mean by *realpolitik*?
2. Attempt to define in specific passages the borderline between "realism" (practical advice, emphasis on military preparedness, etc.) and

"myth" (the ideally equipped leader, the mirage of a unified Italian state). A close analysis of the last chapter, or even only of its last two paragraphs, may be one of many ways to see how the terms of that contrast can coexist, as it were, in the same breath.

3. Taking specific passages from *The Prince*, identify the characteristics that make Machiavelli's style effective.
4. Discuss the extent of Machiavelli's "amorality," and his basic alibi that "if man were good. . . ."
5. Compare and contrast Machiavelli's idea of Fortune with the religious idea of man's free will and, on the other hand, with the meaning of "luck" when we refer to a contemporary political leader as being lucky.

Comparative Perspective

How would Machiavelli judge the actions of some of the rulers depicted in the works you have been studying?

[Candidates for discussion include Agamemnon in the *Iliad*, Oedipus in *Oedipus the King*, Hrothgar in *Beowulf*, Guzmán in *Fuente Ovejuna*.]

Further Reading

See also the reading suggestions in the anthology, pp. 1707–08.

Anglo, Sydney. *Machiavelli: A Dissection*. 1969. A study of Machiavelli's works and political thought through analysis and quotations from his works; with bibliography. Hale calls this book "refreshingly iconoclastic but somewhat too tart."

Bondanella, Peter E., and Mark Musa, eds. *The Portable Machiavelli*. 1979. A good general introduction to Machiavelli's life and works. The introduction is brief and cogent and includes sections on the historical context of *The Prince*, politics and history in Machiavelli, and on Machiavelli today. A good anthology with ample possibilities for further readings.

Hulliung, Mark. *Citizen Machiavelli*. 1983. Separates Machiavelli from the tradition of "civic humanism" and describes him as "the first and one of the greatest subversives of the humanist tradition."

Mazzeo, Joseph Anthony. *Renaissance and Revolution: The Remaking of European Thought*. 1965. See the chapter on Machiavelli.

Pitkin, Anna F. *Fortune Is a Woman: Gender and Politics in the Thought of Machiavelli*. 1984. A study of Machiavelli "in terms of ambivalence about manhood."

Pocock, J. G. A. *The Machiavellian Moment*. 1975. See particularly chapter VI, B, "Machiavelli's *Il Principe*." An attempt to "selectively and thematically define . . . the moment, and the manner, in which Machiavelli's thought made its appearance within the specific historical context of the Florentine republic."

Wilkins, Ernest Hatch. *A History of Italian Literature*. Revised by Thomas G. Bergin. 1974. Chapter 23 deals with Machiavelli and Guicciardini.

LUDOVICO ARIOSTO

Orlando Furioso

Classroom Strategies and Topics for Discussion

In approaching Ariosto's *Orlando Furioso,* perhaps your first task is to establish how adding romance to epic transforms the heroic tradition with which students have become familiar. Placing Ariosto's introductory verses alongside those of Homer and/or Virgil, students should immediately see the difference between the classical poet's conventional deference to the Muse and the Renaissance poet's bolder announcement of his mission. Working in the shadow of many predecessors, including the medieval accounts of Roland and Boiardo's more recent treatment of that same hero in love, Ariosto will nevertheless set "down what has never before been recounted in prose and rhyme." To the somber Virgilian formula, the writer of romance epic adds new themes, not the least his own identification with his hero: like Orlando, once renowned for "his great prudence," the narrator struggles under the burden of an apparently ruthless mistress. Instead of an omniscient Muse, he addresses himself to a patron (yet later on in his long poem, Ariosto will make a number of sly, if apparently complimentary, references to the Este family that he served, of a sort that Virgil could never have dared). To launch their narratives, the classical poets appeal for an informed elucidation of divine motives. Ariosto's declarative self-assurance is a mark of the secularity of the *Orlando Furioso.*

A look at Ariosto's references to armor will underscore his burlesque handling of serious martial themes. The discomfiture of walking around fully armed is frequently noted, especially when one is intent on raping a lady. Ferrau's preoccupation with his lost helmet typifies the petty concerns of these paladins, accentuated by the lineage of their helmets; to demonstrate the debased treatment of the Matter of Troy (and the Matter of France) in this poem, have your students recall the emotional power in the ancient references to Hector's helmet and compare it to Ferrau's concerns.

With the introduction of Angelica, it will be helpful to define the topography of romance epic. As the headnote makes clear, the *Orlando Furioso* covers most of the known world, but no one would consult this poem for information about the real places it mentions. Close attention to the description of Angelica's flight in the opening section of canto I shows how the poem's pastoral terrain mirrors shifting psychological states even as it embodies presumably stable allegorical meanings. If you have taught *Gilgamesh* or Dante's *Inferno,* your students have already been in dark forests; the *Orlando* allows urban and suburban readers familiar with sanitized camping grounds to reconsider why the woods have figured in so much great literature of the past as the site of mental anguish and spiritual crisis.

Angelica's flight is rendered as nightmare, and the telling epic simile that likens her to "a baby fawn or kid who has watched through the leaves of the wood where he was born, and has seen the leopard's fangs close on his mother's throat" will resonate throughout the poem. Her (dubious) virginity is conventionally but significantly imagined in similar terms: once the rose "is plucked from her mother-stalk," she loses all. Callously deciding to use Sacripant as a protector in the dark forest, Angelica announces herself to him, with this result: "Never was such joy, such amazement to be seen in a mother's eyes when she lifted them to look on her son whom she had bewailed and lamented for dead as she heard the troops return without him: such, though was the Saracen's joy, such his wonder on suddenly beholding her angel's face." Three different figures of speech in close succession have identified Angelica as an abandoned orphan. Taken seriously, they seems to suggest that, in the dark wood of life, human beings are existentially alone.

In the same breath, of course, you need to instill in your students an appreciation of Ariosto's exquisitely balanced seriocomic tone. The pathos is (often) real; so (always) is the ridiculousness of the overblown rhetoric. When the narrative shifts to Ruggiero and the rugged hero's unruly mount starts tearing trees apart, other facets of the European pastoral tradition come to the fore. Astolfo is caught in—not by—a tree. You and your students may want to debate how sorry we should feel for Astolfo. From a serious perspective, this image of the Christian soul trapped in the material world might conjure up memories of Dante's Pier delle Vigne; from an entirely different vantage point, Astolfo, who lacks the dignity of this literary precursor, may be closer to Bruin the Bear, farcically entrapped in a tree by Renard the Fox, who has lured him there with visions of a honeycomb. And Alcina's garden evokes other, more ironic pastoral antecedents, drawing both on Ovid and the allegorical geography of the medieval romance.

Without losing sight of Ariosto's way of adapting prior writers' themes and images, you might ask your students to characterize that which is distinctively Ariostan. His treatment of sexuality should be an easy way to introduce this discussion. On the one hand, the poem titillates with surprisingly graphic details: note, for example, the poet's readiness to cede his descriptive office to Alcina and Ruggiero in bed, "the more so as they frequently had a second tongue in their mouth" (p. 1744), or to Richardet, who is the narrator when Fiordispina is led to discover the proof of his sex. This soft porn reaches its apogee in the extraordinary description of the impotent hermit's "flop-eared nag" (p. 1754). On the other hand, Ariosto's symbolic universe takes sexuality, and (as the headnote indicates) the horse as its embodiment, seriously.

One useful way into a discussion of horses and the control of sexual energy is to ask students what term the *Orlando Furioso* uses for "knight." Someone is sure to know the word "cavallo," which opens up an inquiry into the equine vocabulary of "chivalry." Why do we build equestrian statues? Why is horsemanship so central to the idea of knighthood in the Romance languages, while the Germanic languages stress instead apprenticeship and service ("knecht" derives ultimately from the Old High German word for "boy")? A comparative view of the heroic values

represented by *Beowulf* (and embodied in Chaucer's latter-day very perfect knight) would be illuminating here. There is a hint of glamor, if not
outright self-aggrandizement, built into the notion of the cavalier (even
the use of the word in English to mean "disdainful" or "offhand" suggest
this) that the humble knight eschews.

Ariosto's concerns differ from those of the old oral poets in many ways,
of course. If time permits, the *Orlando Furioso* offers a good introduction
to the complexity of Renaissance attitudes towards reason. Alcina's sister,
Logistilla, stands for Reason in one of the clearest allegorical details in
the poem. How logical human action can ever really be remains a question, however. Ruggiero backslides after his immersion in Logistilla's
realm, and neither human reason nor human strength can solve all problems. When pressed, even the bravest must turn to magic. Of the implements most frequently mentioned in the selections available in the
anthology, it is notable that both the shield of Atlas and the ring of Angelica solve dilemmas by transcending reason. The shield gives its bearer
power because it dazzles when uncovered, blinding one's opponent's
eyes, the locus of sight and understanding. Similarly, the ring of Angelica
confers invisibility when the bearer takes it in the mouth, the locus from
which speech—the word, the Logos—emerges.

Another quintessential Renaissance concern is addressed in the poet's
many self-conscious references to his own artistic method. He compares
himself to a musician selecting "different strings, fresh harmonies, as he
seeks effects, now muted, now strident" (p. 1752). Too vigorous a quest
of variety, of course, threatens to leave an audience disoriented and
destabilized. You might want to ask your students why Ariosto's narrative
so often breaks off in the middle of an episode. A ready answer, which is
not to be despised, is "for the sake of suspense."

Recent criticism of romance epic prefers to cite psychoanalytic expla-
nations for the displacement, condensation, interpolation, and fragmentation of narrative in the *Orlando Furioso*. Without discoursing on
critical theory, you may refer your students to the rapid succession of
events in Orlando's dream (p. 1757), which is no more dreamlike than
the episodes that enmesh the poem's many characters when they are
awake. At base this narrative method illuminates the identity crises
through which so many of Ariosto's characters pass. Like most Renaissance texts, his poem is not conceived in terms of the realistic development of character that students brought up on late-nineteenth-century
prose fiction expect. It nevertheless provides a variety of subtle nonlinear
depictions of personality development and, more typically, of neurotic
individuals' failure to establish a secure sense of self.

Adapting the epic simile to such concerns, Ariosto manages to endow a
stock character like Angelia with a modicum of internal life. When we
first meet her, she is adamantine in her scorn for her suitors (see pp.
1731, 1753, 1764). Her fate, fittingly enough, is to be chained to a rock
and all but mistaken for a statue. Likened in the first frenzied canto to a
ewe lamb, as we have seen, she is recalled by Orlando in this mode again
(p. 1756). The narrative suggests, however, that Angelica fell in love with

Medor because he needed her—because for him she served a maternal role. If this is a sign of female maturation, it also is the point at which the poet essentially loses interest—he leaves his characters when they become domesticated and, presumably, boring.

Psychological complexity is also hinted at in romance literature by the doubling of characters. Students familiar with Shakespeare's *Twelfth Night* will see in the twins Bradamant and Richardet precursors of Viola and Sebastian. The unfulfilled yearning so endemic in the *Orlando Furioso* is crystallized in the story of Fiordispina. Significantly, the Spanish princess comes upon shorn, armor-clad Bradamant "asleep in the tender grass" (p. 1779). On the one hand, her appearance declares her masculinity; but on the other, her posture and surroundings betray her underlying softness. Bradamant quickly explains that she is a woman, and Fiordispina has no recourse but to dream. With the appearance of Richardet, who invents an Ovidian metamorphosis to explain "Bradamant"'s new accoutrements, Ariosto suggests how complex are the links between gender and identity, mischievously skirting the porous boundaries of sexual orientation.

The longing for completion that drives men and women to seek for their lost other half (as expressed in the parable of the separated egg in Plato's *Symposium*, to which, you may want to note, reference is made in the debate following Story Eight of Day One of the *Heptameron*) is further complicated when twins mirror each other. The martial woman, like Bradamant, is a figure out of a dream, almost hermaphroditic and supernaturally desirable. Typically, it should be emphasized, Ariosto's poem is conscious of the delicacy of Bradamant's sensibility; yet in detailing Fiordispina's earthier needs, it also coarsens the love theme in the bawdy bedtime scene between Richardet and the disbelieving Fiordispina.

This episode can also lead into a discussion of the fragility of the self in Ariosto' world. Bradamant and Richardet seem to be two versions of the same person; how much worse for two versions to coexist within one frame, as they do in the case of mad Orlando. If flux is frightening, so can stability be a horrifying state in this poem. Too firm a constancy, as Orlando's case makes clear, can be a danger; certainly students should be asked to comment on the brutal physicality of the naked, demented knight. Is every human being capable of acts that we would like to consider subhuman?

Another instance of constancy that leads to brutality may be found in the fate of Isabel. In choosing to die by his hand rather than to be raped, she elicits from Rodomont a definitive enactment of the self-centered attack on her person that he had been planning all along. Even here, in an episode that Ariosto takes as an occasion for a compliment to Isabella D'Este that seems to be deeply felt, he allows himself a moment of comic deflation that inspired no less a satirist than W. S. Gilbert in *The Mikado*: "Her head bounced thrice: from it a voice could be clearly heard pronouncing the name of Zerbin, to follow whom she had found so novel a way to escape from the Saracen" (p. 1785).

In the midst of flux, both personal and narrative, Ariosto is acutely sensitive to the need to provide some sense of continuity, however mockingly. One of the devices that links the poem together, the brilliant introductory stanzas that shift from one set of concerns to another, increasingly deal with the poet's identification with Orlando mad for love. Interestingly, he links Orlando to Ceres in quest of Proserpine, the mother searching for her daughter, as he is searching for the Angelica he views as a motherless ewe lamb (p. 1768). Disabused of the notion that Angelica needs him, he runs mad, and at this point Ariosto forcibly reiterates his kinship with Orlando. This link between the poet and his titular hero suggests how much the human experiences of love and desire depend on literary conventions. Orlando, the most desperate of the poem's lovers, is also the most literate and linguistically gifted of its heroes. Indeed, if not for his command of languages, he would be incapable of deciphering Medor's ecstatic verses, which give the evidence of Angelica's desertion of all other men for this Saracen peasant.

In his very madness, Orlando becomes a link in another literary chain. Rejecting the life of reason and of courtly responsibility, dragging a dead mare in his wake, Orlando (as the headnote suggests) defiles the *cheval* at the root of chivalry. World literature has always found in the distracted hero a powerful sign of the folly of human ambition and pretension; at the same time, it is always the gifted who run mad, thereby accentuating the ironic sense of what is lost when reason and measure become impossible for the human being to maintain. To gauge the range of meanings that may be gleaned from the spectre of talent run amok, you might point to one of the earliest plays of Sophocles, *Ajax,* which explores the suicidal rage of that Greek hero (see the headnote to *Oedipus the King*), and all his dramatic descendants—which include virtually all of Shakespeare's tragic heroes. If you've read Lucian's *A True Story,* remind your students that "a dose of hellebore" has been prescribed to rehabilitate Ajax and earn him a place at "the Heroes' banquet" on the Isle of the Blest (p. 993).

Lucian is a powerful presence in the ending of the *Orlando Furioso,* when Astolfo takes over the poet's role in the concluding movement of the poem by going to the moon and restoring the feckless hero with whom Ariosto has too fully identified himself. Having fallen under Alcina's spell because he mistook a whale for an island (another motif that echoes Lucian's story), misreading flux for stability, Astolfo can finally be trusted to rescue Orlando's missing wits. He alone, perhaps, may have profited from his experience.

Astolfo's literary critical chat with St. John the Evangelist, author of the Apocalypse, provides a fitting ending for a discussion of Ariosto's long poem. Consigning "verses written in praise of patrons" to what one critic has dubbed the "lunar junkyard," and commenting on the power of poets to burnish a hero's reputation beyond merit, Ariosto indulges in one more self-reflective set piece. In the end, anticipating postmodernism, the Renaissance writer seems to say that poetry is really about poetry. Fully clothed in Hector's armor, Ruggiero concludes the narrative by defeating

Rodomont, the embodiment of "rodomontade," and the poem comes to its terse, abrupt end, imitating Virgil at its conclusion as it had in its beginning.

Topics for Writing

1. Landscape description in the *Orlando Furioso*.
2. Angelica as a Petrarchan heroine.
3. The evolution of Ruggiero.
4. The role of the poet in the *Orlando Furioso*.

Comparative Perspectives

1. Roland/ Orlando: what distinguishes the hero as he appears in *The Song of Roland*? How does Ariosto redefine him in *Orlando Furioso*? How does the difference between the two tell us about the different concerns of the early medieval and the high Renaissance periods?
2. Poets and patrons, writers and courts: Ariosto and the Este family, Virgil and Augustus, Machiavelli and the Medici, *The Book of the Courtier*, the *Heptameron*.
3. Defining knighthood and chivalry—compare Ariosto's knights to any of the following: Beowulf, Gawain, Lancelot, Don Quixote.
4. The hero mad for love: how does a comparison of the circumstances that drive Orlando and Othello to distraction clarify the difference between romance fiction and psychological drama?

Further Reading

See also the reading suggestions in the anthology, p. 1726.

Giamatti, A. Bartlett. *Exile and Change in Renaissance Literature*. 1984. A magisterial discussion of the horse motif, with a probing analysis of Orlando's madness.

Quint, David. "Astolfo's Voyage to the Moon." *Yale Italian Studies* I (1977): 398–408. On the "lunar junkyard" and the impossibility of transcendent meaning in Ariosto's epic.

Reynolds, Barbara, trans. *Orlando Furioso*. 2 vols. 1975. A contemporary English verse translation, with excellent apparatus, including maps, charts of characters and devices, and genealogical tables.

Wiggins, Peter DeSa. *Figures in Ariosto's Tapestry: Character and Design in the* Orlando Furioso. 1986. Particularly interesting on Ariosto's female characters, whom Wiggins sees as more than cardboard caricatures.

BALDESAR CASTIGLIONE

The Book of the Courtier

Backgrounds

The Book of the Courtier is a book of etiquette meant to be useful to gentlemen (and ladies) who lived and worked at court in the service of aristocratic rulers of states. Its form, traditional in Renaissance literature, is that of a dialogue, or more precisely of a conversation. Even more specifically, it is a transcription, formalized but nonetheless brilliant and sometimes witty, of after-dinner talk among people well versed in the customs and requirements of court life. Its style in the original has long been regarded as a model of proper Renaissance Italian, classically formal and yet supple and graceful. Its larger setting is one of the states that composed the mosaic of the then-divided Italy, the duchy of Urbino. Its narrower setting may be imagined to be one of the halls in Urbino's splendid ducal palace. The conversationalists, or dramatis personae, are assembled from different parts of Italy and represent some of the most illustrious families in their respective city-states: a Gonzaga from Mantua, a Bembo from Venice, a Medici from Florence. The local ruler, the duke of Urbino, Guidobaldo da Montefeltro, is irremediably ill and has the habit of retiring early. Hence the evenings at court, with their conversations and games, are ruled over by the authoritative but gentle Duchess Elisabetta, who often delegates her authority to the Countess Emilia, née Gonzaga, one of her ladies-in-waiting. One such evening is imagined by Castiglione to have been the origin of his famous work. Various forms of entertainment are suggested by different members of the party; the one chosen, somewhat unexpectedly, is a purely intellectual "game" proposed by a Count Federico Fregoso from Genoa. The "game" will consist in composing, through well-regulated debate, a description of the qualities and functions of a worthy courtier, or indeed of "forming with words a perfect Courtier."

The work is divided into four parts corresponding to the four evenings of the debate. Book I, after the exordium and the choice of the "game," describes the qualities and capacities required of the model courtier, from the indispensable nobility of his birth to his dexterity in his major profession—the handling of arms in war, in dueling, and in peaceful tournaments. There follow rules and recommendations concerning physical and moral virtues, speech, manners, generosity, the ornaments of culture and the arts. Book II (not in the anthology), partially elaborates on and perfects some of the theme of book I, adding details on music, dance, gracefulness, benevolence, humaneness, and the art of conversation, including counsel on how to handle, in the proper measure, wordplay, jokes, irony, witty repartee, and *burle* (practical jokes). Book III (not in the anthology) discusses the *Donna di Corte* or *Donna di Palazzo*, i.e., the lady-in-waiting or other female member of the court. The qualities, education, and norms of behavior appropriate to her are elaborated on in their similarities to and their differences from those of the male courtier. Examples of feminine excellence are taken from all ages and praised; immodesty and ostentatiousness are blamed.

The first part of book IV deals with the ways in which the courtier, who is not only a loyal subordinate but also a wise counselor to his prince, may conquer the latter's good graces by advising him wisely on such varied matters as war and peace, the active and contemplative life, justice, magnanimity, religion without superstition, and the respective merits of different forms of government. The latter part of the book centers on the sentiment and practice of love by the courtier, in youth and in old age, and finds its culmination in Pietro Bembo's discourse on earthly love transforming to divine love, just as the work itself moves from matters of civilized behavior to concerns of the soul. The selections in the anthology contain the most classic and influential passages on the nature and accomplishments of the courtier. Of the "Words" that, according to the announced purpose, shall "form" the ideal picture of the courtier, some are key terms, particularly "grace" and *sprezzatura*, a Castiglione coinage usually translated as "nonchalance." (For further definition, see below.)

The "courtesy book" as a genre was common in Renaissance culture. The form goes back to Plato's dialogues, and "Platonism" in a generic sense is to be found also in Castiglione's aiming at an ideal form (the *perfect* courtier). But the major source of Castiglione's treatise is, of course, his own experience as a courtier. Though much of that experience in its practical results was negative and disappointing (see the biographical data in the anthology, p. 1811), Castiglione continued to pursue his established aim through his long years of labor on the book with an ever-increasing tendency to idealize what was rarely ideal.

Classroom Strategies

A major difficulty in teaching Castiglione is the remoteness of the society and customs he depicts. On the other hand, *The Book of the Courtier* offers a splendid opening for discussions of the practical usefulness of utopias in establishing an ideal, however unattainable, and of the other kinds of "how-to" books that abound in our own age. The *Courtier*'s own description of its courtly milieu may be enhanced by obtaining from your art department illustrations of the place (the ducal palace at Urbino) and some of the participating characters (e.g., the portrait of Castiglione himself by Raphael or Piero della Francesca's portrait of the duke of Montefeltro). You may also bring the participants closer by reminding the class that they are, in their way, simply government officials in an age when aristocrats had the responsibilities of public office.

The other possible stumbling block—the artificiality of Castiglione's dialogue—should not be exaggerated. The custom of orchestrated conversation survives even in modern times, not only in the society represented, say, in the first chapter of *War and Peace* but also in such contemporary institutions as the panel or roundtable or the television talk show. Moreover, since a large part of our selections concerns the courtier's achieving such expertise in the arts of dueling and dance that he can exercise them without apparent effort—i.e., with *sprezzatura*—Olympic sports activities offer a wide range of comparisons.

Topics for Discussion and Writing

1. Discuss the individual qualities given to the main characters in *The Book of the Courtier,* considering also such matters as differences in age and personal history.
2. Attempt a definition of *sprezzatura* more detailed and inclusive than the simple, approximate translation as "nonchalance."
3. How many writers whom you have studied this term would agree with the Count that the artist's goal is "to conceal art"?

Comparative Perspectives

1. If the students have read the Boccaccio selections in the anthology, a clarifying discussion can center on the characters in the *Courtier* as compared and contrasted with those who take turns telling each other tales in the *Decameron.*
2. A parallel topic can center on the function of the "frame" story as an organizing element in both works.
3. If the students have read Machiavelli, a discussion can center on the likenesses and differences in the ideal of the Renaissance man as presented in *The Prince* and the *Courtier.*
4. Compare the aspects of Achilles praised by three masters of political and philosophical discourse to those emphasized by Homer: see the references in *The Book of the Courtier* (pp. 1842–43), *The Prince* (p. 1716), and/or *The Apology of Socrates* (pp. 736–37). What do their different views of the Greek hero reveal about the values espoused by these writers?

Further Reading

See also the reading suggestions in the anthology, p. 1811.

Hanning, Robert W., and David Rosand, eds. *Castiglione: The Ideal and the Real in Renaissance Culture.* 1983. Among the ten excellent essays in this collection, the following are perhaps of greatest relevance to our discussion: chapter 1 (Thomas M. Greene, "*Il Cortegiano* and the Choice of a Game"), chapter 4 (Eduardo Saccone, "*Grazia, Sprezzature, Affettazione* in *the Courtier*"), chapter 7 (Robert W. Hanning, "Castiglione's Verbal Portrait: Structures and Strategies"), and chapter 10 (Louise George Clubb, "Castiglione's Humanistic Art and Renaissance Drama").

Wilkins, Ernest Hatch. *History of Italian Literature.* Revised by Thomas G. Bergin. 1974. See chapter 24, "Castiglione and Other Prose Writers."

Woodhouse, J. R. *Baldesar Castiglione.* 1978. A "reassessment of *The Courtier,*" the book opens with chapters on life at court and the courtly educational ideal. There follow individual analyses of the four books of the *Courtier* and the subjects with which they deal.

MARGUERITE DE NAVARRE

The Heptameron

Backgrounds

For an account of the "frame story" as given in the prologue of the *Heptameron,* see the headnote, pp. 1855–56. A definitive text of Marguerite de Navarre's collection has not been established and probably never will be, owing to the situation of manuscripts (seventeen of them exist, not at all identical in the numbering and ordering of the stories included) and of early printed editions. The first printed edition appeared in 1558, nine years after Marguerite's death, edited by a prominent scholar, Pierre Boaistuau, under the title *Histories of Fortunate Lovers.* The present title appeared a year later in *Héptaméron des Nouvelles,* a printed edition done by Pierre Gruget, who divided the stories into "Days" with ten stories each and gave more space to prologues and dialogues, although he censored some names and passages, as well as three entire stories that had to do with the corruption of Franciscan monks. Among the manuscript texts, the one produced by the scholar Adrien de Thou in 1553 is of particular interest; oddly enough, it "calls itself *Le Décaméron* of Marguerite, and seems to leave empty pages for missing tales to complete the hundred implied in the title" (P. A. Chilton).

Even from these sketchy notes it is clear that a definitive canon of the stories does not exist. Details are available in Chilton's introduction to his translation (see the anthology, pp. 1856–57), which is based on the best available scholarship and contains seventy-two stories, ten for each of seven days and two for a barely started eighth day. Each "Day," in addition to its prologue, has a long title that summarily indicates the type of stories it contains. The First Day, from which the selections in the anthology are taken, announces "A Collection of Low Tricks Played by Women on Men and by Men on Women." It is generally thought to be the most finished of the sequences, and it introduces the narrators well.

Marguerite de Navarre presents a peculiar type of storytelling, as each story is followed by a discussion of its moral and social implications among the storytellers themselves; thus we have something of a mixture of two genres, the short story and the treatise in the form of a dialogue or conversation. A major example of the latter is Castiglione's *Book of the Courtier* (see pp. 1808–54 in the anthology). For the short story as Marguerite handles it, three precedents can be indicated: the medieval *fabliau*—a short tale in verse form, typically with a humorous and bawdy subject; the *lai,* a longer narrative in verse form, exemplified by the work of Marie de France (see pp. 1169–78 in the anthology); and most importantly the *novella,* of which the major medieval exponent was Boccaccio (see pp. 1429–57). Boccaccio's *Decameron* had first been translated into French by Laurent Premierfait in 1414; a new translation, mentioned in the prologue to the *Heptameron,* was commissioned by Marguerite herself and done by a member of the court of Francis I, Antoine Le Maçon; it came out in 1545.

Classroom Strategies

Marguerite's stories present no difficulties in terms of plot development and narrative sequence. As for their content, particularly with regard to the codes implied in the characters' behavior, it may be in order always to keep in mind some basic facts. This is a group of people who belong to the higher echelons of aristocratic society, indeed to the inner circle of royalty, at a time of kings "by divine right" and of extremely classified societies; whether they tell stories about their peers (which sometimes verge on the "juicy piece of gossip") or about characters of inferior social status, they act as people who do not feel bound by common standards of judgment but who have established standards that are valid for persons of their own rank.

Hence the literary qualities of the stories, the naturalness with which they handle potentially shocking situations such as overt matrimonial infidelity, rape, or the bawdiness of the clergy. This general attitude is reflected in the relative simplicity and directness of Marguerite's narrative manner. Discussion of this attitude may present good opportunities to familiarize students with such notions as objectivity in fiction, point of view, and authorial comment. Actually, Marguerite's manner and technique may prove to be more subtle than they appear at first, especially in the relationship between the stories themselves and the commentary that follows each of them. It could be pointed out that the conversations among the characters, all of them narrators in turn, ultimately create a variety of "voices" or "points of view" for the same fictional material; hence Marguerite's narrative, however deceptively simple, may turn out to be quite sophisticated and "modern."

To a significant degree, these debates seem modern because they address serious moral question in regard to sexual behavior. In the *Decameron,* Boccaccio balances three men and seven women, and his book frequently elevates women's concerns to a level of dignity not always typical of the age. Maguerite balances five men and five women, and since many of the women argue against what one might consider feminist perspectives, the tenor of the discussion often undermines the accomplishments of the female characters in the stories.

Consider, for example, the long conversation between the Princess and her lady-in-waiting in Story Four. The old lady's advice to the triumphant Princess is based on admirable Christian principles, but by advocating silence it also undercuts the self-respect that had given the Princess the strength to fight off her assailant. The debate that follows Story Four, which Hircan dominates, demonstrates how hard it is for women to take credit for their own virtues.

In Story Five, the ferrywoman's strength and quick wits are initially applauded, as is the Princess's self-defense in Story Four, but then the emphasis switches to the two humiliated friars, who get off lightly. The conversation that follows somehow turns into an attack on women, and even the pious Oisille contributes to the trivializing of the situation with a knowing pun. Not until the end of Story Eight, in which the wife who has taken her chambermaid's place scolds her errant (and ironically compromised) husband, does a woman really get the last word. Tellingly, it is after this story that Dagoucin, "the most philosophical member of the group" (as the footnote points out), speaks for the first time, articulating an idealistic view of love that Marguerite will pursue in later sections of the *Heptameron*.

Topic for Discussion and Writing

The characters of Parlamente and Hircan are generally identified with Marguerite herself and with her second husband, Henri de Navarre. Take these two characters' words as they appear in the prologue and in the conversation following the third selection, and attempt to describe the implied notions of what constitutes a rational, successful matrimonial relationship in the world of the *Heptameron*. Also use contributions from other characters surrounding this central couple.

Some Comparative Perspectives

1. Compare the handling of "bawdy" materials in the selections from Day One and in Boccaccio's Sixth Story of the Ninth Day (see p. 1447 in the anthology).
2. Compare the attitudes toward cuckoldry in Story Three with those in Chaucer's *Miller's Tale*, or canto V of Dante's *Inferno*, or the frame of *The Thousand and One Nights*. How does each author handle the reasons for and moral consequences of adultery?
3. Referring to Plato's *Symposium*, Dagoucin describes the ideal love: "if she whom you love is your true likeness . . . then it will be your own self that you love, and not her alone." Adam's love for Eve in *Paradise Lost* uniquely illustrates this situation; compare the conversations about love in Milton's poem with the discussions in the *Heptameron*.

Further Reading

See also the reading suggestions in the anthology, pp. 1856–57.

Cholakian, Patricia Francis. *Rape and Writing in the* Heptameron *of Marguerite de Navarre*. 1991. A useful feminist analysis.

Gelernt, Jules. *World of Many Loves: The* Heptameron *of Marguerite de Navarre*. 1966. Views the work as a "Renaissance treatise on love" and traces in its background the "idealistic" line from courtly love to Renaissance Neoplatonism and the "realist" tradition of the *novella*.

Kinney, Arthur F. *Continental Humanist Poetics*. 1989. See chapter 4 on the *Heptameron*.

Meijer, Marianne. "The *Héptaméron*: Feminism with a Smile." In *Regionalism and the Female Imagination*. 1977–78. A short article from a contemporary point of view.

Norton, Glyn P. "Narrative Function in the *Héptaméron* Frame-Story." In *La Nouvelle Française à la Renaissance*, edited by Lionello Sozzi and V. L. Saulnier. 1981.

FRANÇOIS RABELAIS

Gargantua and Pantagruel

Backgrounds

Gargantua and Pantagruel, as we know it now—whatever the history of its composition, the dates of its parts, and the authenticity of its final part—is an immense and seemingly chaotic work of fiction, divided into five books. It is possible, however, to extract an intelligible "story line" from the seemingly haphazard movements of its narrative course. The necessary premise to any successful encounter with it is that it operates on two levels—fantasy and realism—which are variously balanced and merged. The locale at the opening of book I is a kingdom, for which Rabelais borrowed from Sir Thomas More the name of Utopia, but it is at the same time a large French country estate. The gigantic king-squire is Grandgousier. He and his queen, Gargamelle, beget a giant-son, Gargantua, who enters the world from her left ear while she is lying in a meadow and who calls immediately for wine. After this comes the story of Gargantua's education in Paris. It is a story told in semifantastic, often comic terms, but tracing what was then a highly controversial transition from medieval scholasticism (a term whose meaning students should be asked to look up) to the subjects and methods of the "new" learning: see the selections in the anthology from chapters 14–24 (pp. 1885–97).

Later on in book I Gargantua will leave Paris, answering his father the king's summons to war. The so-called Picrochole War is a mock-heroic version of a country brawl between people of two neighboring estates, with, however, many of the characteristics of wars between nations. The cake-peddlers of nearby Linne ("King" Picrochole's domain) have refused to sell their wares to Grandgousier's shepherds, one of whom knocks down a Picrochole baker. The "incident" is used by Picrochole as an excuse to invade Grandgousier's territories, but his overblown "imperialistic" designs are thwarted by Gargantua's gigantic physical stature and power. (There are such vaguely pre-Swiftian details as his combing cannon balls out of his hair and inadvertently eating several pilgrims in his salad.) Another valiant and picturesque war hero is the monk Friar John of the Funnels; after the enemy is conquered and pardoned, he is allowed as a reward to build the monastery of his dreams, the Abbey of Thélème (see chapters 52–57, pp. 1897–1905).

Book II is Pantagruel's book. Like his father, Gargantua, Pantagruel is sent to Paris to study. The new learning now happily dominates, and Gargantua's letter to Pantagruel (pp. 1908–11) is a kind of manifesto of the proud intellectual achievements of the period. Shortly thereafter, a major new character makes his entrance—Panurge, the still-familiar type of student who grows in age without ever getting his degree: poor but generous, astute and malicious, an erudite and practical joker, and as much a proverbial figure in French literature as Pantagruel himself. The two young men become inseparable; their most significant adventure in book II is the war against the Dipsodes (not included in the anthology)—the root of *Dipsodes*, the same as in "dipsomania," is Greek for "thirst"—who are conquered, Pantagruel becoming their king.

Book III (not included in the anthology) introduces a question that pervades the rest of the work: should Panurge marry? To find out, Panurge and Pantagruel make several fantastic journeys to consult a sibyl, a poet, a magician, a doctor, and a philosopher. Finally a madman, Triboulet, advises them to seek the Oracle of the Holy Bottle. For that purpose, they go on further fantastic voyages, which take them, among other destinations—again in a pre-Swiftian manner—to the island of the Papefigues (Protestants or "Pope-snubbers") and the island of the Papimanes (Catholics or "Pope-enthusiasts"). Finally in book V (also not in the anthology), taking a shortcut through the frozen ocean north of Canada, Panurge and Pantagruel reach Northern India and the subterranean location, under a vineyard planted by Bacchus, of the Holy Bottle. Its oracular response is the single word TRINCH ("DRINK!"). The assuaging of thirst, actual and also symbolical, physical and intellectual, proves to be the cultural metaphor of the entire work.

Before Rabelais made them heroes, raising them to a high place in the literary culture of France, Gargantua and Pantagruel existed as characters in French folklore. In other words, they already had the kind of household popularity now enjoyed by some of our comic-strip heroes endowed with exceptional muscle and superhuman powers. In French folk tradition, Gargantua was a gigantic figure famous for his exceptional voracity, while Pantagruel was a pleasant little devil whose favorite work was making men thirsty. It was Rabelais who, among many other innovations, made them father and son. The composition of *Gargantua and Pantagruel* was as leisurely as the work itself. The first of its parts to see the light was what is now book II. This was published in 1532 under the pseudonym Alcofribas Nasier, an anagram of Rabelais's own name, with a long title, as was then the fashion: *The Horrible and Fearful Facts and Brave Deeds of the Renowned Pantagruel, King of the Dipsodes, Son of the Great Gargantua*. It was intended as the continuation of a preceding anonymous book, *The Great and Inestimable Chronicles of the Great Giant Gargantua*. Rabelais' own and quite different *Gargantua*, the present book I, was published two years later. Books III and IV and the spurious book V were published with considerable intervals between them (1547, 1552, 1564).

Rabelais's characters, apart from their folksy lineage, may be related to such previous literary giants as Morgante and Baldus, respective heroes of mock-heroic poems by Luigi Pulci (1432–1484) and Teofilo Folengo (1491–1544). Their attribute of longevity is, of course, traceable as far back as the heroes of Genesis. More generally, the disparate elements assembled in Rabelais's work are a reflection of his unique life experience (see pp. 1881–82), his multiple occupations, and his extraordinary learning. Even a summary biography of the man throws light on the sources of the work: for the Abbey of Thélème, his experience with monastic life; for the education of the giants, his knowledge as a scholarly humanist and practicing physician; and so on.

Classroom Strategies

Like *The Praise of Folly*, Rabelais's work can help your classes learn how to detect serious ideas in comic and, in this case, particularly extravagant garb. The new reader may have some difficulty with the twists and turns that the author gives to such august texts as the Holy Scriptures— typically, for instance, in his handling of the biblical pattern of "begats" in tracing the genealogy of his heroes. The idea to be suggested and elaborated upon in such cases is that a humanist must be well at ease in a tradition (in this case the Judeo-Christian tradition: Rabelais, in however unorthodox a fashion, was a monk) before he can take the liberty of twisting and parodying that tradition. Laughter does not necessarily indicate disrespect, but often an affectionate familiarity. With Rabelais's mixture of realism and fantasy there should be no problem. Young audiences have long been trained in that area by science fiction and films. The selections in the anthology are intended to emphasize both the fundamental seriousness of Rabelais's purpose and the sheer fun to be derived from his method.

Topics for Discussion and Writing

1. In the course of the story Rabelais often seems to forget the gigantic size and superhuman nature of his characters. Find specific examples of this "oversight" and attempt to explain its significance (for instance, in Gargantua's letter to Pantagruel, we hardly think of father and son as supernatural giants).
2. Describe the implications of the fact that Pantagruel's kingdom is named Utopia. Discuss the idea that utopias are useful in showing the way to an unattainable perfection.
3. Discuss the idea that the Abbey of Thélème's orderly, pleasant life depends on an aristocratic sense of honor.
4. Although Rabelais wouldn't have known the phrase, *Gargantua and Pantagruel* can be called in part a "generational novel." What are possible similarities and contrasts with the generation gap as we experience it in our own time? Discuss the role of one single humanistic or scientific change in altering the outlook of our own period.

Comparative Perspectives

1. Discuss possible comparisons between Rabelais's and Erasmus's views of religious practices, comparing passages in which both seem to oppose pompous, exhibitionistic piety.
2. Compare Rabelais and Castiglione on the mental and physical education of a gentleman. Keep in mind that Pantagruel is also a prince, and receives the traditional education for his rank
3. Pantagruel is born "as hairy as a bear," a feature that leads to a prediction of a great future. Heroic characters, serious as well as comic, are often supposed to have been marked at birth in similar ways. Compare the births of Enkidu or Esau, or the appearance of Orlando when mad. What attributes are linked to the hirsute male in each of these cases?
4. The English scholar Thaumaste and Panurge conduct an argument through signs rather than words. Panurge wins because he has a repertory of (obscene) gestures far more imaginative than Thumaste's: obviously, Rabelais intended this scene to be great fun, and it is. In today's "visual culture," however, the power of nonverbal signs is taken very seriously. Discuss the wit of pictorial description in *Gargantua and Pantagruel* (for example, the landscape of Pantagruel's mouth in book II, chapter 32) and in works like *A True Story* (in the belly of the whale, perhaps), which influenced Rabelais, or in the serious iconography of medieval religious poetry (like *A Hymn to Holy Women* or *A Hymn to St. Maximinus*). Why did images have such power when a large part of the population could not read? Why do they have so much power today, when a large part of the population does not read? How would you contrast the signs typical of earlier centuries with those that are current today?

Further Reading

See also the reading suggestions in the anthology, p. 1884.

Bowen, Barbara C. *The Age of Bluff: Paradox and Ambiguity in Rabelais and Montaigne.* 1972.

Coleman, Dorothy G. *Rabelais: A Critical Study in Prose Fiction.* 1971. An in-depth study of "the richness of Rabelais's vocabulary and the galvanizing dynamics of his style," as well as of "some of the general orientations of his work," his characters, choice of form, and so on.

Cruickshank, John, ed. *French Literature and Its Background.* Vol. 1, The Sixteenth Century. 1968. Chapter 2, by G. D. Josipovici, is dedicated to Rabelais.

Febvre, Lucien Paul Victor. *The Problem of Unbelief in the Sixteenth Century: The Religion of Rabelais.* Trans. Beatrice Gottlieb. 1982. A thorough treatment of the question of Rabelais's religious ideas in relation to the time in which he lived, by an important French scholar.

Losse, Deborah N. *Rhetoric at Play: Rabelais and Satirical Eulogy.* 1980. Quite specialized, with quotations in the original French.

Screech, M. A. *Looking at Rabelais.* 1988. An Oxford lecture by an eminent Rabelais scholar.

MICHEL DE MONTAIGNE

Essays

Backgrounds

Montaigne's *Essays* are divided into three books, each containing a different number of essays of widely varying lengths and, of course, subjects (fifty-seven in Book I, thirty-seven in Book II, thirteen in Book III). The essays are designated as "chapters," a term that can be misleading, not only because a collection of essays is not a work of fiction but also because of the ostensibly haphazard way in which the "chapters" follow one another. Each essay, therefore, would lend itself to individual mention and description. Yet some sense of progression and development can be detected.

Montaigne began to work on what was to become his famous collection of essays when he was thirty-eight years old and had already had considerable experience of the world. Retired now to the library of his castle, he had a private purpose in his writing—not, however, that of keeping a chronological diary but rather that of assembling a scrapbook in which to record passing thoughts and memorabilia. Thus the work began as a collection of rambling observations and meditations on Montaigne's readings, on events past and present, on general human attitudes, foibles, qualities, oddities. Many of his chapter or essay titles start with "Of" followed by the name of a human virtue, vice, custom, etc. "Of" sorrow (I, 2), idleness (I, 8), liars (I, 9), fear (I, 17), pedantry (I, 24), friendship (I, 27), sleep (I, 44), smells (I, 55), drunkenness (II, 2), conscience (II, 5), the affection of fathers for their children (II, 8), riding post (II, 22), anger (II, 31). Such titles, as well as those featuring maxims or proverbs—*That the Study of Philosophy Is to Learn to Die* (I, 19), *That We Laugh or Cry for the Same Thing* (I, 37), *That Our Desires Are Augmented by Difficulties* (II, 15), *Cowardice, the Mother of Cruelty* (II, 27), *All Things Have Their Season* (II, 28)—introduce essays showing the same qualities of casual progression as the work as a whole and coming to the justification of their titles in comfortable, roundabout ways. A selection from book I, for instance, the famous essay *On Cannibals*, opens with a little episode from Roman history, then mentions the unnamed friend who had spent a long time in a section of Brazil and relates to the author some observations made there; gradually, but only gradually, the focus shifts to the main subject, cannibals, and to the personal acquaintance of the author with one of them. The author seems able to maintain a detached, often ironical attitude throughout, however bizarre or horrible his material.

That such an attitude may be ascribed to the influence of a particular philosophical system is doubtful; many not entirely successful attempts have been made to formalize Montaigne's thought, usually in terms of a progression from the Stoicism of his much-admired Seneca and an initial confidence in the authority of human reason, to a more balanced, temperate "natural philosophy" and a deep albeit undramatic contemplation of the limits of human judgment. The thirteen long chapters of book III, written at a more advanced age and after new private and public experiences (such as Montaigne's four years as mayor of Bordeaux), would then be the ultimate statement of that wise "natural philosophy," not without touches of "Epicureanism." Though there is some truth in this, Montaigne remains a striking example of his own idea of the changeable nature of man; he has "slipped through the fingers of even the most daring critics," as he himself says of the Emperor Augustus. Hence the safer, simpler, and most obvious way to trace a line of development in the three books of the essays is to see it in terms of increased focusing on the individual self. Our selections, however sketchily, exemplify such a progress, from Montaigne's early eclecticism to a consideration of mankind's "presumption and littleness," to the overtly central purpose of analyzing the exemplar at hand, himself.

The originator of the "essay" as a literary genre, Montaigne can hardly be said to have had predecessors in that form. His mode of writing can be related, however, to a kind of book very fashionable at the time: collections of informative bits of knowledge and wise sayings in all areas from grammar to geography, from mathematics to history, of which Erasmus's *Adagia* is perhaps the best surviving example. One of the major purposes of such collections, besides moral teaching, was to enable one to display one's familiarity with antiquity. They also exemplify a view of history, and particularly of Roman history, as a source of teachings and models of behavior—a view that in his own different way Montaigne entertained as enthusiastically as Machiavelli. Ancient Roman archetypes of the genre were found in such works as *Memorable Deeds and Sayings* by Valerius Maximus, a writer of the first century A.D., or in Aulus Gellius's *Attic Nights* (second century A.D.). In the shaping of Montaigne's thinking in the earlier parts of the *Essays,* a similar role may be attributed to the philosophical writings of the Stoic philosopher Seneca (ca. 50 B.C.–A.D. 40), while the way Montaigne handles historical characters testifies to his knowledge of and professed admiration for Plutarch (A.D. 45–ca. 125). Montaigne's deep familiarity with an enormous number of other possible "sources" is shown in the very abundance of his quotations from, and his opinions on, a wide range of writers. Naturally his most obvious source remains the observation of life and of himself.

Classroom Strategies

Readers new to Montaigne may be disturbed by the large number of quotations from texts with which they are unacquainted. The best way to cope with this reaction is to demonstrate the fitness of the quotation to its context. It should also be remembered that the passages Montaigne quotes were as familiar and commonplace to him as proverbs; memorizing well-turned sentiments from the classics was a normal school exercise at the time, and keeping a notebook of striking aphorisms was the habit of every educated adult male. The quotations supply a further coloring of universality to Montaigne's themes, most of which belong to all times and are demonstrably still very much with us—the relativity of the ideas of civilized and uncivilized behavior; the position of man in an ever more widely explored and yet mysterious universe; the complex, self-contradictory nature of human intelligence; and so on.

Analysis of Montaigne's texts also offers good ground for the discussion of literary style. Montaigne's great influence is due not only to his subject matter but also to his "tone of voice," the gait of his prose, and his tempered, ironical manner, which is both detached and yet very personal. It is an influence that extends even to such writings of our own day as the newspaper feature article and syndicated column, but no contemporary journalist has the range of reference and the elliptical intelligence that particularly distinguish these essays. *Of Coaches* offers an excellent opportunity for classroom analysis; ask your students to outline Montaigne's arguments here, noting especially the way the titular coaches appear, vanish, and then suddenly draw the essay together in its concluding paragraph.

Topics for Discussion and Writing

1. Granted that it is impossible to extract from Montaigne's view of the world a well-organized philosophical "system," examine closely the meanings he attaches to any one of the following: nature, reason, justice, courage.

2. Montaigne writes of the "disorders of our poor country" (p. 1944) and elsewhere states that "it is no slight pleasure to feel oneself preserved from the contagion of so depraved an age." Our present world can hardly be seen as free from tumultuousness and corruption. Discuss whether, and to what degree, Montaigne's position as we deduce it from our readings and from the main elements of his life, would be conceivable and morally justifiable in our own age.

3. Discuss the quotation as a rhetorical device to support an argument and give it authority. Examine five to ten particular quotations in Montaigne and discuss their effect. What examples can you think of in electoral oratory of our own day in which references to respected national figures of the past and quotations from their utterances are used for similar objectives? Discuss, of course, differences as well.

4. Examine Montaigne's attitude toward scientific discoveries and the idea of progress. Make possible comparisons with Rabelais's notions of the betterment of humankind through education.

Comparative Perspectives

1. In urging caution when we presume to judge others, Montaigne offers an important critique of the comparative method of thought. Explain the sensitivity he shows to cultural difference in *Of Cannibals* and the significance of noting that we "are all of patchwork" in *Of the Inconsistency of Our Actions*. Can you think of any occasions during this semester's reading when either of these essays would have been a useful critical guide?

2. Augustine's *Confessions* is the first autobiographical work of the Western world. Montaigne, in *To The Reader*, declares, "I am myself the matter of my book." Yet his *Essays* are not autobiographical. Examine his reasons for writing and compare them to Augustine's.

3. Ovid was an early favorite of Montaigne's, and a line from the *Metamorphoses* (see pp. 1926 and 926 in the anthology) caps a discussion of spontaneous sex change in *On the Power of the Imagination*. Discuss the psychological insights that this essay provides into the nature of sexuality, comparing and contrasting them with fictional examples in Ovid, Ariosto, or other writers whose work you have studied this term.

Further Reading

See also the reading suggestions in the anthology, pp. 1924–25.

Bencivenga, Ermanno. *The Discipline of Subjectivity: an Essay on Montaigne*. 1990. By a philosopher specializing in language analysis.

Cruickshank, John, ed. *French Literature and Its Background*. Vol. I. 1968. One chapter, by C. R. Baxter, is dedicated to Montaigne.

McGowan, Margaret M. *Montaigne's Deceits: The Art of Persuasion in the Essays*. 1974. By a student of French Renaissance aesthetics and rhetoric.

Sayce, R. A. *The Essays of Montaigne: A Critical Exploration*. 1972. A thorough, detailed analysis, with quotations in French.

MIGUEL DE CERVANTES

Don Quixote

Backgrounds

Don Quixote is divided into two parts (the first of fifty-two chapters, the second of seventy-four), published separately with an interval of ten years between. Like *Gargantua and Pantagruel*, *Don Quixote* mixes realism and fantasy, but with the obvious difference that the fantasy is not here external but located in the mind of the hero. He is an impoverished gentleman who owns a small country estate in the Spanish province of La Mancha. As the whole world today knows from the innumerable films, plays, paintings, and sculptures inspired by his story, he is so infatuated with the reading of romances of chivalry and particularly with the image of the knight-errant and his code—heroic adventurousness, helpful generosity toward the weak and the needy, the service of justice, acts of valor for valor's sake and as an offering to a beloved lady—that he decides to equip himself in the proper manner and single-handedly revive the profession of knight-errantry. Quixote's spear and shield are old relics, his horse is the lean nag Rozinante; he leaves home at dawn, unnoticed, through a secret door. To complete his credentials as a knight-errant he chooses for the object of his devotion a peasant girl, whom his imagination transforms into the Lady Dulcinea del Toboso. Stopping at an inn, which he sees as a castle, he compels the crooked innkeeper, in a scene accompanied by much jesting and slapstick comedy, to dub him knight.

After he leaves the inn, Don Quixote's first actions are his pathetically futile defense of a farm boy being lashed by his master, and his unsuccessful attempt to force a group of merchants from Toledo to perform an act of faith, i.e., to swear to the incomparable beauty of Dulcinea without having seen her. In the ensuing brawl Quixote is unhorsed and badly mangled. A fellow villager finds him in this condition and takes him back home on a donkey (chapters 1–5, pp. 1969–89). Since Quixote's troubles are attributed to his mad infatuation with the chivalry books in his library, the local curate and barber proceed to burn them; but this proves to be a futile action, for he resumes his wanderings (chapter 7, p. 1989), now with his newly appointed squire, Sancho Panza. Their first adventure—probably the most famous of them all—is a fight against windmills, which Quixote declares to be giants; their second, an encounter with two Benedictine monks on their mules, whom Quixote sees as enchanters abducting a lady. The consequent scuffles culminate in Quixote's battle with a choleric attendant in the lady's retinue (chapters 8–9, pp. 1991–2000).

After the significant exchanges between Quixote and his squire in chapter 10 (p. 2000), chapters 11–17 (not in the anthology) take us to a pastoral world. There follow some of the more legendary Quixotic exploits: the attack on a flock of sheep, which the Don sees as an enemy army, and the disastrous effort to liberate a chain of galley slaves (chapters 18 and 22, pp. 2003–15).

Chapters 23 through 32 (not in the anthology) are the Sierra Morena chapters. In that region of woods and forests Quixote decides to spend a period of retirement and penance, in imitation of his knightly models; from there he dispatches Sancho to his lady Dulcinea with a letter for her. The squire never delivers the letter but returns to the Sierra Morena with the curate and the barber, their aim of course being to bring the Knight of the Mournful Countenance back to his senses and his home. In the interval between departure from Sierra Morena and return to the village, they spend a period, long and full of incidents (chapters 32–46, not in the anthology), at the place they had left in chapter 17, the inn/castle of which Sancho has dire memories.

Both the Sierra Morena and the inn sequences are enriched by exemplary cases of romantically difficult loves, presented through the technique of the story-within-the-story, of which Cervantes originated the fashion. In the intimate setting of the inn, the intricate vicissitudes of the two major couples—Cardenio and Lucinda, Fernando and Dorotea—have their happy endings. Their connection with the main *Quixote* plot is made through the character of the beautiful Dorotea, who on the urging of the curate and the barber has persuaded Quixote to leave Sierra Morena and return to the inn—to him an enchanted castle—by playing the part of Princess Micomicona, a "damsel in distress." To the outside world (when Quixote and Sancho are in danger of arrest for their attempt to liberate the slaves) Quixote's rescuers use as a plea his insanity, but in dealing with him they use his own visionary notions and convince him that he is himself the victim of enchantments as they carry him back to his village (chapter 52, the last of Part I, p. 2015). Of the curate's and the barber's two aims—to bring Quixote home and to "cure" him—the first has been achieved, but not the second.

The most important thing that happens to Quixote and Sancho at the beginning of Part II is the realization that their adventures have been narrated in a book. Quixote, of course, is not cured (in the first chapter of Part II he has declared to the curate and the barber: "A knight-errant I shall live and die"), nor is Sancho less desirous of becoming "governor of an island," as his master has promised him. It is Sancho who tells Quixote that they have been put into a book, the source of that information being the young Sansón Carrasco, just back from the University of Salamanca, where he has received his bachelor's degree. Chapter 3 (p. 2023) is the point at which Cervantes, through Quixote conversing with Carrasco, amiably glorifies the popularity of his book (i.e., Part I) in other countries as well as Spain and debates the objections of the critics as reported by Carrasco.

From chapter 8 on (chapters 8–11 are not in the anthology), the two adventurers are on their way again. In the country around El Toboso, Sancho saves himself from trouble by assuring Quixote that his failure to recognize the beautiful Dulcinea in the country wench confronting him comes from devilish spells and enchantments. As they move on toward Saragossa, there is a troublesome encounter with a company of players in their costumes—strange apparitions including "the Devil"—on their way to a performance of *The Parliament of Death*. The two most memorable encounters follow (chapters 12–17, pp. 2029–60).

The first is with Sansón Carrasco. Carrasco, having joined the ranks of the would-be rescuers of Quixote from his folly, tries to do something decisive about it by meeting Quixote on his own terms: as a knight (first called the "Fearless Knight of the Mirrors," then the "Knight of the Wood"), Carrasco plans to challenge and defeat Quixote in a duel. The plan fails as the Knight of the Wood is himself unhorsed and vanquished by the fury of the mad Don. Quixote's other significant encounter is with a kind, wise gentleman, Don Diego de Miranda, who witnesses Quixote's courage as he provokes a lion to come out of its cage and fight. Appropriately placed after Quixote's victorious interlude, this episode—a pivotal instance of Quixote's idea of gratuitous valor—has a semicomic ending, which is fully balanced by Quixote's speech on "the meaning of valor," one of his most movingly eloquent speeches. Aroused to a puzzled admiration, Don Diego invites Quixote to be his guest. Chapters 19 through 21 (not in the anthology) consist once more of a story-within-the-story. It tells of the planned marriage between the fair Quiteria, loved by the poor shepherd Basilio, and the rich Camacho; on the day of the wedding Quiteria is abducted by Basilio, her true love, much to her delight and with Quixote's wholehearted support.

From this point on, the four main narratives of *Don Quixote*, Part II, treat the hero's descent to the cave of Montesinos (chapters 22–23, not in the anthology); Quixote's and Sancho's long stay at a castle as the guests of a duke and duchess (chapters 30–63, not in the anthology); their stay in Barcelona, the scene of Quixote's last duel and lamentable defeat (chapters 64–65, pp. 2061–64); and the hero's return to his village and his death (chapters 73–74, pp. 2064–72). The peculiar character of the Montesinos sequence is that it is narrated by the hero himself to his incredulous listeners after he has been lifted from the cave; to all appearances it is a dream in which Quixote has been granted visions of ancient kingdoms and of his enchanted Dulcinea. A dreamlike atmosphere also pervades the long scenes at the castle, but now it is a manipulated illusion, the result of theatrical pranks played by the duke and duchess and their retinue of idle jesters on the knight and his squire, who are now famous everywhere for their drolleries. One of the castle scenes concerns Dulcinea: a prankster, dressed as Death and pretending to be the magician Merlin, reveals as the harsh condition of her disenchantment that Sancho must submit to 3,300 lashes, a sentence that of course will never be carried out. Another scene involves Sancho. Conducted, blindfolded, to a nearby village that he supposes to be the island of Barataria, he is given the promised governorship. Sancho's victory consists in the fact that he will prove to be a good "governor," beloved by the villagers. The crucial Barcelona episode (chapters 64–65) is staged by Sansón Carrasco, who turns up in a new disguise as the Knight of the Moon and this time defeats Quixote. The Don, after flirting with the idea of a new life enacting a pastoral play instead of a romance of chivalry, returns to his village to sicken and die (chapters 73–74).

Three literary traditions make their presence felt in *Don Quixote*: the epic or romance of chivalry, the adventure story of the *picaro* or vagabond, and the pastoral narrative of shepherds and their loves. The qualities of the chivalric epic may be sampled by the student in the selections in the anthology from *The Song of Roland* (p. 1108), and those of the chivalric romance in the tales of King Arthur and his knights of the Round Table, especially such episodes of courtly love as that of Tristan and Isolde or that of Lancelot and Guinevere. The latter, it will be recalled, is so moving to Dante's Paolo and Francesca (*Inferno*, canto V, p. 1315) that it inspires their sinful love and leads to their destruction. The two collections of stories—that centering on Roland and his uncle, the great king Charlemagne, and that centering on Arthur—are combined and subjected to new twists in the major Italian Renaissance poems, *Orlando Innamorato* (Orlando in love) by Matteo Maria Boiardo (ca. 1441–1494) and *Orlando Furioso* (Orlando gone mad) by Ludovico Ariosto (1474–1533). Both of these poems were well known to Cervantes, and the latter is possibly the immediate source of the Sierra Morena episode and other passages in *Don Quixote*.

The "picaresque" tradition is named from the *picaro*, the stock rogue-hero of many popular tales dealing with life in the undergrounds of society, where robbers, tramps, and various eccentrics meet. This tradition contributes to the "realistic" or "Sancho" aspects of Cervantes's story. Its major literary formulation is the anonymous novel *Lazarillo de Tormes* (first published in 1554), the influence of which was enormous at the time and indeed may be traced through eighteenth-century English fiction and down to our own time.

As for the pastoral romance, this tradition has its roots in Greek and Roman antiquity from Theocritus to Virgil and flourished during the Renaissance in such works—known to Cervantes and cited by him—as the *Arcadia* of Jacopo Sannazzaro (1457–1530) and most particularly the *Diana* of Jorge de Montemayor (ca. 1520–1561).

What matters for us, of course, is what Cervantes made of these backgrounds: a work so new and absorbing it is impossible to lay it down, and peopled by two creations, Quixote and Sancho, who have become part of our everyday mental furniture.

Classroom Strategies

Our selections from *Don Quixote* are best handled in three assignments. A first can center effectively on the figure of Don Quixote as a blind hero, fool, and ultimately wise fool, with the contributions of successive attitudes to our complex of feelings about him. A second can focus in similar ways on Sancho and his functions in the story. And a third can deal with the nature and development of the relationship between the two.

Analysis and discussion of *Don Quixote* call for some use of the terms "parody" and "satire." Parody is ordinarily a magnification of the characteristics of a particular style to the point at which its absurdity becomes unmistakable—in the case of *Don Quixote,* the inflated highfalutin style of the chivalric romances. Yet apart from the early quotations from Quixote's readings, obviously inserted to parody that style, his own speeches in the course of the story and the general nature of his eloquence move increasingly away from parody toward a speech that registers both his delusion and the idealism that feeds it. The term "satire" is equally inadequate for describing Cervantes's tone. Satire, in its usual sense, aims to expose an object or a person to ridicule and censure with implicit reference to a higher standard of conduct. In Cervantes the case is more complex. The argument can be made, in fact, that Quixote, far from being an object of satire, unconsciously becomes the satirist—of, say, crooked innkeepers or aristocratic pranksters—by exposing their cruelty, childishness, and vulgarity. In addition, and more generally, Cervantes's complex attitude toward the world of medieval chivalry can hardly be considered unmitigated satire. The serious interest and the underlying importance of Quixote's actions and speech can be demonstrated by observing their effect on other characters, particularly Sancho, whose warm response to Quixote's genuine chivalry of heart should correct any tendency to identify the two men with a superficial polarity between idealism and realism.

Topics for Discussion and Writing

Don Quixote is perhaps unparalleled as a starting point for broad discussions of the art of fiction in general and its place in a literate society. Our first three suggestions are along those lines.

1. We may grow attached to a fictional character in such a way that it becomes a solid point of reference, something "truer than life." Granted that Quixote and other characters in the novel have acquired that kind of "reality," take any number of examples, major and minor, and analyze by what verbal devices Cervantes produces our perception of them. Discussion may be interestingly extended to the differences between our perception of a character in fiction and one on stage or in a film.

2. *Don Quixote* has been and still is held to be "great" literature. Yet one of Cervantes's most respected contemporaries, Lope de Vega, considered it trash. There is evidence of a similar duality of attitude toward the romances of chivalry in Cervantes's time, some readers regarding them with a mixture of overt contempt and secret fascination. Can you think of forms of writing in our own time that are similarly both admired and condemned?

3. What constitutes the hero of a piece of fiction? One way to put it is that he is the one who determines and qualifies the actions and attitudes of the other characters. Show with specific evidence that Quixote is a hero in this sense, examining the characters of Sancho, the curate and the barber, Don Diego de Miranda, Sansón Carrasco.

4. Don Quixote has become a world figure not only as the hero of a celebrated novel but also as one of the main emblems of Spain. Discuss ways in which he can be compared, in his popularity and representativeness, to heroes of ancient epics on the one hand and to modern heroes of fiction, film, and comics on the other.

5. Take the passage in part I, chapter 4, where Don Quixote confronts the merchants from Toledo (p. 1984); the general effect of the episode may be comic or pathetic, yet the underlying pattern of Quixote's speech is nothing less than the theological virtue of Faith. Choose and analyze other passages of Quixote's eloquence where serious concepts raise an apparently comic situation to importance and significance (e.g., the concept of valor in II, 17, p. 2054).

6. Quixote has been described as the most "autonomous" character in
   literature—a supreme example of the phenomenon by which a fictional character acquires a life of its own, independent of its inventor. See how this paradoxical situation is consciously dealt with by
   Cervantes, not only in the first selection from part II, but more generally in the way in which the narrator "reports" on his hero to the
   reader.

Comparative Perspectives

1. *Don Quixote* is the supreme example of the attachment to books
   exhibited in so many of the Renaissance texts in the anthology. How
   do writers as different as (to name only a few) Montaigne and Cervantes and Milton turn their reading into original forms that then in
   turn became reading matter for others? How would you compare
   the concerns of these hyperliterary eras with those of earlier, essentially oral cultures?
2. Discuss episodes in your own experience that suggest how much of
   the way we feel—or think we ought to feel—derives from what we
   read (or see on television or in the movies). In societies like ours,
   heavily influenced by the media that are the contemporary equivalent of the books that drove Don Quixote, can we have "authentic"
   emotions? (What makes Don Quixote need to challenge so many of
   the people he meets to a duel: what is the source of his "violent
   behavior?")

Further Reading

See also the reading suggestions in the anthology, p. 1964.

Bjornson, Richard, ed. *Approaches to Teaching Don Quixote.* 1984. Contains background, critical appraisals, etc., by various expert hands.

Brenan, Gerald. *The Literature of the Spanish People.* 1951. Chapter VIII
is devoted to Cervantes's life and works. Brenan, who is not only a
renowned scholar but also a brilliant writer, has a vast knowledge of
Spanish culture.

Madariaga, Salvador de. *Don Quixote: An Introductory Essay in Psychology.* 1961. A famous view of the novel, by an outstanding Spanish
writer.

Mann, Thomas. *Cervantes, Goethe, Freud.* 1943. Individual appraisals by
one of the major fiction writers and essayists of the twentieth century.

Nelson, Lowry, Jr., ed. *Cervantes: A Collection of Critical Essays.* 1969.
Besides Nelson's enlightening introduction, includes two essays by
authors of great literary stature: Thomas Mann ("Voyage with Don
Quixote") and W. H. Auden ("The Ironic Hero: Some Reflections on
Don Quixote"). Also includes essays by some of the most outstanding
literary critics: Harry Levin ("The Example of Cervantes"), Leo Spitzer

("On the Significance of Don Quixote"), and Erich Auerbach ("The Enchanted Dulcinea").

Predmore, Richard L. *The World of Don Quixote*. 1967.

Riley, E. D. *Cervantes' Theory of the Novel*. 1962.

Unamuno, Miguel de. *The Life of Don Quixote and Sancho According to Miguel de Cervantes Saavedra*. Trans. Homer P. Earle. 1927. (Originally published 1905.) A famous view of the novel, by an outstanding Spanish writer.

LOPE DE VEGA

Fuente Ovejuna

Classroom Strategies and Topics for Discussion

One excellent way to begin your discussion is to ask about the title of this play. Why is *Fuente Ovejuna* not called by the name of its protagonist; or is it? Lope de Vega's emphasis on the community rather than on a single outsized hero anticipates a trend that will become increasingly common, and you may want to either ask your students to name some post-seventeenth-century plays or mention some that you intend to teach in the second semester of your survey. Like *The Cherry Orchard* or *Six Characters in Search of an Author*, *Fuente Ovejuna* has an idea rather than a person at its center.

Before exploring the play itself in detail, it's helpful to look at its broad outlines in order to contrast classical and Renaissance drama. The theaters of Elizabethan England and Golden Age Spain had neither proscenium arches nor architecturally defined backdrops. Eschewing the palace façade and altar of the ancient Greek theater, or the street scene of Roman comedy, Lope (like Shakespeare) confidently shifts the action back and forth from country to city, from royal palace to public square. Verbal clues and portable props suffice to indicate the scene. The resulting juxtapositions encourage audiences to recognize parallels in apparently unlinked situations, a device that typifies popular Renaissance drama.

Although Lope does not observe the classical unities, the structure of *Fuente Ovejuna* deserves attention for its economy. Character is firmly established, but often quite allusively, in fleeting strokes to which you will want to call your students' attention. The dominant figure in the play is the villain, Guzmán, and like Shakespeare's Iago, he sets the terms of the action. Lope begins by focusing on Guzmán's self-serving disquisition on courtesy. Putting the spotlight on the Comendador's multifarious discourtesies, made immediately perceptible in the short, swiftly shifting scenes of this three-act play, shows that he is unfit to rule. You might point particularly to the momentum against the Comendador's power that builds throughout Act II: in one scene, set in Esteban the mayor's house, we see the Comendador "lose" Laurencia to Frondoso; in the next, set in a meadow, we learn that the Order of Calatrava loses Ciudad

Real to Ferdinand and Isabella. The act ends as Guzmán reasserts himself by violating agreements that bind persons together: he arrests the groom as his marriage is performed, he wrests the mayor's staff from his hands, and it looks as if he has won.

This pitting of the one against the many defines the pace and emphasis of *Fuente Ovejuna*; capitalizing on the point made in a consideration of the play's title, you may wish to contrast Lope's celebration of community with Shakespeare's dramatic focus, in *Othello*, on a singular tragic hero. If the treatment of the heroic differs in these two great Renaissance plays, the public backdrop against which personal strife stands out in both cases reflects the same historical moment. Europe's obsessive struggle with Islam took a significant turn with the unifying rule of Ferdinand and Isabella: in 1492, under their leadership, the Moors (and the Jews) were expelled from Spain. By the time in which the play is set (1476), the Order founded in 1158 to defend Calatrava from Moorish incursions had become an outlaw power, personified by Fernan Gomez de Guzmán. As in *Othello*, the Moors are no longer the real enemies. Flores, the more cynical of the Comendador's servants, dryly mentions that men in Holy Orders "are obliged to fight for their emblem of the red cross—provided, of course, that the war is against the Moors" (p. 2082). For Guzmán, the red cross is an occasion for shedding, rather than a symbol of, innocent blood (see his inciting of the young Maestre to fight, on pp. 2077–78). He is in fact an infidel.

You might have students enumerate the many references to his barbarity: he is compares to pagan tyrants like Heliogabalus (p. 2091) and corrupts the good; witness his transforming the medically useful enema into an instrument of pain (p. 2096). Make sure that your students understand that Guzmán is not simply a gallant womanizer, as his inventory of women (p. 2090) may lead the casual reader to believe. When he brags of compelling "the wife of Pedro Redondo" (p. 2086) to surrender to him, we may initially think he has artfully charmed a good woman in the manner of Don Juan; but we later learn that he has turned "her over to his soldiers" (p. 2094), to bestial treatment.

Given the villain's sordid brutality, your students may wonder why *Fuente Ovejuna* is, as the headnote points out, a comedy. Explain that this generic distinction is based not on the evidence of a laugh meter but on the outcome of events; Dante, too, wrote a "comedy." The offstage rape and torture of peasants are graphically represented; indeed, whether Laurencia herself has been raped remains problematic. Certainly her shocking entrance with "dishevelled hair," a conventional stage sign of madness and disgrace, along with the great diatribe against the "half-men" who have failed to protect their women, leads the audience to assume the worst. One measure of the play's comic status is the relief that comes at the final moment, when Frondoso tells Ferdinand and Isabella that Laurencia remains "virtue personified," because she knew "how to protect herself." If some of your more skeptical students wonder whether we should believe what Laurencia has told Frondoso, so much the better—skillful actors can easily suggest that Laurencia has told

Frondoso a face-saving lie. Mulling over the question, you can lead your students to the conclusion that in comedy characters get on with their lives, however they can.

Such doubts notwithstanding, Lope is sophisticated enough to imply that true purity transcends physical assault. In its pastoral setting and its treatment of the progress of its central couple's love, *Fuente Ovejuna* draws on many traditional features of romantic comedy. Indeed, the strength of Laurencia's and Frondoso's union is clearly proposed as a match for that of Ferdinand and Isabella themselves, who are actually represented on stage. Daringly, the echo of Laurencia's query "Are these the rulers?" by Isabella's "Are these the aggressors?" at least momentarily equates the peasant lovers with the royal pair. The dialogue between Frondoso and Laurencia has a cleansing effect on *Fuente Ovejuna*, and in their early exchanges they conduct a merry war somewhat in the style of Shakespeare's Beatrice and Benedict. Students will recognize in their initial gambits a standard model for romantic comedy, for Hollywood as well as for Renaissance playwrights: boy loves girl, girl insults boy, boy wins girl with one heroic gesture.

They, and several of the other rustic characters in this play named for a village, command a rather exalted rhetoric. This marks them as traditional pastoral lovers in a traditional pastoral setting (you can remind your students that Fuente Ovejuna means Sheepwell—as "pastor" means shepherd). If you have read *Orlando Furioso*, recall the obsessive carving of "Medor" and "Angelica" on the bark of trees. This is a textbook illustration of the absurd attribution of poetic inspiration to woodland lovers that gives pastoral romance so much of its fantasy and charm. In her first long speech, Laurencia, promoter of linguistic probity and delicacy of expression, makes the authenticity of simple cuisine a metaphor for the decent life. When Frondoso joins the scene, he deplores the meretricious language of false courtesy ("the blind are one-eyed; the cross-eyed merely squint"). In her riposte, Laurencia exposes the opposite fault, a language that scorns virtue, in which "the faithful become inconstant . . . and the good Christians, frauds."

Among these curiously eloquent peasants is Mengo, an important character who may be a bit difficult for your students to place. In examining his role, reassure students who have had problems understanding him—in a staged performance, Mengo is precisely the kind of figure who comes alive, who does not need explanation because a good actor, well costumed, embodies his whole nature. Reconstructing his pastoral credentials from the details scattered through the printed text, ask your students why he values his boxwood rebec more than a barn (p. 2080). This piece of information virtually defines Mengo as a pastoral icon, the shepherd who loves music and philosophy (although he disclaims the title of philosopher). At the first, in witty dialogue with the play's two principal women, he reduces love to self-interest:

MENGO I don't know how to philosophize; as for reading, I wish I could! But I say that if the elements of Nature live in eternal conflict, then our bodies, which receive from them food, anger, melancholy, phlegm, and blood, must also be at war with each other.

. . . .

PASCUALA What are you trying to prove, then?
MENGO That individuals love only themselves.

(p. 2081)

By the play's end, as he triumphs over his torturers, Mengo's self-abnegating courage disproves his defense of self-interest. Experience, as opposed to theory, shows that individuals can love their community more than themselves.

Fuente Ovejuna further defines its pastoralism by giving dramatic form to a variety of traditional metaphors, most markedly by turning that staple of love poetry, the hunt for the deer, into the crisis that brings Act I to a stunning conclusion. When Frondoso takes up the Comendador's bow, he not only defends the hunter's quarry, Laurencia, but he directly challenges both the masculinity and the rank of a dangerous opponent. Act II begins with a contrasting scene of communal life in which the mayor and the village scholar, in separate conversations, seem to digress on the wisdom of simplicity. You will want your students to see, however, that in denigrating the pompous pronouncements of the "astrologers" and inveighing against the flood of false learning generated by the new invention of "Gutenberg, a famous German from Mainz" (p. 2088), Estaban and Leonelo are actually continuing Frondoso's attach on those who abuse positions of authority. This is another instance of how Lope uses scenic juxtapositions to link expressions of personal concerns to the social, political, and religious issues they mirror.

Finally, as always when teaching a play, ask your students to think about what performance would add to the literary text. The many songs, some of them actual popular ballads of Lope's day, are choral efforts; what is the impact on an audience of the sound of massed voices? How do these songs give auditory force to the central thematic idea of *Fuente Ovejuna*, that proverbial site of human solidarity? Similarly, have your students imagine the visual power of the various flags displayed on stage, from the defiled red cross to the improvised banners of the rebellious villagers, braver than "any Cids or Rodamontes" (p. 2100), to the scutcheon with the royal arms of Aragon and Castile. The shapes and colors of these physical signs help define the location of the action; their content bespeaks the seriousness of the comedy of *Fuente Ovejuna*.

Topics for Writing

1. What is the importance of Mengo, Jacinta, and Pascuala—the figures who really suffer in the play?
2. Where do you see signs that Lope has incorporated literary conven-

tions and/or folk material into staged drama? How do these elements enrich the dramatic power of the play?

3. Are Frondoso and Laurencia overidealized? Why does Lope give a
peasant woman a love sonnet to speak?

Comparative Perspectives

1. Contrast the heroic ideals embodied in "Cids or Rodamontes" with
the kind of heroism demonstrated in *Fuente Ovejuna*.

   [Perhaps especially fruitful for classes that have read *Orlando
Furioso* as well as a serious heroic work like *The Song of Roland*, or
a skeptical review of the tradition like *Don Quixote*.]

2. In *Lysistrata*, Aristophanes finds comedy in a women's revolt against
men and warlike Establishment values; compare and contrast the
treatment of women and the power of the disenfranchised in
Fuente Ovejuna.

3. In comparing Guzmán to Heliogabalus, Lope joins the many
Renaissance writers who draw on their knowledge of the ancient
world to veil or justify their criticism of contemporary political
wrongs. In *Of Coaches*, for example, Montaigne slides from a depiction of Heliogabalus in his coach to a general reflection on the
"pusillanimity in monarchs, and evidence of not sufficiently feeling
what they are, to labor at showing off and making a display by
excessive expense" (p. 1950). Discuss the conclusion of Lope de
Vega's play in these terms: does the murder of Guzmán solve the
larger political problems that *Fuente Ovejuna* uncovers? How does
Lope's attitude towards the relationship between rulers and those
they rule compare to, say, that of Montaigne in the passage referred
to above, or of Machiavelli in "The Roman Dream," at the conclusion of *The Prince* (pp. 1720–22)?

Further Reading

See also the reading suggestions in the anthology, p. 2075.

Yarbo-Bejerano, Yvonne. *Feminism and the Honor Plays of Lope de Vega.*
1994. Interesting comments on "the construction of gender" in Laurencia's scornful Act III speech to the men who have abandoned their
masculinity.

WILLIAM SHAKESPEARE
Othello

Classroom Strategies and Topics for Discussion

Othello is a very popular play; many of your students will have seen a
filmed or staged version. Its subject matter deeply interests students, and
you will want to channel that enthusiasm into a real engagement with
the play as Shakespeare wrote it. With sufficient time, students gen-

uinely come to grips with the play's language and structure. To begin, you might have members of the group read the opening lines aloud. Confused first readers should be encouraged: they are in effect eavesdropping on a conversation-in-progress, and their struggle to understand what has been going on just out of earshot mimics one of the play's central devices, to be noticed again especially in 4.1, when Iago engineers a discussion with Cassio that Othello watches but does not hear.

In the opening scene, also well demonstrated is Iago's gift for telling partial truths that mislead. Note his explanation of why Cassio was chosen to be the Moor's lieutenant: he used his connections ("Preferment goes by letter and affection"). Yet Iago himself indicates that he had tried the same thing, but his emissaries ("Three great ones of the city") were not successful.

Indeed, the entire structure of Venetian society can be deduced from this scene. What kind of neighborhood are we in? What kind of disruption is Iago always trying to provoke? Brabanzio's irritated appearance on his balcony, his famous protest that his "house is not a grange," captures the arrogance of the privileged urban elite. With startling economy, 1.1 prepares us for the issues of class and race that so predominate in *Othello*.

The comparing of contradictory intelligence reports that opens the third scene, in the Venetian Senate, offers another version off Iago's tactics. The public crisis caused by the Turkish fleet sent out to decoy the real object of its ambitions prefigures the personal drama that is to come. At the same time, the realistic political backdrop for this play may be discussed (this is the only one of Shakespeare's major tragedies in a contemporary setting). Presumably, Shakespeare is recalling battle tactics used in 1570–71, when the Turks defeated the Venetians and took Cyprus. Thus, for all the apparent ease with which the Turkish threat is deflected in Act II, Shakespeare's audience would probably have been aware that the Christian cause (like Desdemona and Othello's faith?) had lost.

You will find it helpful to have your students notice how—and how much—Iago talks. He opens and closes the first act, with Roderigo as his stooge. Ask the class to account for the change in diction when Iago confides his lack of iniquity to Othello and for the shifts between verse and prose throughout. Establish how the cynical rationalism of Iago's brutal advice to Roderigo would have struck the original audience, noting the repeated "Put money in thy purse." Make sure that your students understand that, in fact, Roderigo has been putting money in Iago's purse for some time now, and will continue to do so, with nothing to show for it.

With the second act, a full consideration of Desdemona and her relationship to Othello can be broached. Students will readily identify with Desdemona and her balanced defiance of her overprotective father. Typically, Brabanzio has failed to understand the reason for his daughter's rejection of "the wealthy curled darlings of our nations": Desdemona's thirst for adventure is slaked by Othello and she begins the play as "a fair warrior."

When reading Shakespeare, if left to their own devices, students will concentrate on character analysis and try to ignore the language in which the characters live. Close attention to individual psychology yields valuable insights, as we all know. The challenge is to demonstrate that close attention to words and scenic juxtapositions is equally valuable, that Shakespeare and the narrative traditions upon which his plays draw rely on symbolic devices that offer insight into human motivation and action; they were not concerned with scrupulously reproducing the kind of quotidian detail that students who read realistic fiction expect.

Having this comment ready will insulate you from any questions about what critics have called the problem of "double time" in *Othello*: timetables may be produced by clever students who are puzzled by Othello's credulous acceptance of Iago's accusations against Desdemona. When was there time for adultery to be committed? You can point out that Shakespeare very neatly establishes in the opening of Act II that there was in fact no opportunity for this betrayal to have occurred. Iago and Desdemona greet Cassio, already on Cypriot soil, and wait in the harbor for the ship bearing Othello to arrive. Wife and husband have been separated (as the headnote makes clear, their marriage has not yet been consummated). Cassio has travelled in a third ship. The question is not "when could the adultery happen?" Rather, ask your students why Othello never takes the time to think through the circumstances indicating that it did not happen and could not have happened.

To explain the mental space in which such lapses occur, it is helpful to notice the deep suspicion of women that the men in this play so easily entertain. Look, for example, at the misogynistic verse that Iago produces during the wait for Othello's ship and note Emilia's relation to the action at his early point in the play. Her outburst in 4.4 and her courageous persistence at play's end interest students. In the trio of Bianca, Emilia, and Desdemona, the pay offers three representations of women; significantly, they do not remain static but change and evolve and command sympathy in the face of the masculine scorn they each have to face.

Explore how Iago brings about the downfall of Cassio, asking students to explain the figures of speech exchanged when Othello requires an account of the riot Iago has finally been able to achieve: from comporting themselves like "bride and groom, / Devesting them for bed" (2.3.161–62), Cassio and Montano have "turned Turks" (151). Much of the play's imagery and strategy can be identified in 2.3, including the scene's ending with the dominant Iago giving bad advice to another dupe. If time permits, Cassio's elegance merits some underscoring, as does his ultimate, loving allegiance to Othello ("Dear General, I never gave you cause"). He never stoops to race-baiting; but he can be thoughtlessly cruel to Bianca, which might be part of the discussion of gender representation mentioned above. In short, the fall of Cassio makes clear that Iago succeeds by finding his prey's weak point and exploiting it mercilessly while posing as a friend.

Exactly what Othello's weak point may be should be the subject of further discussion, when the long, interrupted seduction scene of Acts III and IV is available for dissection. Students who have read chapter 2 of

Genesis should be advised to watch for Emilia's defense of her mistress: "If any wretch have put this in your head, / Let heaven requite it with the serpent's curse." As in the story of Eden, an appetite for knowledge—the "ocular proof" that Othello demands—bespeaks a loss of faith and leads to carnality and shame.

Reminders that Shakespeare is writing for performance are always worthwhile. Ask students to discuss the significance of the stage picture of Othello in the grips of an epileptic fit. Likewise the handkerchief, a large piece of white fabric with a pattern of red splotches on it, is remarkably evocative of the bloody sheets that declared a bride's virginity, so that Othello's fixation on Desdemona's "linen" may seem not so bizarre after all but a brilliant piece of stage symbolism. Have students analyze as well the various musical interludes in the play, especially the bedtime scene with Desdemona's song about "Barbary." Ask them to consider the sheer visual impact of the final scene's "loaded bed." Othello's murder of Desdemona, of course, reenacts the scabrous sequence of graphic taunts quoted in the headnote to the play; far from imagining the old black ram tupping a white ewe, we seem to be watching it happen before our eyes. What are we to make of this, and of Othello's fixation on her alabaster body as the scene opens? Does he kill her because she is white? How important finally is Othello's race?

If Iago's motives are famously unfathomable, what about Othello's? How nobly does he acquit himself in his final moments, in which he keeps producing a phallic sword despite efforts to disarm him? Is he, in the notorious judgment of T. S. Eliot, "cheering himself up" when he recalls killing the circumcised Turk, or is this nobility regained, a final stage in the experience of the Shakespearean tragic hero (outlined by Maynard Mack in the essay recommended in the headnote)? These questions may be answered in myriad ways: they are the reason why plays are acted and seem different in every performance. If you have access to one of the many videotapes of *Othello* now available, it is worth posing such questions in terms of an actor's embodiment of the role. Selecting a sequence and showing three different versions of it can prompt unending discussion and provide excellent topics for writing.

Topics for Writing

1. Choose one of the songs in the play and analyze the contribution it makes to the atmosphere and content of the scene in which it occurs.
2. How important is (either) Christian allegory or geopolitical tension to our understanding of Othello's acceptance of Iago's version of events? Why does Othello not trust Desdemona?
3. Discuss the importance of one of the secondary characters: how does Emilia, Bianca, Cassio, or Roderigo mirror and clarify actions of the central characters in the drama?
4. Compare a performance of *Othello* with your experience of the play while reading it. What surprised you?

Comparative Perspectives

1. Adultery is a persistent theme in world literature. Compare and contrast the kind of sympathy extended to women accused of adultery in Marie de France's *Laüstic,* Boccaccio's Ninth Story of the Fourth Day, Chaucer's *Miller's Tale,* and *Othello.* Are they in fact guilty? If so, do we understand why?
2. Iago's final boast is "From this time forth I never will speak word." Suppose that Dante had put Iago in the Inferno. What circle would he be in? What words would he speak to Dante and Virgil that would help Othello—and us—understand his evil?
3. Iago sneers at Cassio because he is a "Florentine," and along with his reference to the drinking habits of Germans, Danes, and Englishmen in 2.4, these comments suggest that he has a strong xenophobic streak. As nation-states were first beginning to emerge in Europe, such comparisons became quite common. Look, for example, at the sequence in *The Praise of Folly* on Selflove and its "communal form" (p. 1698) and discuss the tendency of human beings to stereotype nations as well as persons. What is the tone of this stereotyping in Erasmus's work? How do such references sound when Iago is the speaker? Do you believe there are distinct national styles of behavior? Examine the reasons why we look at other groups of people as strange or amusing according to their social, linguistic, or other habits.

Further Reading

See also the reading suggestions in the anthology, pp. 2115–16.

Boose, Lynda. "Othello's Handkerchief: 'The Recognizance and Pledge of Love.'" *English Literary Renaissance* 5 (1975): 360–74.

Eliot, T. S. "Shakespeare and the Stoicism of Seneca." *Selected Essays.* 1950.

McPherson, David C. *Shakespeare, Jonson, and the Myth of Venice.* 1990. Chapter 4 examines assumptions that the Jacobean audience would have made about Venetian courtesans and the loss of Cyprus.

Vaughan, Virginia Mason. *Othello: A Contextual History.* 1994. An excellent survey of "Jacobean Contexts" and stage history.

JOHN MILTON

Paradise Lost

Backgrounds

Milton's epic *Paradise Lost* is divided like Virgil's epic, the *Aeneid,* into twelve books. Its great theme is announced in the proemium (p. 2197) as that of man's transgression and fall and the promise of redemption. Actually, the scope of the poem is vaster. Using a device common to both the

Greek and the Roman epic—the *Odyssey* and the *Aeneid* in particular—
that is, a flashback in the form of a tale told by one of the characters in
the poem (in this case the Archangel Michael in his speech to Adam and
Eve in books V–VIII), *Paradise Lost* encompasses the story of the rebellious angels and *their* fall, the creation of Hell as their eternal abode, and
of man and his earthly habitation surrounded by its celestial universe.
Thus Milton, through Michael, has also undertaken the Dantean task of
"delineating" events occurring in the Empyrean heaven, and in created
Hell, "by likening spiritual to corporeal forms" (V.573, not included in
the anthology).

Immediately after the proemium and the invocation to the Muse, the
curtain rises on the vision of Hell, where the former Lucifer, now Satan,
tells his legions of "a new kind of Creature to be created" and summons
them to a council in his palace, "Pandemonium," which has suddenly
risen from the depths of surrounding Chaos. In book II (not in the
anthology), the infernal parliament debates whether it should engage in a
new battle against God, or whether it should first verify the news of His
having created a new world and a new being, man, possibly susceptible to
Satanic influence. The latter plan is accepted, and Satan leaves on his
exploratory mission. Book III (not in the anthology), shifts to the vision
of Heaven, where God sits on His throne, the Son on His right side. Here
Milton takes up the task of presenting in poetic language the doctrinal
problems of God's foreknowledge, man's free will, and his redemption.
The omniscient God knows that man will fall, but clears Himself of "all
imputation," having endowed man with free will; He declares His "purpose of grace," provided that someone is found who will "answer for"
man's offense and undergo his punishment. The Son offers Himself and
is exalted as the Redeemer.

The last part of book III shifts back to Satan, who in book IV—after
being torn by the passions of fear, envy, and despair—"confirms himself
in evil." His first attempt on Eve, in the form of a dream, is frustrated by
the intervention of the Archangel Gabriel, and he is chased from the
Garden. In book V, after Eve's account of her dream to Adam, Raphael as
God's messenger descends upon Eden; he warns Adam of the imminent
danger of temptation by the fallen angel, thus beginning his long flashback, which will end in book VIII with Raphael answering Adam's questions on the celestial bodies and their movements. Adam in turn confides
to Raphael what he remembers of his own creation and tells of God's
warning about the Tree of Knowledge. At the end the two discourse on
appropriate relationships between man and woman, and the archangel
departs.

Book IX and the second part of book X are the main selections in the
anthology (pp. 2220–55). Raphael has gone (cf. note 9, p. 2220), and the
poet announces a change in tone from "venial discourse" to the tragedy
of the transgression and fall. This is the section that deals with the poet's
theme and purpose as announced in lines 1 and 26 of book I: "Man's first
disobedience," and the justification of "God's ways to man." It ends, at
the close of book X, with the prospect of life on Earth—life as we know

it—and with the first sinners recommending themselves as supplicants to
the Son of God, who in book XI (not in the anthology) intercedes for
them with the Father. God decrees their expulsion from Paradise and
sends Michael with a band of Cherubim to announce the sentence.
Before executing it, the archangel from a hilltop sets before Adam a
vision of the future life of man up to the Flood; his revelation continues
in book XII up to the coming of the Messiah and His incarnation, death,
resurrection, and ascension. They descend the hill, and Adam awakens
Eve from gentle dreams (p. 2256); the two are led by Michael out of Paradise.

Scores of plays and poems on sacred subjects, in English and in Italian (during his visit to Italy, Milton had known local poets and even
wrote poems in Italian) have been mentioned as possibly inspiring Milton's conception; such relationships in general belong to the area of specialized curiosities. Milton was extraordinarily well read in several
languages; and there may be, for example, generic echoes from Dante
(whom Milton greatly admired) in such early lines of *Paradise Lost* as
". . . sights of woe, / Regions of sorrow, where peace / And rest can never
dwell, hope never comes / That comes to all, but torture without end
. . ." (I.64–69, not included in the anthology), or of Tasso's *Jerusalem
Delivered* in Milton's conception of the infernal council in book II. Or
Milton may practically translate a line from Ariosto's *Orlando Furioso*
("Things unattempted yet in prose or rhyme," I.16) and effectively use it
in a totally different context, much as Dante does when on his first
meeting Beatrice he uses a line (*Purgatorio* XXX.46) that in Virgil's
Aeneid is spoken by Dido as she is falling in love with Aeneas. This is
one of the minor ways in which the "great tradition" works.

More important, quite early in life Milton had conceived of a great
work (at first, apparently, imagined as a drama) on the central story of the
Judeo-Christian tradition. This was to constitute the crowning achievement of his variedly active life—an indication of the supreme place that
he reserved for his activity as a poet. Thus Milton's main inspiration for
Paradise Lost was the very awareness of the magnitude and height of his
task. The significant lines 20–47 of book IX also express his notion of the
superiority of his poetic material (to him, accustomed to religious meditation and doctrinal debate, "chivalry" materials were not only inferior,
they were "tedious") and implicitly of his own poetic power. And perhaps
also those lines signal the feeling that he is the last in a tradition of
poetry on a grand scale, which had begun with the Homeric epics and
continued through Virgil and through Virgil's Christian "pupil," Dante.

Classroom Strategies

Experience would indicate that in Milton's case as in others (cf. the
notes on teaching Erasmus, pp. 171–74) a useful first measure is to test
students' knowledge of the biblical events that constitute his material.
There may be surprises in either direction. Specifically for the selections in

the anthology, a supplementary reading and explication of the relevant passages in Genesis may be in order. Young people possessing superficial knowledge and mental images of the story of the fall and its meaning as a *felix culpa* may find in that notion as dramatized by Milton a source of considerable intellectual stimulation and enlightenment. Attention should be drawn to Milton's poetic handling of the story of the temptation, fall, and promise of redemption, in a poetic style alternating between solemn discourse and lively drama. The ideal student should be able to discover that there is fascination in the Adam–Eve dialogue, conducted as it is by the poet both as doctrinal argumentation and as human drama. Also, as in other previous cases, it should be observed in detail how the poet incorporates Greco-Roman material and uses it in handling his biblical story. The footnotes in the anthology attempt to be helpful on all these levels.

Topics for Discussion and Writing

1. Analyze, in specific passages from the selections in the anthology, the ways in which the concept of the fall as a *felix culpa*, a "happy fault," is dramatized by Milton.
2. If the last selections from the *Purgatorio* (p. 1424) have been read, compare the scene and function of the Earthly Paradise in Dante and in Milton.
3. Choose and analyze passages in which pagan and Christian imagery are fused in Milton.
4. In his description of "chivalry materials" in book IX.27–41, Milton seems to ignore the fact that this material also had a Christian world as its background and that the "battles feigned" were also between Christians and infidels. Contrast with the revitalization of that same material in Cervantes. Discuss whether the differences may be due to the diversity in cultural and religious backgrounds of the two writers.

Comparative Perspectives

1. Discuss the way Eve and her flowers are interwoven, and compare the intimate links between other heroines and the natural world. How might we account for this widespread tendency to identify women with the landscape?
2. Compare the attitudes toward epic expressed in the Invocation to book IX with those of Lucian and Petronius in the ancient world, or of Ariosto, to whom Milton pays a kind of backhanded homage in line 16 of book I.

Further Reading

See also the reading suggestions in the anthology, p. 2197.

Broadbent, J. B. *Some Graver Subject: An Essay on* Paradise Lost. 1967. With illustrations and index. A thorough, detailed analysis of *Paradise Lost*, perhaps somewhat extravagant.

Demaray, John G. *Milton's Theatrical Epic: The Invention and Design of* Paradise Lost. 1980. A critical interpretation of *Paradise Lost* with a view to its origins and development, Milton's theories and techniques, influences, and its relation to Renaissance dramatic forms.

Emma, Ronald David, and John T. Shawcross, eds. *Language and Style in Milton: A Symposium in Honor of the Tercentenary of* Paradise Lost. 1967. Eleven essays on the linguistic background, theological language, spelling and pronunciation, Aristotelian notion of ethos and dianoia, grammar, imagery, and style of *Paradise Lost.* With selected bibliography.

Le Comte, Edward S. *A Milton Dictionary.* 1969. A dictionary including "hard" words from Milton's works, entries on the individual works, and biographical data.

Leonard, John. *Naming in Paradise: Milton and the Language of Adam and Eve.* 1990. Particularly appropriate to the selections in the anthology.

Lieb, Michael. *Poetics of the Holy: A Reading of* Paradise Lost. 1981. A religious interpretation, with illustrations and bibliography. Deals with the basic religious context of *Paradise Lost,* the esthetic dimensions of that context, and the aspects of sacral phenomena in the work.

Summers, Joseph H. *The Muse's Method: An Introduction to* Paradise Lost. 1962. Broadbent says that this is the most complete study of its kind.

Wittreich, Joseph Antony. *Feminist Milton.* 1987.

Index

Abulafia, Meir Halevi, 127
Acharnians, The, 58
Adagia, 195
Aeneid, The, 4, 7, 28, 56, **74–82,** 83, 90, 213, 214
Aeschylus, **30–39,** 65, 68
Agamemnon, **30–39,** 43, 56
Ajax, 182
Alexander the Wild, 124
Alfonsi, Petrus, 127, 128
Alone in Martyrdom, 121
Apology of Socrates, The, **62–67,** 99, 186
Apuleius, 73
Arcadia, 201
Ariosto, Ludovico, 85, 95, 96, 126, **178–83,** 201, 214, 215
Aristophanes, 50, **57–62,** 71, 208
Aristotle, 65, **68–69**
Art of Love, The (Daniel), 126
Art of Love (Ovid), 84
Attic Nights, 195
Augustine, St., **97–100,** 168, 169
Austen, Jane, 114

Balade (Charles d'Orleans), 125, 126
Beatrice, countess of Dia, 126
Beowulf, 28, **105–8,** 109, 113, 116, 117, 126, 160, 180
Bergson, Henri, 129, 130
Bible, The, 102–3
  Genesis, 4, **5–11,** 49, 86, 92, 104, 117, 130, 145, 161, 192, 211, 215
  Job, **11–13,** 27
  Jonah, 15
  Luke, **90–94**
  Matthew, **90–94**
  New Testament, the, **90–94,** 103
  Old Testament, the, **5–15,** 92, 103–4
  Psalms, **13–14**
  Song of Songs, **14–15,** 121, 170
Bishop Orders His Tomb, The, 13
Boaistuau, Pierre, 187
Boccaccio, Giovanni, 116, 126, 128, 134, **140–45,** 186, 187–88, 189
Boiardo, Matteo Maria, 201
Book (Le Livre) de Caradoc, The, 148
Book of the Courtier, The, 174, 183, **184–87**
Born, Bertrand de, 126
Brant, Sebastian, 172
Browning, Robert, 13
Butcher of Abbeville, The, 128, 129, 130

Calvalcanti, Guido, 124, 168
Calvary, 123
Candide, 95
Canterbury Tales, The, 105, 121, 128, 145, **151–57,** 161
  General Prologue, 140, **151–52,** 155, 156
  Miller's Tale, The, 128–29, 134, **152–53,** 155, 156, 189
  Pardoner's Tale, The, 128, 134, **154–55,** 156
  Wife of Bath's Tale, The, 96, 114, 126, 134, **153–54,** 156, 160, 163
Canzoniere ("Song Book"), **167–70**
Castiglione, Baldesar, 174, **184–87,** 193

Catullus, 30, **72–74**
Cavalcanti, Guido, 120, 126
Cervantes, Miguel de, **197–204,** 215
Charles d'Orleans, 125, 126
Chaucer, Geoffrey, 15, 105, 114, 126,
    128, 134, 140, **151–57,** 160,
    161, 180, 189
Cicero, 73
Clodia, 73
Confession (medieval poem), 124
Confessions (Augustine), **97–100,**
    168, 169, 197
Cooke, Thomas C., 128
Cult of Love, The, 120, 127
Cursed Dancers of Colbeck, The,
    133–34

Dancing Girl, 124
Daniel, Arnaut, 126, 168
Dante Alighieri, 28, 96, 104–5, 122,
    126, **135–39,** 145, 156, 160, 168,
    178, 179, 189, 200, 214, 215
Daughters of Pelias, The, 50
Decameron, The, 128, 134, **140–45,**
    162, 188
  Eighth Story of the Fifth Day,
      142–43
  First Story of the First Day, **140–41**
  Ninth Story of the Fourth Day, 117,
      141–42
  Sixth Story of the Ninth Day, 116,
      143, 189
  Tenth Story of the Tenth Day, 126,
      143–44
Diana, 201
*Discourses on the First Ten Chapters of
    Livy,* 175
Divine Comedy, The, 28, 105, 122,
    135–39, 168
  Inferno, 122, **135–39,** 145, 156,
      168, 178, 189, 200
  Paradiso, **135–39,** 169
  Purgatorio, **135–39,** 168, 214, 215
Don Quixote, **197–204,** 208
Dronke, Peter, 122, 124–25

Electra (Euripides), 33
Electra (Sophocles), 33
Eliot, George, 114
Eliot, T. S., 126, 211
Encounter, An, 120, 126
Ennius, 76

Ephraim ben Jacob, Rabbi, 9–10,
    122–23, 126
Erasmus, Desiderius, **171–74,** 194,
    195, 214
Essays (Montaigne), **194–97**
Eumenides, The, **31–39,** 42, 81, 119
Euripides, 33, **48–57,** 65, 68, 85
Everyman, 162, **163–65**

Feast of Bricriu, The (Fled Bricrend),
    148
Folengo, Teofilo, 192
Fox, Charles James, 81
Fox, The, 125
Frogs, 50
Fuente Ovejuna, **204–8**

Gargantua and Pantagruel, 62, 134,
    190–94
Gellius, Aulus, 195
Gilbert, W. S., 181
Gilgamesh, **1–5,** 7, 28, 86, 178
Gruget, Pierre, 187
Guinizelli, Guido, 126, 156, 168
Gulliver's Travels, 95
Gwilym, Dafydd ap, 125

Hadewijch of Brabant, 120, 127
Heptameron, The, 145, 156, 181, 183,
    187–90
Hildegard of Bingen, 14–15, 121,
    122, 125
Hippolytus, 85
Histories of Fortunate Lovers, 187
Homer, **16–28,** 33, 42, 65, 79–81,
    86, 96, 178, 186
Horace, 87, 88
Hymn to Holy Women, A, 122, 123,
    193
Hymn to St. Maximinus, A, 121, 193

Ibn Arfa' Ra'suh, 120
Iliad, The, 7, **16–22,** 54, 65, 75, 86,
    93
In Battle, 126
In Praise of War, 126
Ion, 54

Jerusalem Delivered, 214
Judah Halevi, 15, 120, 121

King Lear, 135

King's Tailor's Apprentice, The, 128
Koran, The, 93, **101–5,** 114, 117, 120

Lament of the Virgin, 123, 127
Lancelot du Lac, 160
Lanval, **114–17**
Last Trial, The, 123
Laüstic, **114, 116–17,** 162
Lazarillo de Tormes, 201
Letter from the Grave, A, 127
Libation Bearers, The, **31–39**
Lope de Vega, **204–8**
Love and Nobility, 126, 156
Love and Poetry, 122
Lover's Prize, A, 126
Love Song (Rudel), 120
Lucian, **94–97,** 172, 182, 215
Lysistrata, **57–62,** 134, 208

Machiavelli, Niccolò, 167–68,
    174–77, 183, 195, 208
Mahfouz, Naguib, 121
Malory, Sir Thomas, 56, 114, **160–63**
Mannyng, Robert, 133–34
Marguerite de Navarre, 121, **187–90**
Marie de France, **114–17,** 187
Maximus, Valerius, 195
Medea, **48–57,** 59–60, 69, 85
Medieval Lyric, The (Dronke), 122,
    125
Medieval Lyrics: A Selection, **119–27,**
    168
Medieval Tales: A Selection, **127–35**
Memorable Deeds and Sayings, 195
Metamorphoses, **82–87,** 95, 159
Mikado, The, 181
Miller, Mark, 133, 134
Milton, John, 189, 203, **212–16**
Mitchell, Stephen, 13
Montaigne, Michel de, **194–97,** 203,
    208
Montemayor, Jorge de, 201
Morte Darthur, 56, 114, **160–63**
Muscatine, Charles, 129
My Galley, 169

Naevius, 76
Notker, 122, 123

Odyssey, The, 4, 7, 10, **22–28,** 33, 42,
    54, 55, 65, 79–81, 86, 93, 145,
    213

Oedipus the King, 35, **39–48,** 68–69,
    182
Of Coaches, 208
Oresteia, **30–39,** 69, 119
Orlando Furioso, 85, 95, 126, 170,
    178–83, 206, 208, 214
Orlando Innamorato, 201
Othello, 126, 135, 145, 205, **208–12**
Ovid, 81, **82–87,** 95, 159, 170, 179

Paradise Lost, 170, 189, **212–16**
Peace, The, 58
Petrarch, Francis, 30, 121, 126,
    167–70
Petronius, **87–90,** 215
Phaedra, 85
Pizan, Christine de, 121, 126
Plato, **62–67,** 96, 181, 189
Plautus, **70–72**
Plutarch, 98
Poetics, **68–69**
Pound, Ezra, 126
Praise of Folly, The, **171–74**
Prince, The, 167–68, **174–77,** 186,
    208
Pro Caelio, 73
Pseudolus, **70–72**
Pulci, Luigi, 192

Rabelais, François, 71, 90, **190–94**
Racine, Jean, 85
Rerem Vulgarium Fragmenta, 167
Rime sparse ("Scattered Rhymes"),
    167–70
Ring That Controlled Erections, The,
    130
Romance of Renard, The, 130, 160
Rudel, Jaufré, 120

Sacrifice of Isaac, The, 122–23, 126,
    127
Sannazzaro, Jacopo, 201
Sappho of Lesbos, 14, **29–30,** 74
Satires (Horace), 87
Satyricon, The, 62, **87–90,** 134
Scholar's Guide, The, 127
Scivias, 122
Scorpions, The, 125
Seneca, 195
Seven Against Thebes, The, 43
Shakespeare, William, 68, 126, 135,
    169, 181, 182, 205, 206, **208–12**

Ship of Fools, 172
Singing Lute, The, 120, 121
Sir Gawain and the Green Knight, 28,
    114, 125–26, **146–51,** 156, 160,
    162–63
Socrates, 62–67, 93, 96, 99
Song of Roland, The, **108–14,** 117,
    183, 200, 208
Song of Summer, 120
Sophocles, 33, **39–48,** 54, 68, 182
Spiegel, Shalom, 123
Spring Song, 120, 121
Strabo, Walahfrid, 123, 124
Strawberry Picking, 124, 125
Sulla, 98
Summer (Judah Halevi), 120, 121
Swift, Jonathan, 95
Symphonia, 122
Symposium, 181, 189

Table, The, 120–21
Tacitus, 88
Tasso, 214
Testament, 13, 125, 126
Thorstein the Staff-Struck, **117–19**
Thou, Adrien de, 187

Thousand and One Nights, The, 85,
    119, 128, 145, **157–59,** 189
Three Hunchbacks, The, 129–30
Tottel, Richard, 169
Tottel's Miscellany, 169
Trial of Renard, The, 96, 125, 130–33,
    134
True Story, A, **94–97,** 134, 182, 193
Twelfth Night, 181
*Two City Dwellers and the Country
    Man, The,* 128

Villon, François, 13, 125, 126
Virgil, **74–82,** 83, 170, 178, 183, 214
Voltaire, 95
Von der Vogelweide, Walther, 124, 126

Waste Land, The, 126
Wild Dream, The, 130
William IX, duke of Aquitane, 121
Women of Trachis, 54
Wyatt, Sir Thomas, 169

Yeats, William Butler, 81

Zaabalawi, 121